THE
SELF–MANAGEMENT
WORKSHOP

THE
SELF–MANAGEMENT
WORKSHOP

Donald H. Weiss

*Helping People Take Control
of Their Lives and Their Work*

▶ A TRAINER'S GUIDE ◀

AMACOM

American Management Association

New York • Atlanta • Boston • Chicago • Kansas City • San Francisco • Washington, D.C.
Brussels • Mexico City • Tokyo • Toronto

Special discounts on bulk quantities of AMACOM books are available to corporations, professional associations, and other organizations. For details, contact Special Sales Department, AMACOM, an imprint of AMA Publications, a division of American Management Association
1601 Broadway, New York, NY 10019
Tel.: 212-903-8316.   Fax: 212-903-8083.

This publication is designed to provide accurate and authoritative information in regard to the subject matter covered. It is sold with the understanding that the publisher is not engaged in rendering legal, accounting, or other professional service. If legal advice or other expert assistance is required, the services of a competent professional person should be sought.

Library of Congress Cataloging-in-Publication Data

Weiss, Donald H.
    The self-management workshop / Donald H. Weiss.
        p.   cm.
    Includes bibliographical references and index.
    ISBN 0-8144-0453-7
    1. Time management.   2. Teams in the workplace.   I. Title.
HD69.T54W53   1999
658.4′036—dc21   99–29236
                                                  CIP

Printing number
10   9   8   7   6   5   4   3   2   1

Contents

Acknowledgments

As I always note, I, like Newton, stand on the shoulders of giants. Many people have taught me what I know, many books have informed my ability to provide training to other people, and many colleagues (especially Henry Garcia, Don German, Forrest Adams, and Bill Beane) have helped me refine my tools. Most importantly, participants in my workshops have taught me much that I know about people, about their needs, their interests, and their values. I hope I have represented them well in this book.

Specifically, I need to thank my wife, Sara, for her patience sitting alone while I worked at my computer or was on the road delivering a workshop. I also need to thank Adrienne Hickey for taking a chance on publishing a book like this, and Jacquie Flynn, my most wonderful editor who has helped me tighten and refine and explain everything in this text.

Introduction

How and Why to Train People for Self-Management

The management mantra of "empowerment" rings hollow because most managers themselves are not as empowered as they would like to be, and very few managers really want their employees to make decisions and act on them (which is what empowerment means) without first consulting with management. One reason is that managers are afraid their employees will make mistakes that will get the managers in trouble with higher management or with the board of directors. That's a reasonable fear as people aren't usually prepared to be empowered, even if managers truly believe in the mantra. *It takes self-management to fulfill the responsibilities of empowerment as well as to bask in its privileges.*

Self-management—the ability to make your own decisions, to control your own actions and achieve personal goals, and to be a positive influence in your environment—doesn't come naturally. People need training in the skills that will make them competent for self-management. This book is designed for you, a trainer, to deliver workshops in which people can learn how competent they already are in self-management and how much they still need to learn. The assessments and exercises will be particularly useful in a team-based environment, whether the teams are now semiautonomous (in which a manager is the leader) or they are already self-managed (self-managed teams, in which no one in the team is a manager). To empower people is to help them to become self-managed.

STYLES AND LENGTHS OF WORKSHOPS

You know better than I what kind of learning environment will work best in your organization. These exercises can be used with total immersion—a concentrated workshop compressed into several days—or spaced learning—one or two hour, one or two day sessions spaced over several weeks. You can select the materials to fit your needs. You will probably find it useful to offer employees in your organization the self-assessments in Chapter 2 and then ask them to help you design interactive workshops that concentrate on areas in which people say they need improvement. In addition, it isn't necessary to use every exercise in this book to help people develop self-management skills.

One-day or partial-day workshops work well if a series is offered over a period of several weeks (spaced learning), with follow-up assignments on which trainees work between sessions. A one-day workshop would focus on several aspects of self-management, whereas a partial-day workshop would deal with only one aspect or involve only one exercise. The outline for a short workshop might be:

1. Introduction and expectations
2. Learning objectives and outcomes for the session
3. Self-assessment with regard to a specific competency (Section I)
4. Exercise related to that competency (Section II)
5. Wrap-up and follow-up assignment

A comprehensive, multiday workshop, involving all or most of the exercises in this book, should also be divided into spaced sessions between which trainees would work on their own improvement plans. A possible outline might look like this:

Week 1, Day 1

1. Introduction and expectations
2. Learning objectives and outcomes for the entire program
3. Learning objectives and outcomes for Day 1
4. Self-assessment of the whole person (Section I) and discussion
5. Goal setting and action planning (Section II)
6. Self-assessment with regard to a specific self-management competency (Section I)
7. Exercise with regard to the self-management competency (Section III)
8. Wrap-up for Day 1

Week 1, Day 2

1. Learning objectives and outcomes for Day 2
2. Self-assessment with regard to a specific self-management competency (Section I)

3. Exercise with regard to the self-management competency (Section III)
4. Self-assessment with regard to a specific self-management competency (Section I)
5. Exercise with regard to the self-management competency (Section III)
6. Self-assessment with regard to a specific self-management competency (Section I)
7. Exercise with regard to the self-management competency (Section III)
8. Wrap-up of the two days and a follow-up assignment

You could then bring the participants back for two sessions in the following week or two weeks later and repeat the format for Day 2.

Regardless of how you timeline or sequence the workshops, their style should always be interactive, employing as many self-discovery methods as possible. The style of the workshop is a model for self-management. Chapter 1, Training for Self-Management, will explain how to make your workshops fit that model.

EXERCISE FORMAT

The design of each exercise also encourages self-management and self-discovery. Each exercise generally follows the structure below. When an exercise is divided into parts, I provide instructions and discussion questions in each division.

▶ Instructor's Notes (with some explanation of the purpose and structure of the activities)
▶ Learning Objectives and Outcomes (expressed behaviorally rather than in measurable terms)
▶ Self-management Skills Involved
▶ Requirements
  — Time
  — Materials
  — Equipment
  — Preparation
  — Room Setup
▶ Lecture Notes
▶ Instructions to Participants
▶ Discussion Questions

Each exercise also comes equipped with handouts that may be reproduced for use in your workshops. Do not reproduce them for resale without written permission from the author. Some exercises involve overhead visuals, and the masters are also included in the book.

Finally, you may tailor these exercises in any way appropriate to your organization's needs. However, I strongly recommend that you not lose sight of their purpose: to encourage self-discovery and self-management.

Sources for the Exercises

I have used the exercises reproduced in this book in one setting or another for more than twenty years. Some of them have been used by other trainers as well, and a few of them come from the great library called word-of-mouth. I know how they work in a live environment, and I also know well enough to offer this caution: Not every group will respond to an exercise in exactly the same way as other groups. That's why when I list discussion questions, I also list *typical answers.* There is never one perfect answer for any discussion question.

GETTING STARTED

1

Training for
Self-Management

By reading this chapter, you will be able to:

▶ Explain the basic concepts of self-management.

▶ Identify and describe the six self-management competencies.

▶ Apply the basic principles of experiential learning to the training for self-management.

People learn self-management skills only by and through experiences that allow them to *do* the skills necessary for learning *how* to get control over their lives. For you to facilitate self-management skill workshops, you need to explain self-management and self-management competencies to your students, and apply experiential learning methods.

Using this chapter's materials as lecture notes will help you explain the concepts and skills involved in self-management. When talking about the six self-management competencies, make the presentation interactive by asking the participants to define, explain, or describe what the words wholeness, self-confidence, self-awareness, drive, self-respect/self-esteem, and respect for others mean to them. However, I advise that, if you plan to assign the self-assessments in Chapter 2, do *not* communicate any of these materials in class until the participants have completed the assessments, lest you "program" them as to how to respond.

SELF-MANAGEMENT AND SELF-MANAGEMENT COMPETENCIES

Self-management consists of the personal power to control what happens in our own mental and physical spaces, our ability to control what we do and how we do it; it's our competence and commitment to manage our own lives. In its simplest sense, self-management means satisfying basic needs for food, clothing, and shelter. In a broader sense, self-management is the ability to manipulate ourselves and the things or processes in the world in which we live, to satisfy our wants, needs, and requirements, and to fulfill our loftiest ambitions.

Management of any kind implies more than the exercise of power; it implies *control.* We can control or manage things, processes, and events in our lives even if it appears as if we don't. We choose the processes in which we're engaged, and, even if we feel we can't escape them, we have actually chosen not to try. Choosing to manage what's in our span of control is the first step toward self-management.

It takes a disciplined and systematic approach to develop our personal power. We also need a vision for our lives that focuses our self-management competencies on the pursuit of personal, lifelong goals and objectives. Discipline and self-management competencies, if exercised, engender freedom, but self-management implies *responsible* freedom, taking ownership of our lives, our work, and the consequences for our actions. It requires learning to adapt those competencies to the life we envision for ourselves.

SIX COMPETENCIES OF SELF-MANAGED PEOPLE

Everyone has *the capacity for becoming self-managed,* which involves six competencies that can be learned through training and practice: wholeness, self-confidence, self-awareness, drive, self-respect/self-esteem, and respect for others. Wholeness, the bility to see ourselves as whole persons, supports the other five behavior sets. On the other hand, insofar as we can't learn "wholeness," becoming whole depends on the strength of the other competencies.

Each of the six terms describes the outward signs or outcomes of large sets of skills related to how people take in, organize, and act upon information about themselves and about the world around them. One aspect of being whole, for example, calls for clearly seeing and managing the various processes and connections of our lives. Each of the descriptions we call traits, therefore, are end products of essential abilities to "become something." Contrarily, to "lose confidence" or to "lose self-esteem" means to lose, for some reason, the ability to take in, organize, and act upon information in the way we did previously. The words do signify traits, but they also signify the processes by which the traits manifest themselves.

Wholeness. The whole person (see the illustration entitled "Portrait of a Self-Managed Person") provides the background and support for managing ourselves—for integrating the experiences, thoughts, feelings, emotions, values, and actions that go into making us who we are. At the same time, the more competent we become at integrating those aspects of our lives, the more secure our wholeness becomes.

Wholeness also means pulling together two very different approaches to life in general and to problem solving or planning in particular, distinctions that are very important to a self-management workshop. Many exercises or activities require analytic, linear (left brain) thinking, useful for the step-by-step processes we use for organizing life and work. However, that kind of thinking takes place only within the bigger context of the vision for our whole lives; it manages the details within that context.

Many of those same exercises or activities require dealing with emotions, values, creativity, flashes of insight, and subjective decisions (right brain activities). A self-management goal consists of using both types of thinking to develop "whole brain" living in which we integrate both the linear, analytic side of our lives and the non-linear, subjective side.

Self-Confidence.   Developing a life vision, with long-term goals and objectives, engenders a sense of security, self-confidence, and belief in oneself. Self-confidence requires the ability to:

▶ Act on principle. This means establishing a set of values (a moral code) and living in accordance with them. It also means deciding what we want for ourselves and determining that it is right, that it gives meaning to our lives, and adds value to the lives of other people and to the world in which we live.

▶ Acquire knowledge and decide that our beliefs are accurate and that they are useful for ourselves and for other people.

▶ Develop abilities and translate what we know into what we do, being creative or innovative as well as skilled.

▶ Develop strong opinions and feel a passion or intensity about what we believe, want, or need.

▶ Accept disagreement and negative feedback without defensiveness or a need to explain ourselves; disagree with other people and give negative feedback; be influenced by other people when we see value in their points of view.

▶ Feel and express realistic optimism, having the patience and the insight to follow the lead of other people as well as having patience with events over which we have no control.

▶ Take responsibility and be accountable for getting results.

Self-Awareness.   Completing self-assessments honestly and completely raises our self-awareness. Accepting feedback from other people raises it to a higher level. Self-awareness is essential to self-management inasmuch as it prevents us from being smug and self-satisfied. Self-awareness comes from the ability to look into ourselves and to become self-critical, thoughtfully introspective, and to:

▶ Develop a knowledge of our limitations as well as our strengths, and to acknowledge those limitations.

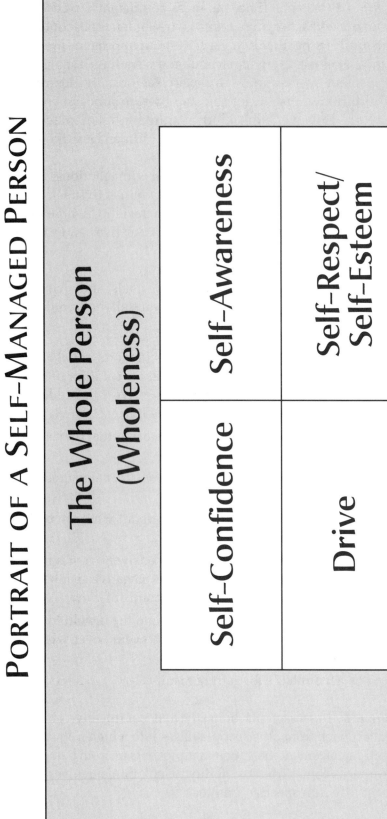

The Whole Person
(Wholeness)

Self-Awareness	Self-Confidence
Self-Respect/ Self-Esteem	Drive
Respect for Others	

- Be *un*satisfied with our present situation and its limitations (that is, be willing to move beyond where we are even if we're happy with it), and see things both as what they *are* and what they *could be.*

- Look for new directions in which to learn and grow, to seek out new and different ways for informing ourselves, for expressing ourselves, for doing what we do, and for perceiving and relating to the world around us.

- Become flexible and adaptable, forming new opinions and ways of doing things when circumstances demand them.

Drive. Drive is the passion to get to where we want to go (not to where life might take us) and to be focused on achieving our goals (to be motivated). Drive means that we:

- Develop the energy and stamina (through diet, exercise, and appropriate forms of rest) to do what we need to do, to be self-starting, and to be strong-willed or tenacious about the vision for our lives.

- Show enthusiasm for our lives and for what we're doing.

- Display vigor of thought as well as deed; develop "sticktoitiveness," staying the course when we believe it's right and on target.

- Develop the daring to take risks and to make the most of our independence and our need to seek out new opportunities for self-expression, for creative expression, and for innovation in both our work and our nonwork life activities.

- Take leadership roles when needed, influencing others to follow.

- Revitalize ourselves regularly throughout each day, renewing our own sources of energy through proper doses of rest, nutrition, exercise, and relaxation.

Self-Respect/Self-Esteem. Self-respect or self-esteem—we use the words interchangeably—allows us to care about both aspects of who we are—mind and body—provisioning both of them, strengthening them rather than depriving them, abusing them, or diminishing them. It requires that we:

- Recognize that we are as valuable as everyone else.

- Find the inner security we must have in order to give ourselves permission to need other people to help us fulfill our dreams as much as they need us.

Respect for Others. Respect is the magic bullet that makes cooperation possible. Developing the skills related to respect for others requires that we:

- Recognize the dignity of other people and avoid judging them.

- Care for and about people; accept them as they are.

- Recognize other people's knowledge, skills, creativity; be open to their ideas, thoughts, or feelings, and contributions to our lives.

- Recognize other people's needs and aspirations.

- ▶ Open ourselves up to other people—listening to them, accepting and acting upon their opinions or suggestions—and learn from and be influenced by them.
- ▶ Give people helpful, honest feedback and act as a positive role model for them.
- ▶ Cooperate and collaborate with other people.
- ▶ Be dependable and credible and contribute accurate information to other people.
- ▶ Communicate openly and honestly, which requires being available and accessible to others, and transferring information to them.
- ▶ Seek group consensus when appropriate, supporting group decisions and acting on them.
- ▶ Be *un*satisfied with the status quo for others as well as for ourselves; encourage them to find new and different ways for adding value to their lives and to the world around them.

TRAINING FOR SELF-MANAGEMENT

The word *training* suggests that an expert of some sort can teach someone how to do something. So, the question becomes, "Who is an expert when it comes to self-management?" To answer this question, we have to distinguish between learning how to be self-managed (form) and the uniqueness of what it means to be self-managed (substance).

As a facilitator you deal only in the process of becoming self-managed (form). You provide explanations as to how to do something and opportunities to do it. The substance of self-management comes from within the people developing their skills, and the substance of what gives one person control over his life may not give another person control over hers.

For example, engineers use analytic methods and linear thinking in most of what they do, whereas artists use expressive methods for doing what they do. Engineers might find expressive methods difficult to grasp or apply, and artists might find analytic methods and linear thinking too difficult. Those differences explain why hard and fast rules are difficult to come by.

Teaching Versus Learning

We really don't teach self-management skills. Rather, we help people *learn* them. Look at how a child learns to ride a two-wheel bicycle. The operative word here is *learn*.

A child learns to ride a bicycle by first riding with training wheels. Then you remove the training wheels and hold on to the back of the seat for a bit, but before the child can learn how to balance and control the bike, you must let go and let her struggle to stay upright. She will fall, get bruised and scraped, but she will learn how to ride the bike.

The child *learns* how to ride the bike; you don't teach him how to do it. Sure, you *help* him learn, which makes you a "learning helper." (Some people like the phrase *performance improvement coach*.) Helping someone to learn is different from the traditional notion of "teaching or training." Helping someone to learn is giving someone information he may or may not ever use or showing someone how to do something he may or may not ever do (or do as well as you can).

Fast forward to the adult-learning classroom. A precourse reading or computer-based training (CBT) or other assignment is the "training wheels." An in-class lecture or demonstration is "holding on for a bit." Exercises and skill practices are "letting go." By tailoring practices to situations, problems, or challenges from their own world ("real-time, as-needed" training), students learn to ride their "bikes" cross country and through rough terrain. Here students work to perfect the skills they need to improve their job performance; instead of role playing, they engage in skill practice. The difference between role playing and skill practice is the difference between making believe you're riding the bike and actually riding it.

As a *learning helper,* you present ideas about self-management to people. You provide them with opportunities to assess their knowledge and skills, and opportunities to apply the knowledge or practice the skills. You give them both positive and negative feedback or reinforcement. If that's teaching, then you teach in that sense, but it's up to the students to learn. Yet, teaching can go on without learning (and vice versa).

An old parable says give a starving person a fish, you feed him for just one day, but teach him how to fish and you feed him for a lifetime. However, self-management workshops assume that teaching the person how to fish does *not* feed him for a lifetime. Instead, it gives him just the *opportunity* to do so. Whether or not the person takes advantage of the opportunity is a matter of personal choice. Choosing from among personal goals and exercising self-management determines whether or not the person will ever use the knowledge and the skill he has for fishing.

No matter what (or if) the students learn, it's up to them to use or not to use their newly acquired knowledge or skills. And, in any organization, it's up to the students' managers to provide them with the opportunities, the challenges, and the reinforcement for applying their newly acquired knowledge or their skills. Otherwise, all the *teaching* you do will come to naught, and no learning will have really taken place.

The Learning Process

Textbooks describe three basic methods of learning: auditory (listening, hearing), visual (seeing, taking in), kinesthetic (feeling, handling). People learn through one of those modalities or through some combination of them. Some people enjoy listening to lectures and absorb much more from them than others. When I was a university professor, I conducted studies on self-directed learning and found that business majors learn more effectively this way; they prefer to learn from lectures tied directly to a reading or to crib notes.

Fine arts majors, on the other hand, are very visual. They have to see things or visualize processes to better understand; lectures without visual aids are for them tedious and boring. Still others need to immerse themselves in doing things; fine arts majors have that in common with math, engineering, and science majors. Liberal arts students, English majors especially, use all three methods—and prefer to work on their own (fully self-directed). A learning environment for teaching self-management skills should maximize all three learning modalities.

You can explain and show subject matter—the *stuff* of learning—but the students have to do things with the *stuff* they take in or they lose it. You can test for knowledge through written or oral exams. They can apply their knowledge through case studies (with written answers or by discussion with others) or they can use the knowledge to understand something else that they hear, see, or touch. They can make things, the way writers, painters, and engineers do. Or they can act on knowledge in interpersonal relations, as they do when they work at self-disclosure or take in feedback or deliver clear and accurate messages, and so on. The doing reinforces the learning and helps retain it for future reference.

Just as the child has to ride to become expert at bike riding, students of self-management have to apply the skills they learn by doing them in order to develop or grow. They can learn *about* self-management by reading about it, as they do if they read my book *Secrets of the Wild Goose,* or by listening to lectures. They can learn how to apply the knowledge they acquire by completing exercises. However, they aren't yet self-management experts. Their expertise comes from experience and practice. Expertise with self-management competencies and skills comes from using self-assessments and feedback from others to enhance or increase self-awareness and from practice that you can facilitate through experiential (or experienced-based) learning.

Self-Assessments

Your students are the only experts when it comes to their own self-management. You can talk about the skills, you can model them, but only the participants can integrate them into their own experience and make the skills work for them. That's expertise.

Self-assessments and feedback assessments help people identify what they think, feel, or do. A Myers-Briggs assessment, for example, examines how you take in information and process it (intuitively, perceptually, judgmentally, etc.); you then compare your responses to the assessment designers' definitions of those methods. Once you've identified how you acquire and process information, you can use that model to keep on doing the same things or for changing your personal methods.

How one person acquires or processes information may or may not be useful information to other people. For example, suppose I know that you're an intuitive person (right-brained) rather than a fact-gathering person (left-brained). That information may encourage me to let you process information in a way that makes you feel comfortable, but, on the other hand, if you require that I never expect you to gather facts before completing an assignment because you're "an intuitive person, not a fact gatherer," you miss the point of self-assessment. An assessment provides the insight that intuition helps you to learn. Knowing that you're intuitive may be interesting, but in many work-related situations intuition may not be an appropriate substitute for fact gathering (or, vice versa).

The self-management self-assessments in Chapter 2 will help your students understand how their behavior fits or doesn't fit with the definition of self-management. Two assumptions are necessary:

1. Your students must accept the definition of self-management and that it will work for them.
2. Your students must assume that the behavior traits and skills of self-management are valuable to them for getting control over their lives or work.

Now, your students can become experts about their own degree of self-management and to what extent they practice self-management skills.

You also can convert the self-assessments into feedback from other people by rewording the instructions and the items in a self-assessment, which I discuss in Chapter 2. Adapting self-assessments into other people's assessments of self-management skills could be useful, especially as 360-degree feedback, which includes the way many different people see the person being assessed. The extent to which their perceptions and the subject's perception agree, the more readily the subject can conclude that her perceptions of her self-management skills are reliable.

The assessments and adaptations for others' perceptions are learning tools, not personality profiles. They simply help people uncover information about their self-management skills. If the subjects like what the assessments say about them, they can take steps to perpetuate what they like about themselves. If they don't like what they read about their self-management skills, they can take steps to change. They now have substance on which to work and that they can transform into a greater degree of self-management.

EXPERIENTIAL LEARNING AND SELF-MANAGEMENT

Since self-management skills can't be learned from books or from a computer, self-management training, especially when interpersonal relations are involved, works best in a classroom- or group-based, facilitated (instructor-led) program. First, people can't learn much about themselves by merely looking in a mirror. Self-assessments are helpful, not definitive. What they see and what other people see usually deviates considerably. They need feedback from others about what they think or feel before they can get a complete image of themselves.

Second, since self-managed people live and work in a world with other people, they need to practice interpersonal relations skills. For a person to understand relationships and to learn how to manage themselves in those relationships, they have to experience them and practice what to do when they run into a variety of challenging situations. Just reading about them won't do. People have to manipulate the information and practice the instructions they receive to make self-management skills work for them.

Third, to have successful learning experiences, your students will need other people to explain *how they respond to what the students say or do and why they responded that way.* Feedback from peers as well as feedback from the classroom leader carry a great deal of weight.

In experience-based learning, the subject matter experts are the participants insofar as only they can tell you what they think or feel about anything that affects them, their thoughts or feelings (the substance of self-management). In an interactive exercise, students test their self-management skills, such as assertive communication. They also test your recommendations for what is effective or ineffective. Only by practicing and testing can a person become an expert.

All this reflects the aphorism attributed to Confucius: "Tell me, and I hear; show me, and I see; let me do, and I understand." Confucius understood that for us to learn *how* to do something, we must *do* it, which would make him the first advocate of experiential learning. Since managing ourselves, especially in our interpersonal relations, requires behavioral skills and are things we do for and to ourselves and for and with other people, self-management skills are best learned through experience in a group setting. Doing may involve some falling off the bike, some trial-and-error, some mistakes or misjudgments, some struggle, but all that experience reinforces the learning and helps us internalize what we're learning, especially when it comes to learning about our own emotions or feelings, which, along with knowledge, are the critical "stuff" of self-management.

THE EIAG MODEL

The Experience, Interpretation, Analysis, and Generalization (EIAG) Model (which implements the Confucian vision at several levels—cognitive, affective, and moral) describes the implicit structure of the exercises in a self-management workshop. This relatively old model consists of learning through a circular process of Experience, Interpretation, Analysis, and Generalization (see the accompanying illustration). The goal of this learning model is to help people fully understand how (and how well) they control their lives.

Experience and Description

Step one of any experiential learning model requires that the students learn by doing, which includes having an experience and *describing* that experience in the most objective terms possible. Looking at any experience is a recollection, and people can only remember and interpret the experience in terms of their values, feelings, emotions, and attitudes; therefore, it's important for students to separate the content, the bare experience, from their emotions, feelings, values, and attitudes. Bertrand Russell, the British philosopher and essayist, said that the most objective expression of an experience is no more than a report of sense data: For example, "Red, here, now." Getting close to that form of expression helps students look at the experience as it was rather than as the interpretation they apply to the experience.

For example, a student says, "The employee asked me to justify my decision." This reflects the *cognitive* aspect of the experience. In the words of Joe Friday, the TV detective of yesteryear, "Just the facts, Ma'am."

Interpretation

After describing the experience as objectively as they can, students look at what they think of and how they feel about what happened. In this second step of the model, it's important for students to surface their values, feelings, emotions, and attitudes, which define and color experience. The definitions and shadings often take on the form of biases, which, especially if kept below the surface, can interfere with people's ability to manage themselves and the relationships they have with others. The students ask: "What did I like about it?" "What didn't I like?" "What worked?" "What didn't work?"

When students interpret what happened, they, not other people or things, become the subject in the sentences of their reports. They describe themselves. Instead of saying, "She made me angry," they say, "I didn't like it when she asked me to justify my decision. I felt angry."

"I didn't like . . ." "I felt . . ." These words express the *affective* (emotional/feeling) aspect of the experience. The student's affect. "Taking ownership of the experience" means recognizing that their report of their experience refers only to how they see it.

Analysis

After a student describes what happened objectively and expresses his interpretation, he then analyzes the experience. "Here's the fact: She questioned my decision. Here's how I feel about that: I didn't like it when she asked me to justify my decision."

In this third step, students question why they responded as they did. The students analyze what happened. "I got angry because I thought that when she questioned my decisions, she questioned my authority. Why did I think that? Why don't I like having my decisions or my authority questioned? Why did she question my decision? Have people questioned my decisions or authority before? If so, how did I react and why?" Answers to those questions lead to a better understanding of the situation. Answers to those questions when they're discussed with a trusted group, including, in our case, the employee who questioned the student's decision, leads to fuller understanding of how (and how well) he or she controls his or her life. That is, of course, the goal of this learning model.

Generalization

The answers to analytic questions help the students to look forward and to talk about what they plan to do in the future: a desired *behavior*. The fictitious student

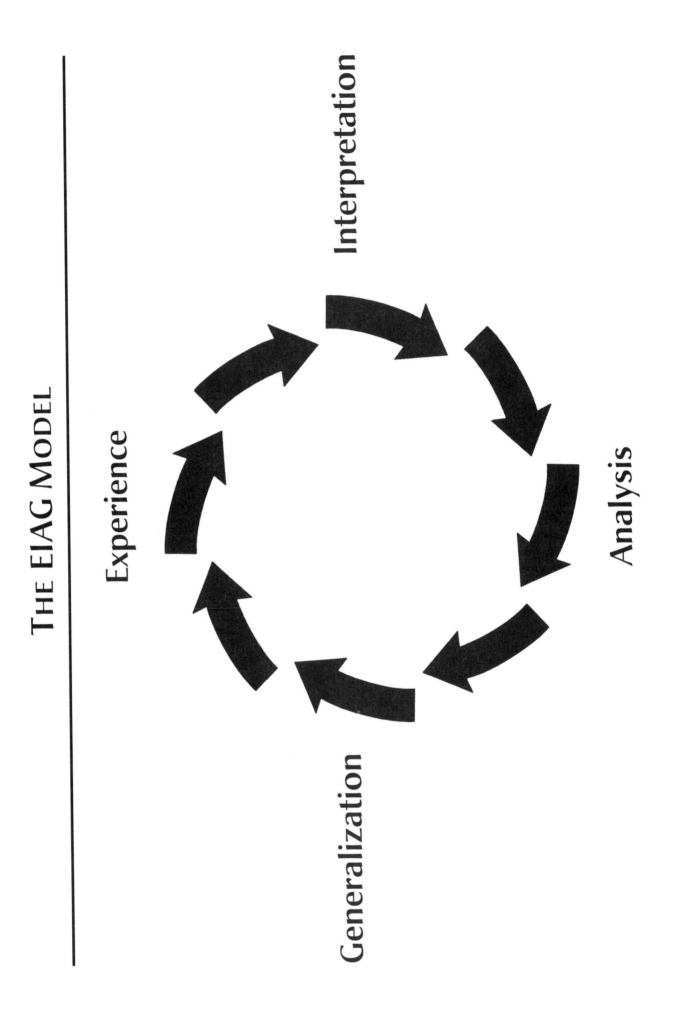

THE EIAG MODEL

Interpretation

Analysis

Generalization

Experience

might say, "Knowing what I now know about myself, knowing how and why I react the way I do when someone questions my decisions or authority, what can I do to change those ineffective reactions or to repeat those that are useful or productive? What would I do differently and what could I expect from the change?" Follow-up activities, with clearly identified goals and steps for accomplishing them, provide a method for applying what the students learn from the experience.

Demands of the EIAG Model on the Instructor

Some instructors find this model difficult to apply. They've been trained to tell and to show, rather than to lead or to facilitate. EIAG methods demand:

▶ *Patience.* You have to let the students learn from their experiences, just as you let a child learn how to ride a bike by letting him or her ride it. When well-intentioned teachers explain everything they know, they jump in before the students can learn from what they do, even if what they do is wrong.

▶ *Restraint—especially restraint from teaching too much.* Not jumping in takes an effort on the facilitator's part. You can't tell someone else what they have learned, although you can ask the right questions that help the students explain themselves.

▶ *Support for learning from mistakes.* Children learning to ride a bike fall. Adult learners have to "fall" also. They won't do everything right, and they'll find that out by getting feedback from their classmates. Whatever corrective action they take must come from "falling."

▶ *Permission for the students to offer information, feedback, and suggestions to one another.* You, the facilitator, are not the only observer in the class. The other observers, adults, have experience, knowledge, and skills they can call on to help other people learn. That makes learning a cooperative or collaborative endeavor rather than a command and control exercise.

Demands of the EIAG Model on Students

Most students aren't ready for this method. It makes extraordinary demands on them. First, they're accustomed through years of classroom experience to being *taught.* They've been trained to be teacher-dependent, passive learners. Seeing and hearing have been enough for them, whether or not they really learn or understand anything. EIAG methods demand the willingness and dedication to:

▶ Prepare for class.

▶ Participate in class activities, exercises, and discussions.

▶ Take risks in a safe environment.

▶ Actively learn rather than passively take in information.

▶ Follow up and take back to the job what they have learned in the classroom.

Second, and most important, they must learn to trust you and their classmates before they can "bare their souls" (if the learning comes to that). People are not accustomed to and are often afraid of opening up to strangers, even if they work with those *strangers* every day. They fear revealing their weaknesses and flaws to themselves; it can reduce self-confidence and self-respect/self-esteem if not immediately followed up with help for improvement. They fear revealing their weaknesses and flaws to other people; they fear that the others might use that information against them. Since experiential learning and the EIAG Model assume that growth occurs when people move from fear and distrust to increasing trust, it's essential to create a safe environment.

A guiding principle of group learning involves a systems approach that we can apply to all formal and informal social systems: The TORI Theory.[1] The letters are an acronym for *trust, openness, realization,* and *interdependence.* Trust tears down and drains defenses of their power. Some of the more obvious defenses are:

▶ *Depersonalization.* Some people find it difficult to talk about themselves or to take ownership of their experiences. It's easier for them to talk about "you," "them," and "they" rather than about "I" and "me." They will often attack the exercise when their own shortcomings or errors are disclosed. The favorite attack: "It's only an exercise; it's not real. Things like that never happen in reality." You, the facilitator, have to keep them focused on themselves.

▶ *Acting on the basis of role prescriptions rather than on principle.* Everyone grows up with scripts provided by parents and other authority figures—what to do and how to do it in given situations. For example, not giving constructive feedback, especially if it's negative, is often excused as politeness. As in the Disney movie *Bambi,* we've been taught "If you ain't got nothin' nice to say, don't say nothin' at all." However, in self-management workshops, that's not much help to the people who need it. You need to encourage self-disclosure and honest, direct, and helpful feedback.

▶ *Hiding behind facades.* A common response to negative feedback is "I was only playing a role. That's not the real me." If the exercise is properly constructed, the person being observed is being himself or herself, and what people see is what he or she really is. You have to encourage people to see exercises as opportunities to learn and to grow and that feedback is *a gift* to be accepted at face value.

▶ *Operating out of hidden agendas or covert strategies.* People in intact groups (e.g., a department or a team) bring into the workshop axes to grind or bones to pick. It's a common occurrence for a team leader to come into the workshop with the intent that *you* will "fix what's wrong with everyone else." You as leader have to hide your true feelings and avoid being put *in the barrel.* Sometimes it's difficult to do, but you have to surface these agendas or strategies when they

[1] J. R. Gibb, "Defensive Communication," *The Journal of Communication* 11, no. 3 (1961), 141–148; see also "TORI Theory and Practice," in *The 1972 Annual Handbook for Group Facilitators,* ed. J. William Pfeiffer and John E. Jones (La Jolla, Calif.: University Associates, 1972), 157–162.

begin to become noticeable (as when people see that the person hiding an agenda is not fully participating).

▶ *Following the rules.* Some people prevent their own growth by hiding behind organizational rules or expectations. Instead of stepping outside of their organizational roles (e.g., team leader), they use them as excuses. People will often say, "I can't change because company policy says . . ." You have to help these students see that company policy isn't an issue where self-management is concerned. They need only give themselves permission to change.

▶ *Doing only what you're told or being persuaded to do something other than you would on your own.* "You made me love you" makes for good song lyrics, but nobody makes you do anything. Even if they put a gun to your head, you choose to do as they say rather than be shot to death. Nevertheless, students often appeal to "*they* made me do it" when they're confronted with negative feedback about their own behavior. You have to help them understand how they themselves are making their own choices.

▶ *Either the need to control or the need to be dependent.* This may be last, but it's among the most common of defenses, especially where managers and their employees or team leaders and their teams are in the same workshop. Managers and team leaders often dominate discussions and give the *right* answers. Anyone predisposed to controlling might do the same. When several control freaks are in the same discussion group, conflicts will inevitably arise. You can use those moments to explore what happened, what the students felt about what happened, why they felt that way, and what they can do about it in the future, that is, apply the EIAG Model.

A large number of people have dependency needs to meet. Employees and team members, often from acculturation, turn to their managers or team leaders for instructions or for the right answers. You need to be aware of when this happens, and, again, explore the situation by applying the EIAG Model.

When you apply the TORI Theory to learning self-management skills, you help your students replace those defenses with:

▶ *Personal, self-determining actions based on principle.* Use positive reinforcement to encourage students to say or do what they themselves believe is right and to take responsibility for what they say or do,

▶ *Greater spontaneity and nonrole behavior.* Use exercises or practices and positive reinforcement to encourage students to react to the moment and from their minds and feelings. The great stage and screen performers are wonderful listeners who *react* rather than act.

▶ *Openness, transparency, and candor.* Encourage through modeling and positive reinforcement what you want from the students. If you hide behind rules, facades, or orders from above, they will too.

▶ *Assertive, self-actualizing behavior.* You have to encourage through modeling, exercises, practices, and positive reinforcement the reality of wholeness—that everyone is entitled to fulfilling his or her own needs and dreams.

▶ *Mutually satisfying interdependence.* You have to encourage through modeling, exercises, practices, and positive reinforcement that self-managed people are social beings who enjoy their relationships with other people. The 1998 baseball sluggers, Sammy Sosa and Mark McGwire, demonstrated, by supporting and cheering each other on, the power of mutual, satisfying, interdependence—in spite of the fact they were *competitors* for the *same trophy*.

In sum, your goal is to encourage students to do on their own what is necessary to develop the behaviors they want. Behavior changes in self-management workshops result from displaying personal feelings, acting on an impulse, or from making a choice. Role playing and skill practices can help your students make the leap from defensive protections to self-management.

Two Experiential Learning Tools

Role Playing

When working with self-management skills and interpersonal relationships, role playing simulates experiences that allow people to try out behaviors to see how they and other people feel about them. As facilitator, you create the entire scenario and have the students act out the roles that fulfill the scenario. The experience has value only if the students examine the activity immediately after the role play. They have to talk about their experiences, process them by talking about and analyzing their reactions or their responses, and generalize as to how to act in future, similar situations.

Many people detest role playing, and I don't blame them. The very name explains the weakness of the method: playing at a role, play acting. In a role play, you explain to the students involved what to do and how to do it in a simulated situation. Then you ask them to act as if they are really in that situation. In some situations—for example, in a simulation or a game in which the students learn such skills as problem solving, decision making, how to run a department, and other technical skills—pretending works well for adults. However, in intensely personal activities, "let's pretend" doesn't work too well; adults need a little more reality than that. One way to take the *pretending* out of role playing is to use what I call Copying a Model.

Copying a Model is a *skill practice* and differs from pure role playing in that the facilitator doesn't tell the student what to say or do. Instead, you have a skill practice after a lecture or discussion of a specific desirable behavior or a reaction to a situation. The students learn about the skill, and if you have a way of demonstrating it (e.g., on a videotape), they see how it is used in a simulated situation (a positive model). Positive modeling can be contrasted by a negative model, but care must be taken not to let the negative one have a large affect on the learning and overwhelm the lesson (as many fun-filled training films do). The rest of the learning process is as real as acquiring any motor skill, for example, assembling an automobile generator.

You create a situation that could happen anywhere at any time. You can also give people roles to play, but not when they are practicing the skill. As the students practice, they are themselves, not a character in a play, and decide how to respond to the situation. They then try to duplicate or mimic what the positive model did or said. This is not playing at a role; rather, it's learning how to apply a skill to a real situation.

Interpretation and analysis then follow the experiential learning to explore how the person practicing felt about the new learned behavior and what made it effective (assuming, of course, that it was). The person practicing also gets feedback from the group as to how well he copied the model and how everyone responded to it.

Being Myself

In this form of skill practice, you don't tell the person practicing the skill how to behave. You don't even demonstrate or model desired behaviors. Rather, you create a situation and ask the student to decide how to respond and to act accordingly. You give other people roles to play, but not the person practicing. You want him to be himself at all times.

Self-discovery learning comes into play most dramatically in Being Myself. Here a person is placed in a situation to which she responds as she ordinarily would. The discussion then explores the person's reactions and self-management skills. As in all such activities, interpretation, feedback, and analysis then follows the experiential learning. The group then explores how everyone reacts to what the person practicing said or did. They discuss what seemed to be effective and what seemed to be less effective. That kind of feedback gives the person practicing an opportunity to build on her own strengths. More importantly, when she gets feedback, she also gets suggestions as to how make her actions more effective (i.e., achieve mutually satisfying experiences with other people). She then has gathered enough information about her behavior to make decisions as to how to act in the future.

That outcome is the goal of all activities and exercises designed with the EIAG Model in mind—to force students to examine their own problems or challenges and to look for answers. Students come together in group activities and ask each other for answers. They dig around in their own minds and feelings for the substance of self-management. All this *before* you answer their questions. Then, your answers should be concise, precise, and accurate. By not dominating the skill practices, you don't divert the students away from peer or team learning.

The material presented in Managing Under Pressure[2] is an example of a "Being Myself" skill practice. In it, the participants confront a contrived situation from their own perspective and with whatever self-management skills they have. The results include learning how they communicate with others, how they manage their body language, and how they help or support other people.

Exercises or practices provide the experience. The feedback the students get from one another as well as from you enhances their descriptions of the experience, their interpretations, and their analyses. The objective of this style of learning is for the students to internalize what they do and the feedback they get. Learning is faster and longer-lasting this way.

---

[2]Adapted from a skill practice used in Citicorp's "Managing People" workshop, which I used when I was a Program Manager for the Citicorp Executive Development Center.

Managing Under Pressure:
Sample "Being Myself" Skill Practice

INSTRUCTOR'S NOTES

This sample consists of a boilerplate design that you can use for developing an exercise appropriate to your own environment. The specifics of the scenario and the roles people play are entirely up to you.

I recommend that you work with teams of five to seven people in breakout rooms, each team in a pair of adjoining rooms.

1. The *practice room*, the participants' office. This room should be furnished with a small table (round or square) and a chair for each member of the team. Recording and playback equipment should be set up in this room. This room is where the skill practice actually takes place, with one person at a time acting as himself or herself in the situation described in the scenario you design. This is also the room in which the group will process (debrief) the experience. In a hotel setting, if two-room suites are not available, the hotel meeting manager usually will agree to move out sleeping-room furniture for this purpose.

2. The *holding room*. Team members use this room when not practicing at the moment to discuss what they individually will do to create pressure on the person practicing. Furniture is a matter of choice. In a hotel setting, the sleeping room furniture can stay in place.

Intact Team

If you're working with an intact team, don't bring real life issues into the classroom and get wrapped up in them until after the students have had a chance to examine the way they themselves behave. Simulate a pressure situation first so students can see their own responses to stress and get feedback from others about how their behavior affected them. The object is for them to plan better ways of dealing with those issues back on the job.

Facilitated Teams

If you have the trained personnel available, assign one person to facilitate the activities for each team. That person operates the equipment during the practice and promotes (not dominates) discussion. She can give feedback, but only if she thinks no one else can or will give the feedback she can offer. The team selects a timekeeper to manage the fair and equitable discussion of each person's practice, in whatever manner you design it, and a scribe to record the team's conclusions and to report those conclusions to the whole class.

Self-Managed Teams

Most adult groups manage any activity you design very well without intervention. However, you should float around the breakout rooms regularly to ensure that the participants are doing the exercise the way you designed it. The downside: Participants sometimes come away feeling they didn't get *professional* help.

I also recommend videotaping each practice and playing it back to debrief that person's practice. That way, each person sees what he or she did as well as hears about it from other people. Often, the person calls out the feedback others would have given him or her as he sees it for himself or herself. "Oh, Lord. Look how I'm waving my hand. It's obvious why you said I was dismissive when we talked." Be sure to instruct the teams on how to use the video equipment (if it is used).

Self-Assessment Instruments

You could use a self-assessment instrument (e.g., 360-degree feedback or a Myers-Briggs or a DISC instrument) in conjunction with the exercise, but it's not required. Three-hundred-and-sixty-degree feedback correlated to behavior under pressure should be discussed prior to the exercise. On the other hand, use a Myers-Briggs or DISC instrument *after* the exercise to prevent interfering with self-discovery learning. People tend to use labels such as, "You're a [something]," instead of focusing on what the person actually says or does.

Learning Objective and Outcomes

One essential skill of self-management is self-awareness, and by the end of this exercise participants will be able to apply their experience and feedback to:

▶ How they communicate with others, especially how they listen

▶ How they manage body language and how their mannerisms affect other people

▶ How they help others improve their ability to evaluate their own values, attitudes, and behaviors, and how they affect other people

Requirements

Time:	Five to six hours, depending on the size of the groups
Materials:	Copies of the scenario you design Giving and Getting Feedback handout
Equipment:	Video recorders and playback equipment (where feasible) Audio recorders (if video is not feasible)
Preparation:	Write scenario and roles to play Copy materials
Room Setup:	Breakout rooms for each team of five to seven participants. For each team, use two adjoining rooms, if possible, preferably with a door between them.

Scenario

You need to create situations and roles for each of the team members to play when they're not practicing. Suggest real-world activities that reflect but don't resemble too closely anything in the students' immediate workplace. The roles should create pressure and produce a fun experience at the same time.

For example, the person practicing a manager has to leave the office in ten minutes in order to catch a plane, and he is already behind schedule. All the other participants need to talk to this person (the manager) about their own issues, which are as important to them as leaving is to the manager. He has to deal with each one of them in that ten minutes.

Here is the structure of the activity.

1. Each person gets up to and no more than twelve minutes "in the box." Since it's her office, she decides what happens and when.

(continues)

2. After all the members of the team complete their practices, everyone on the team gathers in the practice room to watch the tapes and give one another feedback about what happened during the practice.

3. In a self-managed team, with no outside facilitator, one person is assigned to be the timekeeper, another person is assigned to be the equipment operator.

4. Each person has up to twenty minutes to get feedback; therefore, it will not be possible to watch any one person's entire practice on the videotape, just highlights.

After everyone has had an opportunity to be the manager, you debrief the activity as a group. The power of this exercise comes from talking about the experience, describing *what* participants experienced, explaining how they felt about it and why they felt that way, and giving constructive suggestions to one another for how to handle a similar situation in the future. You enhance that power when you videotape the activity because the video gives participants the opportunity to see themselves in action. Coupled with feedback from the rest of the group, viewing a playback punches home the reality of other people's perceptions. But the debriefing process doesn't work unless everyone follows the ground rules and talks about their own experiences during the exercise.

Feedback Guidelines

Use the handout, Giving and Getting Feedback, as your guide for how to discuss each person's practice session.

Instructions to Participants

In classroom training, we can't bring everyday pressures to bear on you. So we will create pressure; perhaps more in a shorter period of time than you would experience on the job. That's okay because we are looking for how you respond to pressure. That's the objective of the exercise; not to mimic your workplace.

Each of you will have an opportunity to practice being yourself as a manager in the situation. You will get only an overview of the situation. Your job is to respond to and manage whatever happens as it happens.

Each of you is also assigned a role to play when you're *not* the manager that explains why you want to see the manager. That script, which you will keep secret from the others, forms the basis for what you do in the situation. For example, you may be told that you are an administrative assistant that worked late the night before to prepare a report for the manager to use this morning in a meeting with his boss. Now you want the afternoon off. However, you won't stop there.

You will have extra instructions for being creative and demanding or challenging when you're not being yourself as the manager. You will also keep these instructions secret. You should use your imaginations to create as much pressure as possible in the shortest period of time. You may make your situation as obvious or as obscure as you wish, especially if presenting a serious personal problem. It's important to the exercise that each person thinks that her problem or issue is important enough to receive the manager's attention now, especially anyone who may have information that affects the manager's meeting with the boss.

Even though the situation is contrived and seems unreal to you, if the *pressure* is real, the person practicing will react as he ordinarily would act when stressed this way. The more pressure you create, no matter how unreal, the better. The object is for you to study your personal reactions to pressure. From this you see what works for you, what works for others, and what you might carry back with you to the job. You will also see or get feedback about behaviors you will want to change because they are ineffective.

GIVING AND GETTING FEEDBACK

FEEDBACK

The function of feedback is to close the gap between what you intended by what you did and what the other person experienced or interpreted you to mean. That gap exists for the obvious reason that no two people experience something in exactly the same way. Self-management includes the ability to communicate, to demonstrate your respect for the other person, and to create a collaborative environment; giving and getting feedback provides a vehicle for increasing those skills.

Many people confuse feedback with what they call "constructive criticism." However, the phrase constructive criticism is an oxymoron, since the word *constructive* means to build and the word *criticism* means to tear down. Giving feedback, on the other hand, whether positive or negative, provides information about how you see a situation and what the other person did or said in that situation. Effective feedback therefore follows this pattern [which follows the structure of the EIAG Model]: what I experienced, how I interpreted that experience, why I felt that way or thought that, and what I suggest you might do that would be more effective in the future or that you might do more often.

Ground Rules for Giving Feedback

Giving feedback enhances your own self-management skills, helping you express yourself in clear, direct, and objective language. It also helps you develop assertiveness (not aggressiveness). Since feedback is effective only if it reflects your experience of what someone else did, the following rules keep processing an activity on track and focused on what it should do: explain how what someone did or said affected you. Only then can feedback be effective as a method for helping someone improve his self-management skills.

1. Focus on what the other person did or said, not on what she is (focus on her behavior, not on her personality or character traits). Contrast these two statements. "You're the most aggravating person I've ever met." "I get angry almost every time we discuss something because regardless of what I say, you say 'Yes, but . . .'" The latter approach not only focuses on behaviors, it also prevents name-calling and gives the other person objective information to use to *reform* her behavior; she can more readily adjust saying "yes, but" than she can adjust "being aggravating."

2. Focus on your own responses, reactions, or feelings. Contrast these two sentences. "You made me angry." "I became angry when you said . . ." The other person may not realize what he said or did, but more importantly he can't know how you feel about it unless you tell him. After a discussion, you might also realize that your reaction was *your* problem. The other person may have done or said something appropriate under the circumstances, and *you reacted hostilely.*

3. Talk about effects, not about intentions. You don't know what another person intended; you know only what you think or feel about something (the effect). Consider this contrast. "I know you didn't intend to hurt my feelings, but . . ." "I don't know if you realized how I felt, but I felt hurt when you said . . ." Even asking the other person to explain his intention misses the point; if his behavior didn't reflect his intent, the objective of the feedback is to help him recognize that fact.

4. Be honest (candid) and direct, but respect the other person's feelings, since, although you don't want to discuss intentions, she may not have intended what you experienced or thought and may not have realized she did anything to disturb you. Another contrast. "You really hurt my feelings." "I don't know if you realized how I felt, but I felt hurt when you said . . ." This feedback also gives the person information to work with; regardless of what she intended, her actions didn't match her intent.

(continues)

5. Give credit where credit is due by explaining what you thought the other person did or said that was effective in the situation. "I felt really pleased when you complimented me on catching the error in that report." It's much easier for a person to accept negative feedback if she also receives positive feedback during the discussion. No, this isn't Mary Poppins's "spoon full of sugar"; rather, it's a way of recognizing a reality: that no one does everything all wrong and shouldn't be made to feel that way.

6. When talking about what you thought wasn't effective or wasn't as effective as it could be, offer a suggestion as to what the other person could do differently or encourage the other person to enter into a dialogue with you to come up with a more effective way of responding. "I became angry when you criticized my work in front of other people because it made me feel like a child. While I agree that I should have caught that error, I'd like to talk about how we can handle a situation like this in the future."

Ground Rules for Taking Feedback

Self-management skills also depend on your ability to accept graciously both negative and positive feedback. The objective of a skill practice is to improve your skills: skills in matching your actions with your intentions, skills in communicating more effectively, skills in closing the gap between what you mean and what others perceive.

1. Listen. Don't just hear the sounds of words; understand what they mean. Clear your mind of other thoughts, and don't mull over your response to what you hear.

2. Ask for clarification. "I don't understand what you're saying. Please explain it."

3. Don't be defensive; what the other person says is designed to help, not hurt. It's hard to say thank you when someone gives you feedback you don't like, but you should say it anyway. Let the other person know that you are really listening.

4. Don't argue. You may not have intended to make someone angry or hurt his feelings, but so what? He was angry or hurt anyway. Instead say, "I didn't intend to make you angry, and I regret that I did. What did I do or say and what do you think I could do to prevent this from happening in the future?"

5. Take in what people tell you as information to use or not. It's not a demand for you to change. It's up to you to decide whether or not you need to reform your behavior. What's ineffective to one person may not be ineffective to anyone else; on the other hand, if there is general agreement in the group that something you said or did didn't work for them, that's a good sign you should seriously consider making the change. Even if there is not general agreement, if you agree with the one person who felt put off that you might do something more effectively, do it.

6. Don't retaliate. When the people who give you negative feedback take their turns to get feedback, resist the temptation to get back at them. The purpose of the exercise is for them to give you helpful feedback; it's now your turn to give them helpful feedback also.

Think of feedback as a gift, one that very few people are willing to give.

2

Assessing Self–Management Skills

Self-management involves six competencies: wholeness, self-awareness, self-confidence, self-respect/self-esteem, drive, and respect for others. The skills associated with these competencies give people the ability to control events that fulfill a self-determined, personal vision. In popular jargon, *self-managed people empower themselves to actualize their potential.*

That type of personal power requires (1) the conscious effort to control how we respond to the experiences that flow into and through our lives, and (2) the ability and the will *to act on* the decisions we make. Since the modern workplace calls upon managers to empower employees, it's essential that both the managers and the employees reporting to them have self-management skills. However, too often people only *assume* that they have the skills they need and are overwhelmed by the responsibilities and authority they get.

Each self-management competency describes the outward behaviors or traits of a large set of skills related to how we take in, organize or process, and act upon information about ourselves and about the world around us. Wholeness, for example, calls for clearly seeing and managing the various processes and connections of our lives. As a trait, it's the end product of essential abilities to "becoming something." The competencies of self-confidence and self-esteem involve the ability to process and accept our own beliefs and actions as *true, good,* or *right.* The expressions "lose self-confidence" or "lose self-esteem" mean to lose, for some reason, the sense that the information we take in, organize, or process, and the actions we take are true, good, or right. So while the words used to identify self-management competencies signify traits, they also signify the processes by which the traits manifest themselves.

One way for people to determine how well they exhibit those traits or competencies is for them to complete the set of self-assessments in this chapter and compare their results with the interpretations. The first self-assessment examines a person's readiness to develop self-management skills.[1] After that, the assessments help a person identify the degree to which he or she may already exercise those skills.

ADMINISTERING SELF-ASSESSMENTS

Preclass Assignments.   Whenever possible, you should make a preclass assignment that the students complete the self-assessment instruments that fit with your workshop, the choice of which depends on the scope of the workshop. If you intend to cover all the skills, distribute all the instruments; if you are covering the skills of only one competency, for example, self-confidence, distribute only the one that relates to that workshop topic. Have the students bring the completed instruments to class, where you discuss the results as early in the session as possible. Preclass assignments save a great deal of time and prevent the class from becoming bogged down in pencil and paper exercises.

You can attach the scoring and interpretative materials to the assessments, or you can withhold the interpretations until you discuss them in class. The advantage in the first method is that students come to class prepared to discuss the issues the assessments raise for them. The disadvantage is that you provide too much information to the students about skills on which they won't work until late in the workshop. The advantage of the second method is that you can control the flow of discussions until you are ready to raise the specific issues of any one assessment. The disadvantage is that students come to class feeling at a loss as to where they are in the process of developing self-management skills. Attaching the interpretations of "Are You Ready for Self-Management?" when you distribute the assessments as preclass materials can help you overcome either disadvantage, since it helps people see where they stand as to their own level of self-management.

In-Class Activity.   If precourse assignments aren't possible, you can administer the assessments in class. Although they take up time with pencil and paper activities (thereby slowing down and interrupting the flow of interaction), the assessments aren't long, and I recommend distributing only one assessment at a time.

If you're covering more than one competency in the workshop, you can distribute the self-assessment for each competency at the appropriate time in the workshop

---

[1] Originally published in Donald H. Weiss, *Secrets of the Wild Goose: The Self-Management Way for Increasing Your Personal Power and Inspiring Productive Teamwork* (New York: AMACOM, 1998).

and discuss the results immediately. If you are dealing with only one competency, distribute only that self-assessment at the beginning of the session and discuss the results immediately.

You should complete the instruments yourself before using them. That puts you on an equal footing with the students, and you will better understand their reactions to certain items and the results of comparing their results to the interpretations.

Instructing Participants. It is very important to explain three caveats when asking students to complete the self-assessments.

1. These instruments were designed for the sole purpose of indicating to the participants completing the self-assessments what self-management skills they already have or which skills they may want to improve.

2. No one but the person completing the instrument will ever see the results, unless he personally decides to disclose them. He should therefore be honest with himself and comfortable with his answers, even if they don't match the interpretations that follow each self-assessment.

3. People often feel conflicted about their lives, themselves, and their goals. Indeed, a person's self-management skills can be influenced by transitory situations. Illness or a personal or professional setback can disturb a person's equilibrium and affect her responses. When discussing the results with the class, point out that their scores aren't written in concrete, that their scores might be different under different circumstances and that low scores will probably be raised by the training. They should look at their answers to individual items in any and all of the assessments to recognize their strengths as well as the areas in need of improvement. If completing more than one assessment, they should also look at the total package of answers to get a more complete image of themselves.

Scoring the Self-Management Person. When you assign *all* the assessments (or distribute them all in class), you can use the Assessment Scoring Guide on page 54, as a way to pull together all the insights the students have gained from their individual assessments.

Interpreting Assessments

If a person responds positively to most of the assessment items, her self-management skills are relatively secure. If she responds negatively or with serious doubt to most of the items, she should consider methods included in this book to improve those skills. Only if people kid themselves will they score perfectly on the instruments.

Perfect or high scores aren't free passes out of class. Self-perceptions are baseline data; the scores only tell people how *they see themselves;* other people may see them differently, and they need to know and compare the two different perceptions. People with high scores need to practice the skills assessed by the instruments in order to *consciously* see themselves in a social setting. They may then see that they don't have the skills they think they do.

People with abysmal scores don't get a free pass out of the class, either, especially if they score low on self-confidence or self-respect/self-esteem. They need the class for several reasons. First, they have the opportunity to see themselves in a different light as well as the opportunity to learn new skills. Redoing the assessments on which they scored low reveals a new and different set of perceptions. Second, they have an opportunity to watch other people, whose skills are better than theirs and to use those people as *role models.* Third, they are given opportunities to develop follow-up plans for working on those skills. In short, whether scores are high or low, anyone registered for the course should stay in it.

One-to-One Discussions

Design your workshop to allow time for one-to-one discussions with people who score low on any of the assessments. In this discussion, you should:

1. Review the scores.
2. Look at specific items with negative or low-score responses.
3. Discuss factors the person thinks could have contributed to the low scores.
4. Discuss personal goals for the workshop.
5. Discuss personal goals for following up on the workshop (back home planning).

Don't try to play psychologist (unless you are a professional therapist). It's better for the student that you ask the right questions and listen well. Asking "What do you think is responsible for this score?" produces a much more effective and personally useful answer than saying "You scored this low because you're experiencing difficulties on the job." In fact, most professional therapists would ask the question rather than offer the answer.

Handling Disagreement With Score Interpretations

When facilitators argue with students, they lose even if they win the argument. Probing offers the best approach to disagreement.

► With what do you disagree?
► What leads you to think the book's interpretation is wrong or off target?
► How do you interpret the scores?
► In your opinion, how is your interpretation more effective than the book's?

Once you get the answers you need, without agreeing with the student's opinion, comment, "That's an interesting way of looking at it." Then redirect. For example, ask "What do the rest of you think of the book's interpretation and what [the student] said?" You can then summarize the results of the discussion with remarks such as "These are all interesting interpretations. Whichever viewpoint you adopt, make sure that it leads you to making improvements in your self-management skills."

SELF-ASSESSMENT:
ARE YOU READY FOR SELF-MANAGEMENT?

INSTRUCTIONS

To respond to these 25 items, mark the space provided with a Yes or No. No also means "not often," "sometimes," or "maybe." If you cannot respond Yes to any one item of a multiple-part question, the answer must be No. Be honest with yourself. No one will see this self-assessment but you.

READINESS FOR SELF-MANAGEMENT

_____ I recognize both my strengths and my limitations.

_____ I communicate and interact well with other people.

_____ I know what I want for myself both in the short term (daily, weekly, etc.) and in the long term (for my life).

_____ I am a good listener, hearing what other people feel as well as what they believe.

_____ I am flexible and competent in coping with change.

_____ I feel in control of myself in all situations.

_____ I feel strongly (even passionately) about what I believe and want for myself.

_____ I feel comfortable when under pressure, prioritizing tasks and completing them.

_____ I am proactive rather than reactive (initiating activities rather than waiting to be told or waiting for things to happen to me).

_____ I am able to get myself going at the beginning of my day and to revitalize myself periodically during the day.

_____ I keep people issues and task issues in proportion to their importance under the circumstances.

_____ I usually solve my own work-related and personal problems effectively.

_____ I motivate myself and do not rely on others to motivate me.

_____ I help other people stay motivated.

_____ I am aware of how I come across to other people.

_____ I have a high regard for other people, that is, I care about how they think and feel.

_____ I recognize that I am as dependent on other people for information, support, and direction as other people are on me.

_____ I encourage people to disagree with me in a constructive dialogue designed to solve problems.

_____ I understand the overall goals and functions of the organization and feel a sense of ownership (commitment) to them.

_____ I feel a sense of obligation to the organization and to the people with whom I associate.

_____ I communicate openly and candidly with people.

_____ I strive to be dependable and knowledgeable.

_____ I am willing to work toward a consensus when resolving disagreements or solving problems.

_____ I can follow the leadership of other people and of the group without feeling that I'm giving up my individuality.

_____ I feel a responsibility to the organization to be an agent for change or renewal.

_____ **Total Score** (the sum of the Yes answers)

INTERPRETATION GUIDE FOR SELF-ASSESSMENT: ARE YOU READY FOR SELF-MANAGEMENT?

This instrument identifies the behaviors or characteristics we expect to find in self-managed people. The higher your score, the greater likelihood that you are prepared to assume responsibilities of self-management. In the workshop, you can use this information as a baseline for evaluating your self-perceptions in relation to the feedback you get from other people. That evaluation will do one of two things: (1) reinforce your perceptions of your self-management readiness, or (2) point out areas in which other people see you differently than you see yourself. Either way, the workshop will give you opportunities to practice the skills you have as well as improve on the skills you need.

25   If you responded Yes to all 25 items, you're either *super* self-managed or you weren't honest with yourself. If your self-perceptions are indeed accurate, you can practice self-managed skills and model them for the people in your training group. On the other hand, feedback from other people could help you see areas in which you need improvement that you didn't recognize exist.

20–24   You're ready to take on the responsibilities of self-management, but in the workshop, work on those items to which you responded No. use this information for setting objectives to improve on your level of self-management.

15–19   You have some work to do before you're completely ready for self-management. Use this information for setting objectives to improve on your level of self-management.

11–14   You need considerable help (training or coaching) before you can become self-managed. It would probably serve you well to have a one-to-one discussion with your facilitator or other counselor to talk about objectives to improve on your level of self-management. Then, during the exercises in the workshop, focus on activities that will help you meet those objectives.

0–10   All is not lost or hopeless, but we recommend you don't join or let yourself be placed on a self-managed team. You need a lot of help before taking on the responsibilities required. The workshop will help, and you should make an appointment for a discussion of your results with the facilitator or some other counselor.

SELF-ASSESSMENT: WHOLENESS

INSTRUCTIONS

Answer each item with either Yes or No. If you're not sure (feel kind of "fuzzy") about an item, place a question mark (?) on the space provided. Be honest with yourself; no one else will see this.

_____ 1. I take my responsibilities at work and at home with equal seriousness.

_____ 2. When I come to work, I never think about situations in my personal life.

_____ 3. When I'm at home, I never think about situations back at work.

_____ 4. My work reflects the values I hold to be important in my life.

_____ 5. I live my life according to the principles I hold to be important in my life.

_____ 6. I try to make decisions based on rational methods and clear, accurate information.

_____ 7. My life is emotionally satisfying, both at work and in personal matters.

_____ 8. I feel good about what I'm doing at all times.

_____ 9. My life and work plans are long term, with an eye to how I want to live my whole life.

_____ 10. The values I hold to be important take into account other people's needs and feelings.

_____ **Total Score**

Scoring

Score one point for a Yes answer to all items except for items 2 and 3. Score one point for each No answer to items 2 and 3. Score all other No answers and question marks as zero (0).

INTERPRETATION GUIDE FOR SELF-ASSESSMENT: WHOLENESS

10   Ten points suggests a good start toward self-management: a broad outlook on life. Or you're kidding yourself. Only you can know which is the case. In the workshop, listen carefully to feedback. Other people may see you differently than you see yourself.

6–9   This score indicates that you have a tendency to compartmentalize your life and deal with events in each compartment separately. This bifurcation can lead to difficulties in either one or the other aspect of your life. This becomes very important if you answered Yes to items 2 and 3. Keeping different aspects of your life separate often can be useful for managing stress, *as long as you don't carry compartmentalizing to extremes.*

        The whole person goes to work, and the whole person goes home. You have a work life, with all the intellectual and emotional issues it involves. You have a life outside of work, with all the intellectual and emotional issues it involves. You can't leave one at the doorstep of the other without creating serious crises.

        Any virtue carried to extremes can become a vice. It's difficult to lock out of your work life that your child is seriously ill. Likewise, it's difficult to block out of your home life that the future of your career depends on completing a project by a specific deadline. Wholeness depends on your ability to harmonize the demands made of you.

0–5   You probably have noticed long before this that you're not satisfied or entirely happy with your life as it is and want to change what's happening in it. You would do well to discuss your situation with the facilitator or other counselor to find ways to pull the different aspects of your life together.

Question Marks

Question marks suggest that you need to look at what you're doing with your life and how you're doing it to eliminate the fuzziness you feel. They indicate that you don't feel confident that what you do in one aspect of your life fits with other aspects. Take for example number 4 ("My work reflects the values I hold to be important in my life"). Questioning how your work values gibe with your values outside of work can lead to living, literally, a double life. Going to church, synagogue, or mosque on the Sabbath, professing the values of honesty and virtue, and then going to work on Monday and cheating your customers is only one illustration of how people stress themselves by fuzziness in what's *good* or *right*. To get control over that struggle, you have to decide to come down on one side of the situation or the other and not try to straddle the fence.

Instructor's Notes: The Importance of Wholeness

After you discuss the interpretations of the answers with the students, you can use this material for a short lecture or summation of the discussion.

Wholeness, represented in the illustration, "Portrait of a Self-Managed Person" (see page 10), provides background and support for managing ourselves—for integrating experiences, thoughts, feelings, emotions, values, and actions that go into making us who we are. At the same time, the more competent we become at integration, the greater extent to which we practice the skills of self-management, the more secure our wholeness becomes.

Wholeness also means pulling together two very different approaches to life in general and to problem solving or planning in particular. Linear thinking, the step-by-step and analytic methods we use for organizing life and work (called "left brain" because that's where analytic thought goes on) takes place only within a holistic, nonlinear context of the vision for our whole life and manages the details within that context. The context of our life's vision is filled with emotional values, creativity, flashes of insight, and subjective decisions (events that go on in the "right brain"). Well-formulated plans for our lives or our businesses provide the details that make vision come to life. The objective of developing the skills associated with the wholeness competency is to integrate both the linear, analytic side of our lives and the nonlinear, subjective side.

SELF-ASSESSMENT: SELF-CONFIDENCE

INSTRUCTIONS

Answer each item with either Yes or No. If you're not sure (feel kind of "fuzzy") about an item, place a question mark (?) on the space provided. Be honest with yourself; no one else will see this.

_____ 1. I always act on principles I consider important to me.

_____ 2. I have an established set of values (a moral code) and live in accordance with them.

_____ 3. I have decided what I want for myself and have determined that it is right and gives meaning to my life.

_____ 4. What I want for myself adds value to the lives of other people and to the world in which I live.

_____ 5. I believe that my beliefs are accurate and that they're useful for me and for other people.

_____ 6. I am skilled and capable, and I can translate what I know into what I do.

_____ 7. I am creative or innovative as well as skilled.

_____ 8. I have strong opinions and feel a passion or intensity about what I believe, want, or need.

_____ 9. I can accept disagreement and negative feedback without defensiveness or a need to explain myself.

_____ 10. I can disagree with other people and give them negative feedback.

_____ 11. I can be influenced by other people when I see value in their points of view.

_____ 12. I feel and express realistic optimism.

_____ 13. I have the patience and the insight to follow the lead of other people.

_____ 14. I have patience with events over which I have no control.

_____ 15. I take responsibility, which means I hold myself and let others hold me accountable for getting results.

_____ **Total Score**

Scoring

Score one point for each Yes answer and zero for each No or ? answer.

INTERPRETATION GUIDE FOR SELF-ASSESSMENT: SELF-CONFIDENCE

15   If you answered Yes to each and every item, you have a high degree of self-confidence, which suggests that you have a vision for your life, with long-term goals and objectives that bring you a sense of security and self-confidence. A vision for your life provides you with a recipe for believing in yourself. Your high score could also mean that you're kidding yourself and need feedback from your classmates in the workshop to help you see yourself through their eyes.

11–14   Some self-confidence is better than none under some circumstances. You need, however, to work on those items about which you are unsure or have said, "No, I am not this." In the workshop, set objectives for becoming more self-confident and identify steps for getting there.

5–10   You need to work at lifting your self-confidence. A lack of self-confidence in the workplace or in your life in general will lead to stagnation and depression. Set an appointment with the facilitator or other counselor to discuss what you can do to raise your self-confidence.

0–4   You need a great deal of help, some of which you can get from the workshop. However, you should have a one-to-one discussion with the facilitator or other counselor to focus your thinking on ways to improve your self-confidence.

Items 9, 10, 11, 13, and 15 tie your self-perceptions to your relationships with others. Answering No to any combination of these items could mean you carry a good thing to an extreme: You have *too much* self-confidence, and you may come across as being what people refer to as "too full of yourself." It's important to check your perceptions with reactions of other people to you.

Answering Yes to items 4 through 8 reflects on both your self-confidence and your potential for leadership. When you exercise self-management skills, you feel confident in what you think or do, and you believe that what you do adds value to other people's lives as well as your own. On the other hand, if you answered No to items 4 through 8, think about them in conjunction with your experience with other people. Has their feedback agreed with your own opinions?

If you answered No or placed a question mark to an aggregate of four items, this reflects a reasonable amount of self-doubt. Answering No or a question mark to an aggregate of five to eight items suggests a shakiness, and answering No or a question mark to an aggregate of eight or more items reflects a large amount of self-doubt that calls for closer examination.

Instructor's Notes: The Importance of Self-Confidence

After you discuss the interpretations of the answers with the students, you can use this material for a short lecture or summation of the discussion.

Successful people believe in themselves and in their abilities. Brian Tracey, a motivation speaker, has a mantra: "Something wonderful is going to happen to me today." The self-management *mantra* is, "I'm going to *make* something wonderful happen today."

Many competent people fail or get stuck in personal and professional ruts because they lack self-confidence, which shows up in behaviors that push people away. Ask participants if other people look to them for leadership? Do they seek out their advice? If they consider themselves to be knowledgeable and competent, yet not a leader or a stand-out person in their group, their inability to influence other people or to gain their respect may be a result of lack of self-confidence. Other people may see that in the way they conduct themselves in their company. Some people who lack self-confidence may retreat and hide from leadership roles; other people compensate for their lack of self-confidence by coming on too strong—as full of themselves.

SELF-ASSESSMENT: SELF-AWARENESS

INSTRUCTIONS

Answer each item with either Yes or No. If you're not sure (feel kind of "fuzzy") about an item, place a question mark (?) on the space provided. Be honest with yourself; no one else will see this.

_____ 1. I am conscious of my limitations as well as of my strengths.

_____ 2. I am willing to acknowledge my limitations to other people.

_____ 3. I am aware of my feelings and emotions.

_____ 4. I am willing to disclose my feelings and emotions to other people.

_____ 5. I am aware of how what I say or do affects other people.

_____ 6. I am able to see things both as what they *are* and what they *could be*.

_____ 7. I look for new directions in which to learn and to grow.

_____ 8. I look for new and different ways to inform myself and to perceive or relate to the world around me.

_____ 9. I look for new and different ways to express myself, to do what I do.

_____ 10. I am flexible and adaptable, forming new opinions and ways of doing things when circumstances demands them.

_____ **Total Score**

Scoring

Score one point for each Yes answer and zero for each No or ? answer.

INTERPRETATION GUIDE FOR SELF-ASSESSMENT: SELF-AWARENESS

10   If you answered Yes to each item either you're an extraordinary person, or you might be kidding yourself. Feedback during the workshop may help you recognize areas in which you are as human as everyone else, especially with regard to items 2 through 5.

5–9   You are reasonably self-aware and willing to identify areas in which you need improvement. Activities and feedback in the workshop will help you increase your self-awareness.

0–4   Unless you are truly not aware of who and what you are, this score admits of too much modesty. However, you might ask the facilitator or other counselor to discuss your results with you and set some goals for increasing your self-awareness.

If you answered Yes to items 1 and 3 but No or ? to items 2, 4, and 5, you *are* aware of yourself, but you may not have the self-confidence to admit to other people that you have limitations or feelings and emotions—and what they are. Your hesitation or inability to self-disclose affects your honest relationships with other people. Skillful self-management includes the ability to express your limitations, feelings, or emotions and to disclose them to others without a loss of self-confidence.

Other aspects of self-awareness lead you to search for and enjoy new ideas, skills, and directions in life. Yes answers to items 6 through 10 indicate that you are aware that whatever your place or station in life, that doesn't signal an end point. It's a stage of development. Likewise, it shows a willingness to move forward in your work. A No or ? to one or more of these items may suggest an unwillingness (for whatever reason) to risk change. Only by practicing self-awareness can you move forward toward achieving new or different goals.

Instructor's Notes: The Importance of Self-Awareness

After you discuss the interpretations of the answers with the students, you can use this material for a short lecture or summation of the discussion.

Self-awareness comes from ongoing, honest self-assessment; it prevents us from being smug and self-satisfied. Self-awareness involves the ability to look into ourselves, to become self-critical, thoughtfully introspective. Introspection leads to identifying what we like about our lives, but more importantly it helps us to become *un*satisfied with present circumstances and limitations. No matter how well our lives are going, they probably can be better.

At the same time, we can carry the virtue of self-consciousness to extremes, until it becomes a liability. If we overdo introspection, if we dwell on our limitations, we can undermine our self-confidence and our ability to succeed in what we do. Likewise, a constant outpouring of *mea culpa* can becoming cloying and inappropriate. Frequently putting ourselves down or frequently criticizing our own actions (or our lack of knowledge or lack of skill), will cause other people to soon agree with us.

Know to whom it is safe to disclose limitations. The reality is that some people may use our own disclosures to hurt us. It's a competitive world, and some people will do anything to get a leg up on others any way they can. To identify when it is safe or unsafe to disclose limitations or weaknesses requires that we know our environment well, that we recognize who has something to gain from our weaknesses, such as people competing for the same promotion or people who have the authority to downsize the organization. No general rule covers all possibilities, but the better we know the people around us, the more likely we are to protect our own interests by keeping appropriately quiet about self-doubts and unsureness.

SELF-ASSESSMENT: DRIVE

INSTRUCTIONS

Answer each item with either Yes or No. If you're not sure (feel kind of "fuzzy") about an item, place a question mark (?) on the space provided. Be honest with yourself; no one else will see this.

_____ 1. I eat a well-regulated diet, exercise regularly, and get appropriate forms of rest.

_____ 2. I am self-starting and need little or no outside stimulation to get on with my daily life.

_____ 3. I am strong-willed or tenacious about the vision for my life.

_____ 4. I feel and show my enthusiasm for my life and for what I am doing.

_____ 5. I display vigor of thought as well as deed.

_____ 6. I am willing to move beyond the conditions of my life or work even if I'm happy with what they are.

_____ 7. I am willing to take risks and to take advantage of my freedom or independence.

_____ 8. I have a need to seek out new opportunities for self-expression, for creative expression, and for innovation in both my work and my nonwork activities.

_____ 9. I am willing to take leadership roles when needed, influencing others to follow.

_____ 10. I am willing to revitalize myself regularly throughout the day, renewing my own sources of energy through proper doses of rest, nutrition, exercise, and relaxation.

_____ **Total Score**

Scoring

Score one point for each Yes answer and zero for each No or ? answer.

INTERPRETATION GUIDE FOR SELF-ASSESSMENT: DRIVE

10   You have enough drive for everyone if you answered Yes to all the items. On the other hand, if this is an accurate assessment, you may overwhelm other people with your energy. Feedback from other people in the workshop can help you see if that's the case.

6–9   Depending on the items you marked with a No or ?, you have little concern about your own drive. However, you may be experiencing some frustration as to how much you can get done or accomplished in a short period of time. Set objectives during the workshop for increasing your drive.

0–5   Lethargy, procrastination, and exhaustion mark the feelings of people without drive. They don't get much done in the course of the day, and sometimes, they don't care. You need to look at yourself in this light: What do I care about and how much do I want it? Without drive, you won't achieve your goals. You might ask the facilitator or other counselor to discuss your results with you and set some goals for increasing your drive.

A No or ? answer to either item 1 or 10 (concerning energy, stamina, and vitality) coupled with Yes answers to the other items indicate that what you do may not fulfill your desires. You need energy and stamina to do what you need to do and want to do; a lack of energy, stamina, and vitality undermines a person's drive and creates frustration and anger. Additionally, a No or ? answer to any of the items 2 through 9, coupled with one or more items to which you answered Yes, suggest that your level of drive is not as high as it should be if you want to be strong.

Instructor's Notes: The Importance of Drive

After you discuss the interpretations of the answers with the students, you can use this material for a short lecture or summation of the discussion.

Drive is the passion to get to where we want to go (not to where life might take us) and to focus on achieving our goals (to be motivated). Drive requires the energy and stamina, the "sticktoitiveness" for staying the course when we believe it's right on target, to meet the challenges of everyday living, as well as to achieve the goals set in the vision for our lives. The desire and commitment to achieve our own and our organization's goals are embodied in that slogan, "I'm going to make something wonderful happen today."

SELF-ASSESSMENT: SELF-RESPECT/SELF-ESTEEM

INSTRUCTIONS

Answer each item with either Yes or No. If you're not sure (feel kind of "fuzzy") about an item, place a question mark (?) on the space provided. Be honest with yourself; no one else will see this.

_____ 1. I believe that I am as valuable as anyone else.

_____ 2. I allow myself to need other people to help me fulfill my dreams.

_____ 3. I believe other people need me to help them meet their goals and fulfill their dreams.

_____ 4. I believe in my own dignity.

_____ 5. What I think, feel, and do fits with my principles and moral values.

_____ 6. What I think, feel, and do will not debase me in my own eyes and in other people's perception of me.

_____ 7. I keep my body and my mind clean and well-ordered.

_____ 8. I give myself room to make mistakes from which I can learn.

_____ 9. I accept myself for who I am although I am willing to change for what I call the better.

_____ 10. I feel pride in my accomplishments without bragging or boasting.

_____ **Total Score**

Scoring

Score one point for each Yes answer and zero for each No or ? answer.

INTERPRETATION GUIDE FOR SELF-ASSESSMENT: SELF-RESPECT/SELF-ESTEEM

10   A score of ten indicates that you have a very high level of self-esteem, but as with any virtue, you must be careful not to allow it to turn into a vice. In the workshop, get feedback from other people as to how you come across to them. You could appear to be very self-centered.

6–9   These scores pretty much reflect a *normal* level of self-esteem. You need to check with others in the workshop to see how you appear to them.

0–5   The lack of self-esteem indicated by these scores is of some concern. You might ask the facilitator or other counselor to discuss your results with you and set some goals for increasing your self-respect/self-esteem.

Answering No or ? to any of items 1, 8, 9, and 10 makes a yes to any other statement suspect. Unless you feel as valuable as anyone else or take pride in what you achieve (1, 9, and 10), you may find it difficult to sustain a sense of self-esteem. If you don't allow yourself room to make mistakes (8), you could beat up on yourself for making them rather than learning from them.

Instructor's Notes: The Importance of Self-Respect/Self-Esteem

After you discuss the interpretations of the answers with the students, you can use this material for a short lecture or summation of the discussion.

Without self-respect or self-esteem, we may give the appearance of self-confidence and inner security, but the appearance is a facade. Our self-confidence and our self-respect/self-esteem are complementary; one supports the other. The more self-confident we become about our capabilities, knowledge, or skills, the more self-esteem we develop, and vice versa. The key to keeping self-respect/self-esteem in harmony with other self-management skills is well summed up by author Albert Terhune: "Win without boasting. Lose without excuse."[2]

If we don't care about ourselves, who will? Self-respect allows us to care about both aspects of who we are—our minds and bodies—provisioning both of them: strengthening rather than depriving, abusing them, or diminishing them. Take this self-assessment in context with all the others, because many of the other competencies reveal our level of self-respect/self-esteem.

---

[2] Quoted in Arthur F. Lenehan, ed., *Leadership . . . with a Human Touch* (Caldwell, N.J.: The Economics Press, 1998), 2.

SELF-ASSESSMENT: RESPECT FOR OTHERS

INSTRUCTIONS

Answer each item with either Yes or No. If you're not sure (feel kind of "fuzzy") about an item, place a question mark (?) on the space provided. Be honest with yourself; no one else will see this.

_____ 1. I recognize the dignity of all other people; I accept them as they are.

_____ 2. I avoid judging other people, even when I don't agree with them or don't like what they do.

_____ 3. I recognize other people's right to their thoughts, feelings, and actions as long as they do not harm or interfere with my rights or those of other people.

_____ 4. I give people my trust willingly until someone earns my distrust.

_____ 5. I care for and about other people.

_____ 6. I recognize other people's knowledge, skills, creativity, and contributions to my life.

_____ 7. I recognize other people's needs and aspirations.

_____ 9. I am open to other people's ideas, thoughts, or feelings, listening to what they have to say and learning from them as well as about them.

_____ 10. I allow myself to be influenced by other people (that is, I accept and act upon their opinions or suggestions when I think they are right or useful).

_____ 11. I give people helpful, honest feedback.

_____ 12. I accept helpful, honest feedback.

_____ 13. I try to act as a positive role model for other people.

_____ 14. I am available and accessible to other people who need or rely on me.

_____ 15. I cooperate and collaborate with other people.

_____ 16. I try to be dependable and credible, meeting obligations and checking out the accuracy or value of my beliefs.

_____ 17. I contribute accurate or useful information that benefits other people.

_____ 18. I communicate openly and honestly.

_____ 19. I seek group consensus when it's appropriate, and I support and act on the group decisions.

_____ 20. I am *un*satisfied with the status quo for others as well as for myself, encouraging them to find new and different ways to add value to their lives and to the world around them.

_____ **Total Score**

Scoring

Score one point for each Yes answer and zero for each No or ? answer.

INTERPRETATION GUIDE FOR SELF-ASSESSMENT: RESPECT FOR OTHERS

20   A Yes answer to all twenty items indicates more awareness of and respect for others than most people exhibit. How accurate do you think this score really is? Listen to feedback from people in the workshop. You may not have as clear a perception of yourself as you think.

15–19   Depending upon what you answered No or ? to, you probably exhibit as much respect for other people as anyone else. Set objectives during the workshop to work on those items you rejected or considered to be fuzzy.

10–14   You may be treating people as you would *not* like to be treated, and you may not even know it. Seek feedback from people in the workshop as to how they feel about working with you. Do they feel that you respect them? If so, your score may not reflect the real you. Set objectives for getting a clearer picture of yourself or, if necessary, for working toward giving more respect to others.

0–9   Take these scores in the context of your relationships. If you find yourself alone a lot, these scores might be quite accurate. You might ask the facilitator or other counselor to discuss your results with you and set some goals for increasing your self-awareness.

A No or a ? answer to any one item doesn't mean that you don't respect other people. Instead, look at the aggregate of answers to this long list of items. If the majority of your answers are Yes, you probably get along and work well with most people. If the majority of your answers are No or questions marks, you may want to reassess your relationships with others. Self-managed people learn from other people, they support them, they collaborate with them, and they value their lives.

Instructor's Notes: The Importance of Respect for Others

After you discuss the interpretations of the answers with the students, you can use this material for a short lecture or summation of the discussion.

Respect is the magic bullet that makes cooperation possible. No matter how highly we score on the other skills, in the workplace a lack of respect for others destroys our careers as well as any possible teamwork. Likewise, a lack of respect for other people undermines our own self-confidence and self-respect because people won't care for or about us, which reflects back to our lack of respect for them. Two versions of the Golden Rule, taken together, provide a well-defined path increasing our ability to treat others with respect.

▶ Do unto others as you would have others do unto you.

▶ Do not unto others anything you would not have them do unto you.

ASSESSMENT SCORING GUIDE

Complete this scoring guide to determine the strength of your self-management skills, which is the average of the five separate skills plus your score for wholeness.

Self-Confidence total score   _____

Self-Awareness total score   + _____

Drive total score   + _____

Self-Respect total score   + _____

Respect for Others total score   + _____

       Grand total   = _____ ÷ 5

                        = _____

     Wholeness score   + _____

Total Self-Management score   = _____

Interpretation

23   It isn't *im*possible to have a score of twenty-three. If you do have a score of twenty-three, that would mean you have absolutely no doubt as to who you are, where you're going, and what you're about. It would also mean that you have absolutely no difficulty collaborating with other people, you admire them, and respect their dignity at all times. You listen to people and never misunderstand them, and . . . . Well, you get the idea. If you're that perfect, you're an extraordinary person. On the other hand, other people may have a different impression of you; you should take seriously the feedback they give you and, if they don't agree with you, you should make appropriate adjustments to your self-perceptions.

21–22   This possible score is not very common and indicates that you have a strong sense of your-self and your ability to manage your life. You should listen to feedback from other people and, if they don't agree with you, you should make appropriate adjustments. At the least, use the skill practices to reinforce the positive aspects of your self-management.

15–20   Most people score between fifteen and twenty. It indicates that you have a strong sense of control but that specific self-management skills need improvement. Listen to the feedback you get from other people and set objectives for making changes in your weaker areas.

0–14   These scores suggest that you have much work to do to develop self-management skills. Discuss your situation with the facilitator or other counselor and set goals for change.

At any level below a score of twenty-one, practice should help raise your scores. Therefore, you might want to retake the self-assessments after you have worked on your skills for six months.

Instructor's Notes

After you discuss the interpretation of the Scoring Guide for the Self-Managed Person with the students, you can use this material for a short lecture or summation of the discussion.

Our strength as self-managed persons depends on integrating all the skills we've just assessed. By building on where we are strongest, we can improve the quality of our self-management. By using our strengths, we can also increase our skills in areas in which we need improvement. But we cannot despair if we never achieve the ideal of total self-management.

Self-management is a matter of degree, not one of perfection. In fact, self-managed people realize that they'll have up days and down days. They'll achieve maximum effectiveness sometimes, and they'll barely reach their minimum expectations on other days. In fact, they know they'll become richer for the failures they experience. We quickly forget our successes, but we learn from our mistakes.

THE PYRAMID OF CONTROL

The *pyramid of control,* a metaphor, describes an action (see the accompanying overhead illustration). The base (actions) supports the whole structure, and the structure gives the base its purpose and direction (vision and action planning). The pyramid represents the power of self-management to achieve the goals of your personal visions for your lives and your work.

The power of the pyramid is at the apex where goals direct (in a sense, "pull") how you live your life (objectives and activities). The process of getting control follows this pattern:

Peak of the Pyramid.   The vision for your life. This is the "top" to which you aspire. Working with values, hopes, and desires, you do the following at this level of the pyramid:

▶ Create the vision.
▶ Organize your life into interactive, sometimes interdependent, dimensions that will satisfy the demands of your vision for your life.
▶ Prioritize the dimensions.
▶ Set goals that satisfy the demands of the dimensions.
▶ Prioritize the goals.

Midsection of the Pyramid.   Action planning. Here you describe the intermediate steps toward reaching the top. You:

▶ Identify objectives/milestones for how to achieve goals.

- ▶ Prioritize the objectives.
- ▶ Design action plans to achieve those objectives (what to do to achieve objectives).

Base of Pyramid. Action. The base is the arena where your life takes place and consists of:

- ▶ Doing what is necessary for achieving objectives
- ▶ Living your daily life in accordance with your vision for your life
- ▶ Evaluating your progress toward goals and taking corrective action where necessary

SELF-MANAGEMENT COMPETENCIES AND THE EIGHT STEPS TO THE TOP

Chapter 2 provides self-assessment instruments that by their content identify the skills associated with self-management. Identification is only a beginning. Application brings the skills to life, and it gives a person more control over his personal life, the work he does, and the management of an organization. The eight steps to the top, another metaphor, consists of applying the skills in eight activities that make increasing self-management possible.

- ▶ Step 1: Sort out your values.
- ▶ Step 2: Organize your values into life dimensions.
- ▶ Step 3: Write a vision statement.
- ▶ Step 4: Prioritize your life dimensions.
- ▶ Step 5: Goal setting.
- ▶ Step 6: Prioritize goals and performance ranges.
- ▶ Step 7: Write an action plan (objectives and activities).
- ▶ Step 8: Evaluate progress and take corrective action.

The chapters of this section are essentially a "script" that lays out the eight basic steps you can use to get more control over your life. Develop this material to suit your training situation. You can use the subheadings as the contents of handouts, and/or overheads, 35mm, or computerized slides. Use the examples here or create your own. Whatever you do, be sure to provide the students with illustrations of what to do or what to say or write.

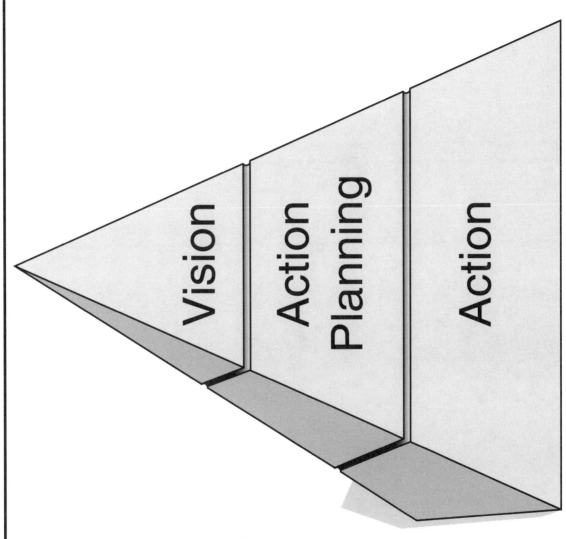

Vision

Action Planning

Action

3

Sort Out Your Values (Step 1)

A vision for life is constructed from the values that are important to us. That's why we begin with exercises that help identify those values. Self-management begins by deciding which activities and returns or payoffs give our lives value. For example, "being loved" is a personal value, whereas "having managerial authority" is a business value, and "having a successful career" combines both personal and business values. Identifying those values creates a life vision that each individual sets for himself or herself that not only consists of the values he or she holds most dear but that also describes the whole person he or she wants to be. The vision then forms the broad outline and the motivation for becoming that person.

The long, three-part activity—Where Am I on My Journey?—is designed to help participants evaluate how well their current situation aligns with the values they find most important and what to do to change direction to reach their goals. Part 1 consists of a tool for identifying and ranking twenty-five specific life values, the self-assessment called "What Drives You?" concerning work and personal goals. Part 2 consists of the self-assessment called, "What Am I Doing to Achieve My Goals?" and "What Can I Do to Change What I'm Doing?" is the planning guide that makes up Part 3.[1]

---

[1]Adapted from *Secrets of the Wild Goose: The Self-Management Way for Increasing Your Personal Power and Inspiring Productive Teamwork* (New York: AMACOM, 1998); *Managing Stress* (New York: AMACOM 1987); *Successful Delegation* (Watertown, Mass.: American Management Association, 1978, 1987), all by Donald H. Weiss.

Exercise 3.1. Where Am I on My Journey?

Instructor's Notes

You can use class time to have participants complete this activity, if you have that much time available. However, independence suggests you use this exercise as one of three possible activities:

▶ A precourse assignment to be brought into class for discussion

▶ An Evening Learning Opportunity (ELO), which is what my friend and associate Sid Nachman calls an after-class assignment between daily sessions of a workshop

▶ A follow-up tool to a seminar as part of participants' planning for the future

In any of those activities the participants can take their time to give serious consideration to their answers. If you assign all three parts of the exercise as a follow-up activity, go over the instructions for each part of the assignment before leaving the topic. If you are doing this exercise in class, read the instructions before starting each part.

Learning Objectives and Outcomes

By completing this exercise participants will be able to:

▶ Identify their most important personal and work-related values.

▶ Describe where they are in relation to fulfilling their most important values.

▶ Create a preliminary plan for changing what they are doing in order to better fulfill their most important values.

Self-Management Skills Involved

▶ Honesty

▶ Openness

Requirements

Time:	Two or more hours
Materials:	Self-Assessment: What Drives You? Work and Personal Goals
	Self-Assessment: What Am I Doing to Achieve My Goals?
	Self-Assessment: What Can I Do to Change What I'm Doing?
Preparation:	Photocopy the self-assessment handouts.
Room Setup:	If exercise is used in class, any individual seating arrangement will do.

Discussion Points After Completing Part 1

What follows are just basic questions; there are no "book answers." The discussion must be spontaneous (i.e., not programmed to reach specific answers) and directly tied to the participants' values if it is to help them understand their own personal and work-related issues. You need not require everyone to answer each question. Instead, let a small group of volunteers answer them. Follow-up questions could include, "What makes that goal important to you?" You may also redirect with, for example, "That's very interesting. What do the rest of you think of that answer?"

1. Relative to the entire list, where did you rank your top five personal values?
2. Relative to the entire list, where did you rank your top five work-related values?
3. Which of your personal values do you find among your work-related values as well?
4. How do your work-related values and your personal values mesh? Do they conflict with each other?

Discussion Points After Completing Part 2

You could turn this into a small group discussion, especially if participants seem reluctant to talk about their evaluations in a large group.

▶ Form small groups of up to four people.
▶ Give the groups up to twenty minutes to complete the discussion.
▶ Have the groups elect a timekeeper to allow each person up to five minutes to explain his or her answers to these questions:
   1. What are you doing most effectively with respect to the top five personal values?
   2. What are you doing least effectively?
   3. What are you doing most effectively to realize your top five work-related values?
   4. What are you doing least effectively?

Discussion Points After Completing Part 3

1. What did you decide you have to do differently and why?
2. What do you think you can do immediately to begin making the changes to your life needed to maximize your values?

Self-Assessment: What Drives You?
Work and Personal Goals

LEARNING OBJECTIVE

By completing this part of the exercise you will be able to identify your most important personal and work-related values

EXPLANATION

Every action produces some kind of result, whether you know the reason you're doing it or not and whether you plan for it or not. Unless you plan for the result you want, the one you get may not satisfy the (deliberate or unconscious) reason for which you took the action. To align your organization's goals and your work or personal goals, it's important for you to know what results you want from the effort you put out.

Organizational goals are all very compelling, while some personal goals that act as motives are more compelling than others. The goals that motivate you most forcefully are your drivers—your most important reasons for doing what you're doing. Satisfying those drivers becomes your most important activity because reaching those goals means getting the payoffs you want for yourself. So, what goals drive you?

The list consists of twenty-five possible reasons for doing anything. Each word or phrase can be used to answer the question, "What do I want to get out of the effort I'm putting into my life?"

INSTRUCTIONS

Step 1. This is important. Read the entire list of possible payoffs before continuing. Don't write anything down at this time. Simply read the list. Then follow the instructions that appear after the list.

_____ 1. **Knowledge:** To pursue and learn about new things and ideas; to search for truth, or information; to be know by others as an intelligent person and to feel intelligent.

_____ 2. **Wisdom:** To understand and frame for myself a meaning of life, perceiving experience from a broad frame of reference.

_____ 3. **Power:** To lead and direct others; to influence or control others, that is, to get them to do what I want them to do.

_____ 4. **Aesthetic pleasure:** To enjoy and respect the things from which I derive pleasure—art, nature, work, people.

_____ 5. **Ethical standards**: To believe in and maintain a code of ethics, a sense of right and wrong; to be moral; to conform to the standards of society, my family or spouse, my profession, and my personal or religious ideals.

_____ 6. **Independence:** To achieve my own goals in the manner best suited to me; to have freedom to come and go as I wish; to be myself at all times; to control my own actions.

_____ 7. **Accomplishment:** To achieve my personal objectives with a sense that I've done something as well as, if not better than, someone else would have; to experience self-satisfaction when I rise to a challenge, accomplish a task or a job, or solve a problem.

_____ 8. **Recognition:** To receive attention, notice, approval, or respect from others because of something I've done; to generate a feeling in others for who I am and what I achieve.

_____ 9. **Friendship:** To have many friends; to work with others, enjoying their camaraderie; to join groups for companionship; to look forward to and enjoy social relations.

_____ 10. **Responsibility:** To be held accountable to others or to organizations to which I belong for a job or task; to possess something and care for it.

_____ 11. **Creativity:** To be free to and have the ability and desire to develop new ideas, solutions to problems, improvements in products or procedures, or designs of things or plans; to be mentally challenged; to be first to innovate or create.

_____ 12. **Security:** To possess the basic wherewithal for living; to feel safe; to have self-confidence; to have job security and continuity of income.

_____ 13. **Dedication:** To be loyal to a company or to a supervisor, my family, social and political groups, and others; to give devotion, commitment, or friendship to others.

_____ 14. **Justice and parity:** To receive rewards and recognition for my contributions and achievements in proportion to my effort and comparable to those received by other people.

_____ 15. **Growth:** To advance, to expand my life through a job, through the improvement of my status at work or in the community; to increase my work- and nonwork-related knowledge or skill; to find fulfillment in the groups in which I work or live; to mature personally and professionally.

_____ 16. **Self-esteem:** To be someone of value in my own eyes and in the eyes of others; to be accepted as a person rather than as a nonentity or as a means to an end; to feel useful and wanted by other people; to be a leader; to be appreciated by others.

_____ 17. **Religiousness:** To believe in a supreme being; to relate to others on a spiritual or personal basis with respect to some faith or set of beliefs.

_____ 18. **Love:** To experience warmth, feelings of affection, a sense of caring, enthusiasm for, attachment to, devotion to, and interest in something or in another person, especially someone to whom I can make a commitment.

_____ 19. **Challenge:** To feel good about what I do, its degree of difficulty, and the complexity or demands on my creativity; to have opportunities to apply my knowledge and skills effectively and easily.

(continues)

_____ 20. **Faith:** To have self-confidence and to believe in my abilities and skills, in the goodness and value of life, and in the goals and objectives of my company or social organizations; to feel secure in the availability of help from others and to recognize help received.

_____ 21. **Helpfulness:** To provide assistance, support, empathy, or protection to others; to be open, responsive, and generous.

_____ 22. **Health (physical/mental):** To feel energetic and free of physical pain from injury, disease, or infection; to feel free of worry and anxiety and of emotional blocks to success in all aspects of my life; to have peace of mind.

_____ 23. **Money:** To have sufficient income or other assets to use as I wish; to be materially comfortable or well-off.

_____ 24. **Good times/pleasure:** To have fun; to enjoy myself; to do things I like to do rather than only things I have to do.

_____ 25. **Being loved:** To experience warmth, feelings of affection, and a sense of caring from other people, especially from someone from whom I can expect a commitment.

Step 2. Return to the beginning of the list. Slowly review each item, _ranking_ each payoff as to its _importance to you_. In the spaces provided, write one for the most important and up to twenty-five for the least. For example, if you feel that **knowledge** is important but not the most important reason for doing things, you might write an eight on the line next to number one. It may make things easier if you hunt out the item that represents the most important reason before you rate the rest.

Step 3. From the list of twenty-five goals, transfer the top five you want from your _work_ to the chart at the end of this handout. For example, you could list **recognition** as the most important work-related goal even if it ranks as the fourth most important goal on your list.

Step 4. Transfer the top five _personal_ goals you want to satisfy outside the workplace. These help you harmonize and maintain your well-being and your relationships with other people, for example, your family.

Use the accompanying model as a guide. When you complete the list of goals in _each_ group, compare the two columns. Note which side of the chart contains the highest ratings in the master list—work-related or nonwork-related.

In some cases, goals may be both work- and nonwork related. For example, many people seek **Friendship** at work as well as outside of work. The model shows you that you can list a driver on both sides of the chart.

When you finish, you'll have a personal profile, a picture of your own most important reasons for doing things. Check your lists of goals to see which of them you think you should pursue most vigorously. Future decisions you make should fit with your goals. Integrating your goals will help you become more effective at achieving them and help reduce frustration and stress.

MODEL

Rank	Work-Related Drivers	Rank	Nonwork-Related Drivers
2	Recognition	1	Love
4	Friendship	3	Being loved
5	Accomplishment	4	Friendship
15	Money	20	Religiousness
9	Responsibility	8	Aesthetic Pleasure

YOUR GOALS

Rank	Work-Related Drivers	Rank	Nonwork-Related Drivers

SELF ASSESSMENT:
WHAT AM I DOING TO ACHIEVE MY GOALS?

LEARNING OBJECTIVE

By completing this part of the exercise you will evaluate what you are doing to achieve the payoffs you identified in Part 1.

EXPLANATION

The expression "walk the talk" means simply, live what you believe. Only talking about values reduces your personal effectiveness and creates frustration and stress. A goal's real value is determined by the amount of effort you put into pursuing it. This part of the exercise will help you evaluate how much of your talk you actually walk.

INSTRUCTIONS

For each item in the list of twenty-five values, write a sentence or two to explain what you are doing at this time to maximize that value. For example, **Knowledge:** I spend at least one hour every day reading a piece of nonfiction that is not related to my work.

_____   1. Knowledge

_____   2. Wisdom

_____   3. Power

_____   4. Aesthetic pleasure

_____   5. Ethical standards

_____   6. Independence

_____   7. Accomplishment

_____   8. Recognition

_____   9. Friendship

_____ 10. Responsibility

_____ 11. Creativity

_____ 12. Security

_____ 13. Dedication

_____ 14. Justice and parity

_____ 15. Growth

_____ 16. Self-esteem

_____ 17. Religiousness

_____ 18. Love

_____ 19. Challenge

_____ 20. Faith

_____ 21. Helpfulness

_____ 22. Health (physical/mental)

_____ 23. Money

_____ 24. Good times/pleasure

_____ 25. Being loved

SELF-ASSESSMENT:
WHAT CAN I DO TO CHANGE WHAT I'M DOING?

LEARNING OBJECTIVE

By doing this part of the exercise you will begin developing a change plan that helps you achieve the payoffs you identified in Part 1.

EXPLANATION

The frustration that follows from unfulfilled goals often leads to depression, a loss of self-respect/self-esteem and self-confidence, and stress induced by a sense of "failure." Only doing something can change the situation, but it's a mistake to follow the old adage, "Do something, even if it's wrong." Instead, reviewing the actions you described in Part 2 of this exercise will help you take *directed action*, doing something with a purpose and with a plan.

INSTRUCTIONS

Enter the top five personal and top five work-related values from your list in Part 1 on the worksheet. Determine how much effort you are putting into maximizing those values by comparing how much attention you pay to them now with how much attention you are paying to other values. For example, if **love** is a high personal value and you're not doing anything that allows you to love someone else, you're probably putting time and effort into something of a lesser value to you. If **growth** is a high work-related value, and you spend only a fraction of the time on it that you spend pursuing **aesthetic pleasure**, you're putting yourself at a disadvantage with regard to your own values.

Consider also the possibility that, after doing the first two parts of this exercise, you may want to change your perceptions of what you value most or least (or anything in between). You may want to admit to yourself that one or another of the twenty-five goals are not as important to you as you thought, and that perhaps one or another of them is more important to you than you originally believed. A review of the list and your rankings in Part 1 would therefore be in order.

Use the worksheet to list immediate action steps that can help you align what you are doing with your important goals.

TOP FIVE PERSONAL VALUES

1. Goal: _____

    _____

    Immediate Action Step(s) _____

    _____

    _____

    _____

2. Goal: _____

    _____

    Immediate Action Step(s) _____

    _____

    _____

    _____

3. Goal: _____

    _____

    Immediate Action Step(s) _____

    _____

    _____

    _____

4. Goal: _____

    _____

    Immediate Action Step(s) _____

    _____

    _____

    _____

5. Goal: _____

    _____

    Immediate Action Step(s) _____

    _____

    _____

    _____

(continues)

TOP FIVE WORK-RELATED VALUES

1. Goal: _____

    _____

    Immediate Action Step(s) _____

    _____

    _____

    _____

2. Goal: _____

    _____

    Immediate Action Step(s) _____

    _____

    _____

    _____

3. Goal: _____

    _____

    Immediate Action Step(s) _____

    _____

    _____

    _____

4. Goal: _____

    _____

    Immediate Action Step(s) _____

    _____

    _____

    _____

5. Goal: _____

    _____

    Immediate Action Step(s) _____

    _____

    _____

    _____

Exercise 3.2. The Million Dollar Inheritance

Instructor's Notes

Whereas Exercise 3.1 is very long and could be done on the students' own time, The Million Dollar Inheritance is an in-class exercise that is quick, fun, and revealing. The objective is to identify the participants' most important values. The students then use these values to produce a vision for their lives. After distributing the instructions, read them aloud and then conduct a discussion as described in the following text.

Learning Objective and Outcome

By the end of this exercise participants will have identified their most important values.

Self-Management Skills Involved

▶ Openness to thinking in a new way
▶ Self-disclosure

Requirements

Time:	Thirty minutes
Materials:	Instructions for The Million Dollar Inheritance Exercise handout
	Pencil and paper
Preparation:	Photocopy the handout.
Room Setup:	Wherever the training is done. In step 2, participants should be arranged in pairs. If you have an odd number of students, arrange one group in a triad.

Discussion Items After the Exercise

Have each person in the class tell you the first item on his or her list, and write the items on a board or chart that everyone can read. In an extremely large group, you can modify this step by asking for a sampling of first items, which you then chart.

Explore what the results seem to indicate by asking what the lists mean to the participants and how they reflect people's highest values.

Lecture Notes to Sum Up Discussion

The first item most people list usually reflects their highest value. If the first item is "Distribute the money among my family," it puts family at the highest point. If the first item is "Pay cash for a $500,000.00 house," it puts material goods highest on the list. If the first item is "Donate the money to charity," it puts social values at the top of the list. By identifying these values, the participants can now develop a vision for their lives.

INSTRUCTIONS FOR THE MILLION DOLLAR INHERITANCE EXERCISE

LEARNING OBJECTIVE

By the end of this exercise you will have identified your most important values.

Step 1. Individual Exercise

You have just inherited one million dollars from a great aunt, but she has placed several stipulations on the inheritance.

► You must spend all of the money in one year.

► You may spend it in any manner you want, but you cannot invest the money in the stock market, certificates of deposit, or other income-producing activities, nor can you put the money into a savings account.

Take five minutes to write a list of ways you will spend the money. After the five minutes are up, proceed to step 2.

Step 2. Interactive

Taking five minutes for each person, discuss with your partner the choices you each have made. Read aloud your list of the ways you will spend the money and briefly explain the rationale for each decision.

4

Organize Your Values Into Life Dimensions (Step 2)

People experience a great deal of confusion and frustration in their lives in part because experience is a great deal like a picture puzzle without a completed picture for guidance. They have difficulty sorting out the pieces into the proper patterns (e.g., background images and foreground images). You can help your students sort out the pieces with exercises designed to provide some patterns (dimensions) for creating their own temporarily completed picture. That's the advantage of puzzling out a life over puzzling out a portrait; a life's not over 'til it's over.

Exercise 4.1. The Important Dimensions of My Life

Instructor's Notes

Before completing this exercise, participants must have completed the first part of Exercise 3.1, "What Drives You?". If you haven't administered Exercise 3.1, do so now.

Learning Objectives and Outcomes

By the end of this exercise participants will:

▶ Have categorized their most important personal and work-related values into several or all of the seven dimensions of a life.

▶ Be able to explain the relationships between the dimensions of their lives and how they interact (if at all) with one another.

Self-Management Skills Involved

▶ Honesty

▶ Openness to looking at one's life in a new or different way

Requirements

Time: Thirty minutes

Materials: Results of "What Drives You?" assessment from Chapter 3
                 Sample Dimensions Model overhead
                 Dimensions Model worksheet

Equipment: Overhead projector and screen

Preparation: Create an overhead of the Sample Dimensions Model.
                 Photocopy the Dimensions Model worksheet.

Room Setup: Any individual seating arrangement will work.

Lecture Notes

Although you may think of your life as a continuous line of events taking you from birth to death, life itself doesn't take a straight or linear path leading directly from one point to another that you can plot on a line graph. Rather, a life looks like a kaleidoscope in which currents of colors swirl together to form a whole experience. You can use your power of linear thinking to freeze the swirl into categories or dimensions that you can isolate from one another, but only for the purpose of thinking about them. In truth, they can't really be untangled.

▶ Some event currents flow parallel to one another (e.g., a volunteer activity and your job).

▶ Some event currents interact (work and family relationships).

▶ Some event currents are dependent on something else (e.g., your ability to possess the material things you want may depend on the income you earn).

On their own, your values or goals seem to have no discernible pattern or connection to one another. You have career-oriented values or goals, such as earning a large income or entering into management. You have family-oriented values or goals, such as having a large number of children and being a good parent. You also have values or goals that are strictly personal and involve no one else, such as being a moral person, being spiritual, and being healthy. The pyramid of control helps you organize your values or goals into interactive, sometimes interdependent, paths for fulfilling them. Each path or dimension is an aspect of anyone's life, most commonly referred to as the seven listed alphabetically below.[1]

1. Career (the work you want to do and where you want to do it)

2. Community (your roles and the degree of influence you want)

3. Family (which refers to both your family or origin and your acquired family or families)

4. Financial (income from all possible sources and how you spend your income)

5. Material goods (things you want for yourself and/or your family)

6. Personal values (morality, spirituality, health, etc.)

7. Social relations (friends, acquaintances, neighbors, etc.)

You can and should add categories to the list. Often people add specific job-related aspects of their lives, such as the department they manage. Sometimes, however, you will find that what you add is actually a subset of one of the categories already listed, which you can break out as a separate dimension if you wish to concentrate on it or emphasize it. Examples: A "spiritual" dimension is a subset of personal values that you can break out if you feel it's an extremely important part of your life. You can divide career into current job, career aspirations, and other aspects of your worklife. You can separate finances into wages or salary, income from investments, and expenses of various kinds. You can also isolate material goods into home, vehicles, and so on. It is important that you recognize the connections among the different dimensions of your life regardless of how you separate them for the purpose of planning.

One way to do that is to categorize your most important personal and work-related values or goals into several or all of the seven dimensions of a life. This next exercise will help you do that.

[Facilitator: Put up the Sample Dimensions Model overhead and distribute the Dimensions Model worksheet now.]

---

[1]From *Secrets of the Wild Goose: The Self-Management Way for Increasing Your Personal Power and Inspiring Productive Teamwork* (New York: AMACOM, 1998) and *Get Organized: How to Control Your Life Through Self-Management* (New York: AMACOM, 1986), both by Donald H. Weiss.

Instructions to Participants

Using the Dimensions Model worksheet, categorize the values in your "What Drives You?" assessment into the seven dimensions of your life. Concentrate on the top five personal and top five work-related values, but divide the others as well (if time allows).

The Sample Dimensions Model overhead gives you an idea of how to complete the Dimensions Model. Under each dimension, I have included the example in the handout and other values or goals taken from my own analysis of what drives me and that are very important to me. You do the same now.

Discussion Questions

1. Into what categories did the most important of your values fall?

   Typical answers: Career, Family, Financial, Personal. (Not necessarily in rank order.)

2. How do those dimensions relate to one another? For example, do any of the dimensions depend on your success in another dimension?

   Typical answers: My family goals depend on my personal values. Material goods depend on financial.

SAMPLE DIMENSIONS MODEL

Dimension	Values
Career	Example: Growth
Community	Example: Justice and Parity
Family	Example: Being loved
Financial	Example: Money
Material Goods	Example: Aesthetic pleasure (as in art work)
Personal Values	Example: Knowledge
Social	Example: Friendship

DIMENSIONS MODEL

Dimension	Values
Career	
Community	
Family	
Financial	
Material Goods	
Personal Values	
Social	

5

Write a Vision Statement (Step 3)

In any self-management workshop, the participants must complete a vision statement for themselves that encompasses all seven (or more) dimensions of their lives. They can use any number of tools for writing a vision statement. The sample Vision Statement illustrates a formal approach that describes several dimensions as distinct from one another. Your students can follow the format in this example. Some people call this formal, linear method of writing vision statements too confining and prefer to think more globally and to write statements in a form of free association; for those people, a popular method called Eulogy: Writing a Vision Statement for Your Life gives them the freedom they need (as long as they cover all seven dimensions).

At the same time writing a eulogy can help anyone begin the process of creating a life's vision. Many people, once they've written their eulogies, write formal vision statements, as in Exercise 5.2, The Vision for My Life: A Formal Statement.

Exercise 5.1. Eulogy: Writing a Vision Statement for Your Life

Learning Objectives and Outcomes

By the end of this exercise participants will:

▶ Be able to explain how they want to live their lives.

▶ Be able to explain how they want people to see the person they are or will become.

▶ Have written a narrative vision statement they can use as is or that they can use to produce a more formally structured statement.

Self-Management Skills Involved

▶ Openness to looking at one's life in a new or different way

▶ Self-disclosure

Requirements

Time:	Not less than sixty minutes (You could make Exercise 5.1 an Evening Learning Opportunity—an ELO—which is recommended only if you end the day at this point and schedule writing the formal vision statement early the next morning. If you are making this an ELO, tell the participants to bring their eulogies back with them the next morning.)
Materials:	Instructions for the Eulogy Exercise handout Pencil and paper
Preparation:	Photocopy the handouts.
Room Setup:	Classroom style. In step 2, arrange students in pairs. If you have an odd number of students, arrange one group in a triad.

[Facilitator: Distribute the exercise instructions and read them aloud.]

Lecture Notes After Exercise Ends

Your eulogy points out what dimensions in your life you think are most important to you at this time. It also describes the ways in which you want to fulfill the values you consider important in each of those dimensions. Pin it up on a wall in front of you to refer to whenever you can. After all, it's your eulogy. Nevertheless, don't be afraid to make changes in it over time. What's important to you now may not be as important to you five years from now. Remember, in the words of Yogi Berra, the famous baseball catcher and coach, "It ain't over 'til it's over."

Instructions for the Eulogy Exercise

Learning Objectives and Outcomes

By the end of this exercise you will:

► Be able to explain how you want to live your life.

► Be able to explain how you want people to see the person you are or will become.

► Have written a narrative vision statement you can use as is or that you can use to produce a more formally structured statement.

Step 1: Write Your Eulogy

Write a eulogy you would want someone to read at your funeral. By the time all is said and done, how do you want your résumé or vitae to read? Writing in the past tense, develop a broad picture of how you fulfilled the life you now think you want to live. Think in terms of the seven dimensions (or more, if you added any) and the priorities you set for them: Career, Community, Family, Financial, Material Goods, Personal Values, and Social. Dream a little, but don't fly in the face of reality. When you finish, you'll have produced a broad vision statement that will guide you when you set goals for your life and work. You have thirty minutes to complete this step in the exercise.

Step 2: Listen to Your Eulogy

1. Have your partner read your eulogy to you.

2. Listen to how it sounds.

3. Decide if that's what you want to hear people say about you when your life is over.

4. If not, make changes to it now.

Exercise 5.2. The Vision for My Life: A Formal Statement

Learning Objective and Outcome

By the end of this exercise participants will have a structured vision statement defining the dimensions in their lives they most want to fulfill.

Self-Management Skills Involved

▶ Using structured methods for creating a vision statement
▶ Openness to discussion in a classroom environment

Requirements

Time: Not less than thirty minutes

Materials: Sample Vision Statement
                   My Vision Statement worksheet

Preparation: Photocopy the sample and worksheet.

Room Setup: Classroom style

Lecture Notes

[Facilitator: Distribute the Sample Vision Statement and the worksheet.]

Instructions to the Participants

Using the Sample Vision Statement and your eulogy as a guide, write a vision statement for your life. You can omit any dimension you want or add dimensions if you wish. Use extra paper if needed, but be sure to able the dimensions in which you're working.

Discussion After the Exercise

1. Ask for volunteers to read their vision statements.
2. Ask all participants to discuss how the vision statement could produce goal conflicts, in which goals compete for immediate action. For example, career demands competing with family demands.

SAMPLE VISION STATEMENT

Career: I want to be successful at my life's work, in my career, in my job. I want to learn all I can about the world in which I live.

Community Relations: By living a moral, principled life, I want my life to set an example and be influential in my community.

Family: I want my life to be filled with love, me for others and others for me. I want a family (spouse and children, as well as parents and siblings) to hold and to hold me.

Financial: I want to earn enough money through regular income and investments to make me and my family comfortable and secure.

Material Goods: I want to house, clothe, and provide things for me and my family that are considered important to a "good life."

Personal Values: I want to live a moral, principled, physically fit life and be an influential model to my family and my coworkers.

Social Relations: I want friends whose lives I treasure and who treasure mine.

MY VISION STATEMENT

Dimension	Desired End Results
Career	
Community	
Family	
Financial	
Material Goods	
Personal Values	
Social	

6

Prioritize Your Life Dimensions (Step 4)

Sorting our lives into dimensions adds an advantage for planning we wouldn't otherwise have: If we lay out the dimensions and the goals we want to achieve in them side by side, we can easily recognize where goals conflict with one another. However, those conflicts don't demand that we eliminate one or another; rather, setting priorities permits us to achieve as many of the goals in the different dimensions as we can.

Chapter 6 contains exercises designed to help participants manage goal conflicts by setting immediate priorities, looking down the road five years from now, and down the road twenty-five years from now. These three separate rankings will allow the students to emphasize one set of goals at one time and different sets of goals at other times, thus allowing for conflicts and resolutions without abandoning one or another.

Exercise 6.1. Prioritizing Dimensions

Learning Objectives and Outcomes

By the end of this exercise participants will:

▶ Be able to explain how the dimensions of their lives may create goal conflicts.

▶ Be able to explain how to harmonize conflicts when they arise.

▶ Have created a table in which their dimensions are prioritized for the immediate future, for five years from now, and for twenty-five years from now.

Self-Management Skills Involved

▶ Openness to looking at one's life in new or different ways

▶ Openness to talking about one's vision in a classroom setting

Requirements

Time:	Not more than thirty minutes
Materials:	Instructions for Prioritizing Dimensions handout Sample Setting Priorities worksheet Setting Priorities worksheet
Equipment:	None
Preparation:	Photocopy the handout, sample, and worksheet.
Room Setup:	Any classroom style

Lecture Notes

People's goals bump up against each other and conflict when two or more life goals compete for immediate attention. Why does this happen? Because people try to *balance* or *juggle* too many dimensions at one time.

Sometimes goal jugglers do that out of the mistaken belief that everything in their lives always has equal *value*. However seriously we take all the dimensions of our lives and believe that they all require attention, we don't need to assign equal value to each of them at any one moment in our lives. Sometimes we may find it important to focus more on one dimension than on others. For example, young couples, starting in a marriage or committed relationship, find themselves at odds because they haven't prioritized the dimensions they should attend to for themselves individually and the dimensions they need to consider as a couple.

Rather than balance or juggle dimensions, harmonize them. That means, make the different dimensions work together to benefit you *in the long run*. Exercise 6.1, Prioritizing Dimensions, is designed to help you rank the dimensions that you mentioned in the formal vision statement you wrote in Exercise 5.2. You will rank them in terms of: (1) their importance to you right now; (2) the importance you would like them to have five years from now; and (3) their importance to you as you would like them to have twenty-five years from now. These three separate rankings will allow you to emphasize one set of goals at one time and different sets of goals at other times, thus allowing for conflicts and resolutions without abandoning one or another. The Setting Priorities Sample will help you understand the process.

The illustration is from a young, single, recent college graduate who is looking at the dimensions of her life now, in five years, and in twenty-five years. Notice the emphasis on Career and Financial. They definitely go together at this point in the person's life. Likewise, Personal Values stay important and harmonize with all other values throughout the person's life. Family, Community, and Material Goods don't mean as much to her as does Social, which is another arrangement you might expect from her at this stage of her life.

Look how the priorities change over time. In five years, Financial and Personal Values are still of equally high importance. But now Family has joined this lofty priority, and discussion revealed that the person wanted to get married and start a family at this time. Those three number one dimensions can work together very well. Notice, however, that Career has dropped down a notch, probably because Family and Career tend to conflict at this stage. At the same time, the dimension Material Goods has jumped several levels of importance, which is not at all uncommon among young couples. Social also drops at this time, but look at the third column.

After twenty-five years, this person doesn't think that she will be as concerned about Career as she was earlier. Family and Personal Values still top the list of priorities, but now Community has climbed to the number two slot, along with Financial. Material Goods will not be as important to this person by then as it was twenty years earlier.

[Facilitator: Distribute the instructions, sample worksheet, and worksheet. Read the exercise instructions aloud. Then refer to the following notes for the discussion and afterwards.]

Lecture Notes for After Discussion

Two or more dimensions may have the same ranking, but when they do, they may conflict. Ranking all your dimensions as one suggests you could have many goal conflicts that pull you in different directions. To harmonize competing dimensions, look first at the relationships among them.

How does your Career dimension interact with your Family dimension? If, for example, your family relationships are taking a back seat to your current career demands, depending on the current stage of your career, that would be natural and understandable. If you're just starting out, as in the case of a young couple, recognizing that your family will benefit *in the long term* by what you do now in the Career dimension helps you *harmonize* that disparity. When other people are involved, as in the case of conflict between Career and Family, it's essential that you involve those other people in examining the conflicts and the steps that must be taken to harmonize those dimensions.

So much for looking at your rankings *now.* Be aware that emphasizing one aspect of your life more than the others over a long period of time and in spite of life changes can create an untenable dissonance in your life. That's why you want to look at the dimension's importance five years from now as well as right now. You need to ask yourself if you should be as deeply engaged in, for example, Career activities five years from now as you are now. If you think you should, consider the adjustments that you and the significant others in your life have to make to accommodate that emphasis. Another example: What if you plan to have two children in the five-year period? How should you rank the priority of Career at the end of that time? You may want to deemphasize Career and emphasize Family.

INSTRUCTIONS FOR THE PRIORITIZING DIMENSIONS EXERCISE

Review your vision statement and rank the seven (or more) dimensions in the Setting Priorities table in terms of: (1) their importance to you right now, (2) the importance you would like them to have five years from now, and (3) the importance to you as you foresee them twenty-five years from now. Use one to denote the most important, two the next in value, and so forth. Ties are likely.

It's important to consider these same dimensions five years from now. How do the rankings of the dimensions change? You need to ask yourself that if rankings are the same as now, how come? If you decide that identical rankings are appropriate, that's fine, otherwise you may want to think further about what it means to keep the same priorities over time? Then, do the same for your rankings of your life dimensions twenty-five years from now. If they remain the same, again think further about what that means. Once the priorities of your life's dimensions are aligned with one another, it's easier to set and prioritize the goals within each dimension.

Discussion Items After the Paper and Pencil Exercise

1. Circle the dimensions ranked at the same level (tied) in the first five years.

2. What are the relationships between the tied dimensions?
   - Are they connected, as in the sample in the overhead (Career, Financial, Material Goods)?
   - If not, which dimensions compete with one another for immediate attention?
   - Consider at least one way you can manage that competition to make them harmonize, make them work together. If they can't be made to work together, reset the priority of one dimension or the other.

3. Circle the priorities of your life's dimensions that stay of equal importance over time.
   - How harmonized do they remain over time?
   - If they don't remain harmonized, consider what will happen—the kind of goal conflicts you might have or the frustration you might experience—when trying to accomplish more than you are capable of accomplishing.

SETTING PRIORITIES SAMPLE

Dimensions	Now	In 5 Years	In 25 Years
1. Career (work you want to do and where you want to do it)	1	2	4
2. Community (your roles and the degree of influence you want)	4	4	2
3. Family (family of origin and acquired family or families)	3	1	1
4. Financial (income from all sources and how you spend it)	1	1	2
5. Material Goods (things you want for yourself or family)	5	2	3
6. Personal Values (morality, spirituality, health, etc.)	1	1	1
7. Social Relations (friends, acquaintances, neighbors, etc.)	2	3	2

SETTING PRIORITIES

Dimensions	Now	In 5 Years	In 25 Years
1. Career (work you want to do and where you want to do it)			
2. Community (your roles and the degree of influence you want)			
3. Family (family of origin and acquired family or families)			
4. Financial (income from all sources and how you spend it)			
5. Material Goods (things you want for yourself or family)			
6. Personal Values (morality, spirituality, health, etc.)			
7. Social Relations (friends, acquaintances, neighbors, etc.)			

7

Goal Setting
(Step 5)

Once the participants divide their lives into dimensions and see the relationships between them, they can decide on how they should fulfill the values in each of those dimensions. Exercise 7.1 is designed to help them set goals and design action plans for getting to where they want to go.

Before the students can complete the exercise, however, you have to prepare them with a rather extensive lecture because very few people have training in and experience with writing well-formulated goal statements. Although people talk about developing action plans, they refer mainly to one of two activities: (1) writing a list of goals, or (2) writing a list of things to do. However, an action plan consists of goals, objectives, and activities—all expressed as statements (goal statements, objective statements, activity statements). A complete plan also identifies the resources needed for executing the plan and the barriers that can be foreseen that could prevent a person from achieving his or her goals. The existence of a plan doesn't ensure success, but it does help.

Exercise 7.1. Writing Goal Statements

Learning Objectives and Outcomes

By the end of this exercise participants will have:

▶ Learned how to write well-formulated goal statements.

▶ Produced well-formulated goal statements for themselves in whatever dimension(s) they want to use to begin action planning.

Self-Management Skills Involved

▶ Linear thinking

▶ Openness to discuss goals and objectives in a classroom environment

Requirements

Time:	Not more than sixty minutes
Materials:	Sample Goal Statements With Targets
	Sample Goal Statements With Means and Conditions
	Instructions for Writing Goal Statements handout
	Pencil and paper
Preparation:	Copy the samples and handout.
Room Setup:	Any classroom style

Lecture Notes

A goal is an end point, what you want to accomplish. A goal statement describes the end point, when you hope to accomplish it, and, in general, how you want to get there. When you get there, activity toward the goal comes to an end. You move on to achieving a new or different goal. To simplify the language, use the words *goal* and *goal statements* interchangeably. Let's look first at how to develop well-formulated goal statements.

Criteria of Well-Formulated Goal Statements

The values that constitute each dimension of your life are just words until you do something to fulfill them, that is, use them to direct the goals you want to achieve. You begin by asking yourself how you might fulfill an important value; for example, "How can I fulfill the value of having managerial authority?" One answer might be, "Earn a promotion to management." This answer is the first step in writing a well-formulated goal statement.

A well-formulated goal statement is *specific, measurable, observable, realistic,* and *time bound* (though inelegant, the acronym is SMORT).

Specific.   Goals must be specific to be useful. "Earn a promotion to management in three years by succeeding as the team leader, attending management classes, receiving high ratings on my performance reviews." Not only is that example specific, it's also simple. It obeys the KISS principle: Keep it Simple and Straightforward. Eliminating ambiguity helps identify the priorities you want to achieve and reduces goal conflicts.

Measurable or Observable.   As for being *measurable* or *observable,* some people say that in management, if you can't measure it, it never happened. I won't go that far, but I will say that unless you can observe a result, you can't measure it. If you can't observe it, you can't know if you ever reached our target. However, some observable events are not measurable or at least not easily measured. You can observe that a person is angry or that she is happy, but you would have to have special devices to measure the degree of anger or happiness. Supposing a person achieves his goal or gets a promotion to manager. The promotion is observable, and the raise that comes with the promotion is measurable, whereas the promotion itself is not.

Realistic.   A note about *realistic.* The word's standard definition, in *Webster's Collegiate Dictionary* (10th Edition), says that to be realistic means to refer to facts and to reject the impractical and the visionary. Rejecting the impractical means that a realistic goal is achievable. If a goal is realistic, a person should be capable of achieving it; contrarily, if it isn't realistic, it isn't achievable. At the same time, the standard definition of achievable is to be capable of successful completion, which is to say that an achievable goal is realistic.

"Rejecting the visionary," however, is another story. I don't know why *Webster's* definition includes that notion. Goals can and should reflect one important sense of the word *visionary*: having or being marked by foresight or imagination, invention.

Targets.   For a goal statement to reflect a realistic target, the target should:

▶ Fit with previous experience.

▶ Fit within accepted bounds of knowledge.

▶ Recognize personal physical, emotional, and psychological limits.

▶ Recognize limits placed on you by the world in which you live.

Realism is a matter of degree. The more a goal falls outside the parameters listed above, the more you risk achievability. That doesn't mean you can never achieve a goal that doesn't fit with previous experience or fit within the accepted bounds of knowledge. By no means. No discovery, no new horizons, no new paradigms would ever exist if we use the criteria that define "realistic" to straightjacket our minds and spirit. So-called "stretch goals" are a minimal recognition that you must try to exceed the probable in order to achieve the possible.

Three Elements of Well-Formulated Goal Statements

When writing a well-formulated goal statement, you need three elements: (1) a target, (2) a time frame in which the target is to be reached, and (3) means and conditions that will help you reach the target. Let's examine the goal statement: "Earn a promotion to management in three years by succeeding as the team leader, attending management classes, receiving high ratings on my performance reviews."

Targets. To guarantee expressing a goal statement's target with a measurable or observable event, use an *active verb* and *object* that together describe an end point. Express the target as a description or as a description and a quantity. "Earn a promotion to management." That's the descriptive target of the goal that states what you want to accomplish; the result is *observable.* Getting promoted is the observable outcome that determines whether or not you achieved the goal.

Since a goal is an end point, when you reach the target, all activity toward it ceases. "Earn a promotion," "Earn a salary," "Increase productivity by 12 percent." Once you're promoted to manager, or earn $50,000, or increase productivity by 12 percent, you have to start another active process by setting another goal.

Express a target both descriptively and quantifiably. A quantifiable target states both what you want to accomplish and how much value that target has. For example, "Earn a salary of $50,000." In this example, "earn a salary" is the *what,* $50,000 is the *how much.* Another example: "Increase productivity by 12 percent." Increase productivity = the what; 12 percent = the how much.

[Facilitator: Distribute Sample Goal Statements With Targets now.]

Time Frames. The most obvious quantifiable expression of a goal, the time in which you wish to achieve it, is also the second element of a well-formulated goal statement. The target of a goal pulls you toward the future. The time frame that you set for achieving it, pushes you. Every goal statement should therefore include a realistic time frame, with a start date and an end date, that you use as one measure among others of success.

Likewise to satisfy the criterion of achievability, you need some idea of by when you will achieve it. A deadline provides a *measurable outcome* that, like a target, has to be realistic to be achievable. "Become a millionaire in one year" may be realistic for someone, but it isn't realistic for most people. "Earn a promotion to management in three years" may be realistic for most people who aspire to move from a line position to management. It depends on conditions.

Means and Conditions.   Let's examine the goal-statement we've used to illustrate the third element of a well-formulated goal statement: "Earn a promotion to management in three years by succeeding as the team leader, attending management classes, receiving high ratings on my performance reviews." In the Sample Goal Statements With Means and Conditions we see how the statement sets the planning process in motion. In effect, the list of the means or conditions is an outline of steps that you need to achieve before you can reach your target. The target guides how you decide on the steps for reaching it. In the case of the illustration, those three conditions have to be met before the person reaches his or her goal.

That doesn't mean you can't change the statement to meet new conditions. Nothing in writing is ever written in stone unless you make it so.

[Facilitator: Distribute Sample Goal Statements With Means and Conditions now.]

Write Down Goals

When working on achieving greater self-management, you have to write down your goals. It's also a good idea to tell someone about them. Written goals become a document you can use to contract with yourself to fulfill. Telling someone about them gives you an ally with whom you can consult or call upon to collaborate with you when you need support.

[Facilitator: Open the floor to discussion.]

Handling Discussion Issues

Issue: Some people may not see value in writing down goal statements. They often don't like to plan their lives. A common response: "I'd rather be spontaneous."

Possible Response: Long-range planning doesn't prevent spontaneity. In fact, it helps keep you focused on the broad outlines of your life while letting you freely explore the details.

Issue: Some people may not see the value in writing complete, well-formulated goal statements.

Possible Response: Unexpected events can sidetrack you from your goals. By laying down a time frame and by identifying means and conditions, you can stay focused on what you have to do regardless of whatever else may happen.

[Facilitator: Distribute the exercise instructions and read them aloud.]

Discussion Questions

1. What is the value to you of writing down your goal statements?

   Typical answer: I have a better idea of what I really want to achieve.

2. What is the value to you of writing means and conditions as well as target and time frame?

   Typical answer: It gives me some idea of how to get to where I want to go.

SAMPLE GOAL STATEMENTS WITH TARGETS

Example 1
"Earn a salary of $50,000."   Earn a salary = the *what* $50,000 = the *how much*

Example 2
"Increase productivity by 12 percent."   Increase productivity = the *what* 12% = the *how much*

SAMPLE GOAL STATEMENTS
WITH MEANS AND CONDITIONS

Target	Time Frame	Means and Conditions
Earn a promotion to management	In three years	1. By succeeding as the team leader 2. Attending management classes 3. Receiving high ratings on my performance reviews

INSTRUCTIONS FOR THE WRITING GOAL STATEMENTS EXERCISE

Using this model, write at least one goal statement in one dimension. If you have enough time, write a goal statement in two dimensions.

Goal Statement: Earn a promotion to management in two years by finishing my degree, leading the cross-functional team to its goals, and receiving highest possible performance appraisals.

▶ Target: Earn a promotion to management.

▶ Time Frame: Two years.

▶ Conditions/Means: Finishing my degree, leading the cross-functional team to its goals, receiving highest possible performance appraisals.

8

Prioritize Goals and Performance Ranges (Step 6)

Most people aren't very patient. They want everything, and they want it now. So, goal conflicts happen because they don't prioritize their goals and pursue those of relative immediacy or importance. The result is frustration, which sometimes leads to feelings of despair resulting from failure.

The exercises in Chapter 8 are designed to help the participants create action plans that avoid goal conflicts and the feeling of despair they engender. The first part of action planning is to prioritize goals and set performance ranges that allow students to feel good about whatever progress they make toward their goals. This chapter deals only with prioritizing goals; Chapter 9 deals with objectives and activities. The two chapters should therefore be taken together.

Exercise 8.1. Prioritizing Your Goals

Learning Objectives and Outcomes

By the end of this exercise participants will be able to:

▶ Assign priorities to their goals.

▶ Use one well-formulated goal statement as the starting point of an action plan.

Self-Management Skills Involved

▶ Linear thinking

▶ Openness to discussing action plans in a classroom environment

Requirements

Time:	Not more than thirty minutes
Materials:	Action Plans overhead
	Criteria for Prioritizing Goals handout
	Decision Criteria handout
	Assigning Priorities overhead
	Pencil and paper
Equipment:	Overhead projector and screen
Preparation:	Photocopy the handouts.
	Make overheads.
Room Setup:	Any classroom arrangement

Lecture Notes

[Facilitator: Put up Action Plans overhead now.]

Action Plans

In brief, an action plan is a road map, complete with a destination, milestones, and things to do to get you through the milestones to the ultimate end point. The Action Plans overhead provides a schematic of action plans designed to fulfill a vision for one's life or work. The vision gives a broad picture of what you want and why you want it. From there you separate your visions into dimensions—broad aspects of your life or work: for example, career, community, family, financial, personal values, or social relations. In each of those dimensions you set goals for yourself and conceive of the steps or milestones and activities it will take to get to those goals. You identify the resources you'll need, and, in some cases, you'll anticipate barriers or obstacles for reaching your milestones. If possible, you'll set up a plan for overcoming or getting around the barriers as well.

Prioritizing Goals

Setting goals is the first and most important step in designing an action plan for developing satisfactory dimensions in your life and work. On the other hand, not every goal is equally as important or as immediate as every other goal. Timing and circumstances often dictate what you want or should achieve at any given time. And, sometimes you can't achieve one goal unless you achieve others first. Three criteria, summarized in the table in the Criteria for Prioritizing Goals handout, will help you decide how vital goals are.

[Facilitator: Distribute Criteria for Prioritizing Goals handout now.]

When prioritizing, consider three key points. What is important to you, what is immediate or urgent, and what depends on other things to happen.

Importance. A goal is important to you when you think it's a good thing to achieve, that it's desirable, that its outcome is "good." A goal that says "Stay debt-free by paying all bills," for example, becomes important only if you think it's good to do so. Goals important to someone else, say your boss, become important to you *only* if you think it's desirable or good that you want them too.

"Good" and "desirable" (value words) signal emotional aspects of decisions you make, even if they are defined in measurable or observable terms. Numerical outcomes are "good" only if you say they are.

Immediacy. A goal gains immediacy when it becomes urgent to achieve it. In the example, if in order to remain debt-free it is urgent that you earn a specific level of income, then that income goal becomes immediate as well as important. Goals important to your boss may never become important to you, but they can achieve a high level of immediacy if failing to achieve your boss's goals will interfere with you achieving yours.

Dependency. A goal becomes a high priority when another high-priority goal depends on you achieving the first one, even if you don't consider it all that important or immediate to you. The boss's goals may not seem important or immediate to you, but building a career is one of your high-priority items. Since your boss is partially responsible for determining how your career progresses, you may want to take on his or her goals, help him or her achieve them, in order to serve the greater purpose you have set for yourself.

Decision Criteria

To decide if a goal is important, immediate, or essential for something else to happen, you need to answer three sets of questions.

[Facilitator: Distribute the Decision Criteria handout now.]

Importance. The first question you must ask and answer is, "Just how badly do I want this?" Then, ask:

▶ If I or others around me don't accomplish this goal,
— What would happen?
— Who would be affected and how?
— What consequences of inaction—positive or negative—could affect my other goals or those of other people or the organizations to which I belong or in which I work?
▶ If I or others around me don't accomplish this goal, and if nothing bad or of consequence would happen, why work for it?
▶ Does this goal fit with or complement other goals? If not, why pursue it?
▶ If achieving this goal produces desirable results, why not put everything necessary into doing it and doing it right?

Immediacy. New goals present themselves with changing circumstances, and when they do, you need to examine them for how urgent they really are.

▶ If I or others around me don't accomplish this goal *now,*
— What would happen?
— Who would be affected and how?
— What consequences of inaction—positive or negative—could affect my other goals or those of other people or the organizations to which I belong or in which I work?
▶ If I or others around me don't accomplish this goal *now,* and if nothing bad or of consequence would happen, why work for it?
▶ If achieving this goal *now* produces desirable results, why not put everything necessary into doing it and doing it right?

Dependency. When you set a goal that doesn't seem important or immediate at the moment, you need to determine if other goals depend on it for their fulfillment. Ask:

▶ What other goals depend on the achievement of this goal?
▶ Which goals have to be reached first before this goal can be achieved?
▶ What is *the price of inaction?*

Assigning Priorities to Goals

A goal that is important and urgent to you or to someone else with whom you are closely related (e.g., your boss), or on which other goals depend, is an *A* goal. It should get your greatest amount of immediate attention.

A goal that is important but not urgent is a *B* goal. A goal that is urgent but not important is also a *B* goal.

A goal that is neither important nor urgent, and on which nothing else depends, is a *C* goal. A *C* goal could be struck from the list and no one would miss it—unless it has significance as a long-term goal, one you plan to achieve *someday.*

Instructions for Prioritizing Your Goals

This exercise is the first step in creating an appropriate, realistic road map for yourself. Write at least three goal statements. They can be in one dimension or in several different dimensions. Use the three criteria (importance, immediacy, dependency) to determine which of the goals has the highest priority for you at this time. Use the capital letters *A, B,* and *C* in the following manner:

[Facilitator: Put up the Assigning Priorities overhead now.]

▶ *A* indicates a goal that is both important and urgent to you. If other high-priority goals are dependent on achieving this goal, you could designate the goal *A+.*

▶ *B* indicates a goal that is, to you, important but not urgent or urgent but not important. You can recognize the goal as a *B* priority if it is important or urgent *and achieving other goals depends on it.*

▶ *C* indicates goals that are neither urgent nor important to you. However, you may not be able to simply discard or ignore a *C* goal. Other, longer-term goals may depend on achieving a *C* goal.

If you assign the letter *A* to two or more goals, make a list of reasons why they are both important and immediate.

Group Discussion

1. What did prioritizing goals do to help you sort out what you are trying to achieve?

   Typical answer: It helped me to see what is really important to do now and what I can put off.

2. How did prioritizing goals help you resolve goal conflicts?

   Typical answer: By putting off some goals until later, I can concentrate on goals I need to achieve now.

ACTION PLANS

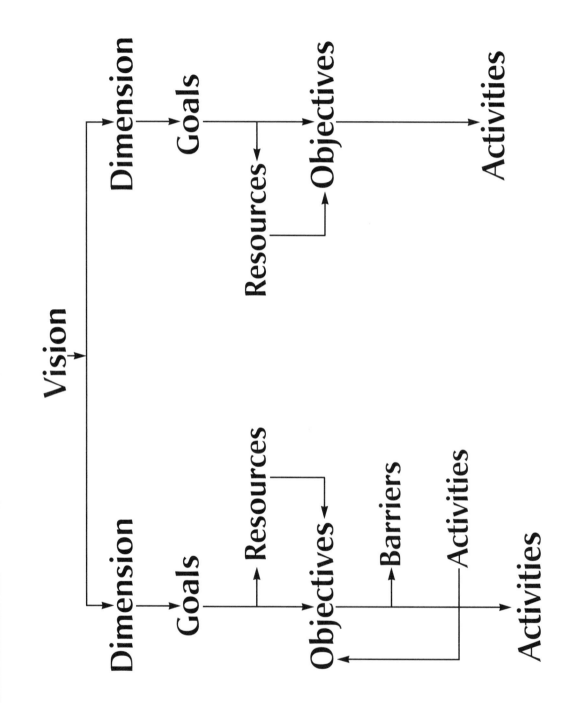

CRITERIA FOR PRIORITIZING GOALS

Priorities	Definitions
Importance	A goal is important to you when you think it's a good thing to achieve, that it is desirable, that its outcome is good. Goals important to someone else, say, to your boss, become important to you *only* if you think it's desirable or good that you want them too. "Good" and "desirable" (value words) signal emotional aspects of decisions you make, even if they are defined in measurable or observable terms. Numerical outcomes are good only if you say they are.
Immediacy (Urgency)	A goal gains immediacy when it becomes urgent to achieve it. Goals important to your boss may never become important to you, but they can achieve a high level of immediacy if failing to achieve your boss's goals will interfere with your achieving your goals.
Dependency	A goal deserves a high priority when another high-priority goal depends on your achieving the first one, even if you don't consider it all that important or immediate to you. The boss's goals may not seem important or immediate to you, but building a career is one of your high-priority items. Since your boss is partially responsible for determining how your career progresses, you may want to take on his or her goals, help him or her achieve them, in order to serve the greater purpose you have set for yourself.

DECISION CRITERIA

Priorities	Tests of Priorities (Questions to Answer)
Importance	Just how badly do I want this? ▶ If I or others around me don't accomplish this goal, What would happen? Who would be affected and how? What consequences of inaction—positive or negative—could affect my other goals or those of other people or the organizations to which I belong or in which I work? ▶ If I or others around me don't accomplish this goal, and if nothing bad or of consequence would happen, why work for it? ▶ Does this goal fit with or complement other goals? If not, why pursue it? ▶ If achieving this goal produces desirable results, why not put everything necessary into doing it and doing it right?
Immediacy (Urgency)	▶ If I or others around me don't accomplish this goal *now*, What would happen? Who would be affected and how? What consequences of inaction—positive or negative—could affect my other goals or those of other people or the organizations to which I belong or in which I work? ▶ If I or others around me don't accomplish this goal *now*, and if nothing bad or of consequence would happen, why work for it? ▶ If achieving this goal *now* produces desirable results, why not put everything necessary into doing it and doing it right?
Dependency	▶ What other goals depend on the achievement of this goal? ▶ Which goals have to be reached first for this goal to happen? ▶ What is *the price of inaction*?

Assigning Priorities

A = Both important and urgent to you.

A+ = Both important and urgent; other goals depend on it.

B = Important but not urgent or urgent but not important. If important or urgent and achieving other goals depend on it.

C = Neither urgent nor important to you. However, long-term goals may depend on *C*'s.

Exercise 8.2. Setting Performance Standards as Performance Ranges

Learning Objective and Outcome

By the end of this exercise participants will be able to establish performance ranges for their goals.

Self-Management Skills Involved

▶ Openness to a new or different way of setting goals
▶ Openness to discussing goals in a classroom environment

Requirements

Time:	Not more than fifteen minutes
Materials:	Performance Ranges overhead Achievement Over Time overhead Pencil and paper
Equipment:	Overhead projector and screen
Preparation:	Make overheads.
Room Setup:	Any classroom arrangement

Interactive

After the participants select one or more goal statements and divide their targets into performance ranges, the group discussion should focus on how setting performance ranges helped reduced some of the anxiety associated with achieving important goals.

Lecture Notes

People often set themselves up to fail by reaching beyond their grasp or by not recognizing their own limitations (e.g., insufficient training or experience).

You can head off such obstacles by establishing performance ranges for your goals rather than setting one inflexible performance standard for each of them. Decide in advance what would be the optimal standard for a goal, what would be the least you would accept, and what would be realistic (i.e., the point between the two that you could honestly believe you could achieve). If you get no other benefit from setting performance ranges like these, you will find your anxiety or stress levels going down. The Performance Ranges overhead illustrates the matter.

[Facilitator: Put up Performance Ranges overhead now.]

The overhead suggests getting to where you want to go, starting from ground zero: no education, training, or skills for achieving your goals. As you learn or gain skills over time, you can reach higher and higher toward your goals. At the same time, the model only figuratively represents a person's efforts. Progress toward achieving a goal usually involves setbacks and little failures. Little or nothing ever happens in a straight arc, the way it appears in the overhead.

[Facilitator: Put up Achievement Over Time overhead now.]

The Achievement Over Time overhead applies the performance range model to an actual goal. Here you can see what I mean by the fact that little or nothing ever happens in a straight arc. Assuming that you are starting at ground zero, the minimally acceptable goal reflects early learning stages. The realistic goal is what you believe that you can achieve with training and practice or experience. The optimal goal is what you'd like to achieve over time. Accepting these performance levels helps you accomplish what you're capable of without feeling terrible that you haven't achieved the highest possible level immediately.

Reducing stress or anxiety levels is a double-edged sword. Eliminating all forms of stress or anxiety can lead to complacency, yet too much stress or anxiety can lead to apathy. The result of both complacency and apathy is the same: not trying to reach the optimal level of performance. Both complacency and apathy encourage people to settle for the minimum acceptable performance.

At the same time, for those who truly want to achieve the most and the best, stretching for the optimum (reaching for the stars) is sure to land them where they want to be (on the moon).

Instructions to Participants

Select one goal statement and divide the target into minimum acceptable, optimal, and realistic possibilities. Start by identifying the optimal target first (e.g., "Earn a promotion into management in one year"), then the minimally acceptable (three years), and then the realistic (two years).

Discussion Question

If you experienced any anxiety at all about achieving a specific goal, how did setting performance ranges help you resolve those feelings?

Typical answer: I could see that a range of targets is possible, rather than one, maybe unrealistic, goal.

PERFORMANCE RANGES

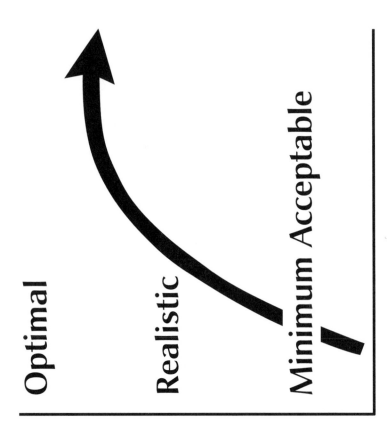

Optimal

Realistic

Minimum Acceptable

Level of Performance

Time

ACHIEVEMENT OVER TIME

Level of Performance

Optimal
Promoted to manager
in one year

Realistic
Promoted to manager
in two years

Minimum Acceptable
Promoted to manager
in three years

Time

9

Write an Action Plan (Step 7)

The lack of a plan is the enemy of action.
The lack of action is the enemy of a plan.

The exercises in Chapter 9 provide the tools necessary for the participants to complete their action plans. The explanation and practice in Exercise 9.1 will result in laying out the steps or a path toward accomplishing a goal. The explanation and practice in Exercise 9.2 will result in identifying what things have to be done to complete each step and reach the goal.

Exercise 9.1. Design an Action Plan, Part 1

Learning Objectives and Outcomes

By the end of this exercise participants will:

▶ Be able to explain how to design objectives (milestones) that lead to a goal's target.

▶ Have a list of steps toward achieving a specific goal.

Self-Management Skills Involved

▶ Openness to a new or different way of looking at life planning

▶ Openness to discussing goals and action plans in a classroom environment

Requirements

Time:	Not more than thirty minutes
Materials:	Finding Objectives in a Well-Formulated Goal Statement overhead
	Action Plan, Part 1 worksheet
	Pencil and paper
Equipment:	Overhead projector and screen
Preparation:	Make the overhead.
	Photocopy the worksheet.
Room Setup:	Any classroom style

Lecture Notes

Maybe you don't have to plan everything you do. Spontaneity has great merits. However, especially in business, failing to plan can lead to disaster. Visioning and goal setting set you in motion. The directions in which you move depend on planning on how to get to where you want to go and how to fulfill our vision.

A basic action plan describes the objectives, also referred to as milestones, necessary for achieving your goals (arriving at destinations) and outlines the steps you'll take to make the objectives happen.

Objectives (Milestones)

Objectives have been called *minigoals* because in all respects, save one, they resemble goal statements. A well-formulated objective statement consists of:

▶ A specific, measurable or observable, realistic target

▶ A time frame (a start date and an end date)

▶ Conditions or means by which the target will be achieved

The only difference between a goal statement and an objective statement is that a goal statement describes an end point that, when reached, puts an end to all steps toward it, and an objective statement describes a means toward an end (a goal's target). It's only a step in the plan for achieving a goal. In fact, the dependence of a goal on the objective can give the objective a very high priority.

[Facilitator: Put up the Finding Objectives in a Well-Formulated Goal Statement overhead now.]

You find objectives in the third part of a well-formulated goal statement, in the means and conditions. Let's take the example: "Earn a promotion to management in two years by finishing my degree, leading the cross-functional team to its goals, receiving the highest possible performance appraisals." The goal gives the action plan its direction. One route toward promotion in this case has the target "finishing my degree." That's one objective in the process toward earning the promotion. The next objective has the target of "leading the cross-functional team to its goals." The target in the third objective is "receiving the highest possible performance appraisals." You need only add the time frames and the means or conditions for achieving the objectives' targets, as we did in the overhead. Once you identify the objectives or milestones required for reaching your goals, you can plan the actions necessary for reaching the milestones.

Most people leave out this link between goals and action. Once you see your destination and think about what it takes to get there, instead of leaping right from goals to a list of activities (things to do) to achieve them, you must identify the steps for getting there (milestones or outcomes) that keep you on track and give you a yardstick for measuring your progress as you go.

Resources

Most plans succeed or crash on the status of resources for achieving objectives. Anything or anyone contributing to or adding value to your work and your life is a resource or a means for achieving objectives: Contacts (work place associates, prospects, clients, customers, vendors, family, friends), equipment, capital goods, cash, facilities, or other assets. When planning, make a list of resources you may need and do not have, as well as those you do have. You may come up with a need for additional resources later, but you have a starting place and can plan for acquiring resources you need but don't have.

Obstacles or Barriers

The absence or lack of resources is only one kind of barrier. Others include lack of management support, defective materials, inadequate planning, and other conditions in the way of achieving objectives or that remove value from your objectives. When planning, think about the possible barriers to getting to where you want to go.

To identify barriers and to decide what to do when an obstacle gets in the way of progress toward goals, play "what if . . .?" and use "worst case" scenarios. Example:

"What if supplies I need are not available?" Then turn the barrier into a goal. "Supplies replenished by tomorrow at a cost of $2,500.00." Continue action planning by listing what you have to do to overcome the barrier and meet objectives.

Instructions to Participants

[Facilitator: Distribute the Action Plan, Part 1 worksheet now.]

Select a goal statement and, using any method you want (Pass Backward, Pass Forward), complete Part 1 of the Action Plan.

Discussion Questions

1. How will planning to achieve goals in this manner help you achieve your goals?

   Typical answer: I'll get all my "ducks in a row."

2. If you experienced any anxiety at all about achieving a specific goal, how did setting up a list of steps help you resolve those feelings?

   Typical answer: I know what I have to do and I can alter the plan if I need to.

Finding Objectives in a Well-Formulated Goal Statement

Target	Earn a promotion to management
Time Frame	In two years
Means or Conditions	Finishing my degree
	Leading the cross-functional team to its goals
	Receiving the highest possible performance appraisals

Objective 1	Within two years, finish my degree by . . .
Objective 2	During this next year, lead the cross-functional team to its goals by . . .
Objective 3	During the next two years, receive the highest possible performance appraisals by . . .

ACTION PLAN, PART 1

Well-formulated Goal Statement:

Objective or Milestone:

Objective or Milestone:

Objective or Milestone:

Objective or Milestone:

Objective or Milestone:

Objective or Milestone:

Objective or Milestone:

Objective or Milestone:

Objective or Milestone:

Exercise 9.2. Complete the Action Plan, Part 2

Learning Objectives and Outcomes

By the end of this exercise participants will:

▶ Be able to describe their entire action plan for achieving a specific goal.

▶ Have a complete "road map" toward a specific goal.

Self-Management Skills Involved

▶ Openness to a new or different way of looking at one's life

▶ Openness to discussing action plans in a classroom environment

Requirements

Time:	Not more than thirty minutes
Materials:	An Action Plan overhead Day Calendar overhead The Complete Action Plan worksheet Pencil and paper
Equipment:	Overhead projector and screen
Preparation:	Make the overheads. Photocopy the worksheet.
Room Setup:	Any classroom style

Lecture Notes

Whereas objectives are steps in the direction of reaching a goal, activities are the things you do to achieve objectives or to overcome barriers. By writing an action plan designed to produce desired results, you anticipate what you have to do. At the same time, no list of activities is set in concrete. Regardless of when you plan to do something, you can always change dates and times.

When planning activities, tie them to the goals and objectives you need to achieve. Focus yourself by asking, "What goals or objectives do I want to achieve?" Then decide on what you have to do to reach the goal(s) or objective(s) you've tabbed for attention. As you apply your plan to your daily activities, do the same thing. Ask "On what goal(s) or objective(s) do I want to work today?" Then decide on activities for the day that will help you achieve the results you want to achieve. Let's look at some examples.

[Facilitator: Put up An Action Plan overhead now.]

In this first overhead, we have an action plan related to getting that promotion in two years. The activities listed under Objective 1 are things you have to do to get the degree. The statements are incomplete since they don't have any time frames. However, in the next overhead, which contains one day's calendar, you see some of the activities related to the objective's target, "Earn a degree."

[Facilitator: Put up the Day Calendar overhead now.]

As you can see in the overhead, activities have targets: "Attend stats class," for example. The target is the outcome you want from your effort. Outcomes can be quantified or not, depending on what you are doing. Actions can also have three specific kinds of outcomes, as they do in the overhead:

1. *Information Only.* In the activity of attending class, the outcome, or what would be accomplished in the activity, would be information only.
2. *Productive, that is, producing a tangible outcome.* The activity "Meet with the professor to decide on degree plan" would have a productive outcome because decisions would be made.
3. *Mixed, a combination of both Information and Productivity.* Going to the library to research materials for a term paper would result in getting information and being productive.

Or, an activity can have no outcome at all. We could stretch a point by saying that going to dinner with your spouse is productive, or, perhaps, mixed, but for the most part, we could just let it be a visit, with no material outcome of any kind.

[Facilitator: Distribute the Complete Action Plan worksheet and read aloud the instructions.]

Discussion Questions

1. How will planning to achieve goals in this manner help you achieve your goals?

   Typical answer: I will have more direction with the plan, and it will even provide some motivation to get up and get going.

2. If you experienced any anxiety at all about achieving a specific goal, how did setting up a "road map" help you resolve those feelings?

   Typical answer: I feel as if I have more control now.

An Action Plan

Goal Target

Earn a promotion to management

Time Frame

In two years

Objective 1: Finish my degree

Activities:

Attend classes

Turn in term papers

Pass final exams

Day Calendar

Desired Results: Earn a degree by attending classes, etc.

Times	Activities
8:00–9:00	Attend stats class
9:00–10:00	
10:00–11:00	Attend economics class
12:00–1:00	
1:00–2:00	Meet with professor to decide on degree plan
2:00–3:00	
3:00–4:00	Go to library to do research for my economics paper
5:00–6:00	
7:00–8:00	Go to dinner with spouse

COMPLETE ACTION PLAN

INSTRUCTIONS

Take the goal and objectives you wrote in Exercise 9.1 as the basis for completing the Complete Action Plan worksheet. Although we made space for three activities in each row, you can add as many activities as you wish on extra pages. If you can identify due dates for the activities, add them also. When you are through you will have a complete action plan for achieving the goal you identified at the top of the chart.

Well-formulated goal statement:

Objective 1:	Activity:
	Activity:
	Activity:
Objective 2:	Activity:
	Activity:
	Activity:
Objective 3:	Activity:
	Activity:
	Activity:
Objective 4:	Activity:
	Activity:
	Activity:
Objective 5:	Activity:
	Activity:
	Activity:
Objective 6:	Activity:
	Activity:
	Activity:

10

Evaluate Progress and Take Corrective Action (Step 8)

The exercises in Chapter 10 will provide participants with simple tools for measuring progress toward goals. The participants will need to complete the exercises in Chapter 9 to apply the tools in this chapter to their actual requirements.

Exercise 10.1. Definitions of Success as Observable or Quantifiable Targets

Learning Objective and Outcome

By the end of this exercise participants will have identified the observable to quantifiable measures of success in their action plans (other than time frames).

Self-Management Skills Involved

▶ Linear thinking
▶ Openness to monitoring one's own efforts

Requirements

Time: Fifteen minutes

Materials: Pencil, paper, and participants' previously written action plans

Instructions for Definitions of Success as Observable or Quantifiable Targets Exercise handout

Preparation: Photocopy the handout.

Room Setup: Any classroom style

Lecture Notes

How do you define success? No one doubts that *any* answer is debatable. Wealth. Position. Status. Happiness. What drives you may not drive the person sitting next to you.

How do you measure success? In terms of the amount of wealth you have? In terms of the roles you play in your communities? In terms of the number of people you manage? In terms of the degree of satisfaction you express? What works for you may not work for someone else.

By the definition of self-management, any answer is correct as long as it expresses your values, your vision for your life, your goals, and your action plans. And, all those values—vision, goals, and action plans—are subject to modification, change, or replacement. It's not the plan that matters, as Dwight Eisenhower reportedly had said. It's the *planning process.*

[Facilitator: Distribute the instructions handout.]

Discussion Questions

1. What is your definition of success?
2. How well does that definition fit with your vision for your life or work?

Lecture Notes: Summary of the Exercise

Measures are built into well-formulated statements that include observable or quantifiable targets, time frames, and the means and conditions by which you reach your targets. When you fulfill the vision for your life, satisfy the goals you set for yourself, and meet the terms of your action plans, you can call yourself successful.

INSTRUCTIONS FOR THE DEFINITIONS OF SUCCESS AS OBSERVABLE OR QUANTIFIABLE TARGETS EXERCISE

Using your previously written action plans, list the observable or measurable targets in all of your well-formulated goal and objective statements. Do not count time frames in the list yet. If you find any target that doesn't fit the criteria of observable or measurable (that is something you can experience or quantify), rewrite the target to fit. If you don't specify a target you can experience and/or measure in some way, you can never know if you've achieved it. For example, defining success as "being happy," without specifying what "being happy" entails, makes it difficult to decide whether or not you've achieved the goal.

Once you have listed all the targets, summarize them in one sentence. That becomes a definition of success. Does that sentence jibe with the vision statement for your life or work?

Exercise 10.2. Time Measures

Learning Objective and Outcome

By the end of this exercise participants will have identified the time measures of success in their action plans.

Self-Management Skills Involved

▶ Linear thinking
▶ Openness to monitoring one's own efforts

Requirements

Time: Fifteen minutes

Materials: Pencil, paper, and participants' previously written action plans
Sample Gantt Chart Structure handout

Preparation: Photocopy the handout.

Room Setup: Any classroom style

Lecture Notes

Simple Tools for Measuring Success

You don't need elegant formulae and elaborate charts to determine your degree of self-management and your levels of success. The chart of your own action plan and a Gantt Chart should suffice for most personal plans.

Checklists. Use your action plans as checklists to track progress toward goals. Just check off each activity you complete, each objective or milestone you reach, and each goal you achieve.

Gantt Charts. Meeting or exceeding your deadlines is one observable way to measure your progress. If you're not satisfying the time frames in your well-formulated action plan statements (goals, objectives, activities), you can get yourself back on track.

[Facilitator: Distribute the Sample Gantt Chart Structure handout now.]

If you lay out a chart of your action plans, like the one in the sample Gantt Chart, you can determine how and when to achieve various parts of your action plan. You reproduce your action plans in the left hand column, and divide the time line whatever way you want (in the handout, the time line is divided into four equal parts only for illustrative purposes). For long-term goals, you could separate the time into years. For very short-term goals, you can separate the time line into days. The xs represent planned start and stop dates.

A start date is as important as an end date. In the goal statement, "Get promoted to manager in two years by . . ." you have clearly determined the duration (two years), which provides you with a specific end date only if you say two years from a specific start date. For example, "starting today." Place an x in the column that represents the start date and another x in the column that represents the end date.

Once you lay out the chart, you have a way to determine whether or not you are at least on schedule, if not on target. Compare where you are with what you planned and marked in the Gantt Chart and decide whether or not you are satisfying the demands of your action plan. (Some people use a color code, marking the plan in one color and drawing actual progress with an overlying line in a different color.) If you aren't on your planned schedule, you can take steps to bring yourself into synch with your plans.

Instructions to Participants

Using your previously written action plans, identify the time frames in all your well-formulated statements. All goal statements and objective statements should include tentative start and end dates, and any activity statements that describe immediate actions should have tentative time starts and ends as well.

Discussion Questions

1. What is the greatest value of setting both start and end dates or times?

   Typical answer: Not only do I have a deadline, I know when I should start to give myself the maximum amount of time I need.

2. How does a time measure help you measure success?

   Typical answer: A deadline is a target to achieve.

SAMPLE GANTT CHART STRUCTURE

Action Plans	1	2	3	4
Dimension 1				
Get promoted to manager	x _____	_____ x		
Earn a degree	x _____ x			
Attend classes	x _____ x			
Complete research project	x _____	x		
Lead team	x _____	x		
Improve processes	x _____ x			
Reduce costs	x _____ x			
Increase income 10% a year	x _____	_____	_____ x	
Earn raises	x _____	_____	_____	x
Improve skills	x _____	x	x ____	x
Learn new skills		x _____ x		
Build relations	x _____	_____	x	
Improve holdings		x _____	_____	x
Stock purchases		x _____	_____	____ x
Buy property			x _____	____ x

Exercise 10.3. Means and Conditions

Learning Objectives and Outcomes

By the end of this exercise participants will be able to:

▶ Say whether or not their action plan statements will help them lay out the steps for achieving success.

▶ Explain how identifying means and conditions in an action plan helps to achieve success.

Self-Management Skills Involved

▶ Evaluating or assessing one's work

▶ Openness to making changes in one's work

Requirements

Time: Fifteen minutes

Materials: Pencil, paper, and participants' previously written action plans

Room Setup: Any classroom style

Lecture Notes

This simple exercise is a way to check if your goal statements and objective statements contain all the information you need for identifying whether or not you can use your plans to succeed in reaching your goals.

Instructions to Participants

Using your previously written action plans, underline the means and conditions you have included in all your well-formulated goal and objective statements. The means and conditions listed in goal statements will help you plan your steps or objectives, those listed in objective statements will help you plan your activities. If any statement seems incomplete, add the appropriate means and conditions to it.

Discussion Questions

1. What is the value of listing means and conditions?

   Typical answer: It provides some direction as to how to get to where I want to go.

2. How do means and conditions contribute to your ability to measure your success?

   Typical answer: You know what to look for as a realistic outcome.

Follow-Up Activity: Taking Corrective Action

Instructor's Notes

The purpose of this activity is to give the participants a tool for helping them follow up on what they do in the workshop. It's important that they have a way of adjusting if the preliminary plans they take away from the class don't work out just right.

Learning Objectives and Outcomes

By doing this activity, participants will take steps to:

▶ Evaluate or assess their action plans.

▶ Take corrective action when needed.

Self-Management Skills Involved

▶ Evaluating or assessing one's goals and work

▶ Openness to making changes in one's goals or work

Requirements

Time:	Five minutes for instruction plus discussion time
Materials:	Elaboration on Questions to Answer for Taking Corrective Action handout
	Questions to Answer for Taking Corrective Action worksheet
Preparation:	Photocopy the handout and worksheet.

Distribute the handout of the Elaboration on Questions to Answer for Taking Corrective Action, and use it to explain how participants should apply the questions to evaluate their progress and determine if corrective action is needed, and to prompt discussion. Then distribute the Questions to Answer for Taking Corrective Action worksheet and instruct the participants to take it home for use later.

ELABORATION ON QUESTIONS TO ANSWER
FOR TAKING CORRECTIVE ACTION

What you do and how you do it to keep yourself on plan depends on you. Basic questions you need to ask yourself if you find yourself missing deadlines or floundering along the path to your goals are:

Are your targets realistic? Sometimes, when people find they're not reaching the targets in their objectives or goals, it comes simply from expecting too much of themselves. Even what they call their realistic target is out of reach. They need to adjust performance ranges to get them closer to the desired conclusion over a longer period of time. Sometimes they need to set new or different targets because those they previously set are totally unrealistic.

Are your time frames realistic? Sometimes the performance ranges are okay, but the time lines are unrealistic. Actually, most people set longer time lines than they need. On the other hand, some people put themselves under too much pressure by not allowing enough time for reaching realistic targets in a realistic amount of time. Regardless of whether they set too much time aside or not enough, they need to consider new or different deadlines.

Are expected resources available? This is a common failing; people not looking ahead to decide what resources they need—and if they're accessible. Let's say that getting a degree will require $5,000 a semester. What if your company doesn't have a tuition reimbursement plan? Do you have that kind of money? If you determine the resources you need are not immediately accessible, what do you do then? Have you looked into grants or scholarship funds?

Have you accounted for obstacles that you could have predicted? The lack of resources so often creates barriers to success that it's remarkable that people don't look for such obstacles as they plan. You need to make an accurate and thorough environmental scan to examine what barriers could prevent you from reaching your goals.

Are obstacles you thought you could overcome insurmountable? Since people don't always predict barriers that could get in their way, they fail to see that one or another barrier could permanently prevent them from reaching a goal. They don't have a plan *B*. "What if this goal turns out to be impossible? What can I do to change direction to get around those obstacles and to achieve more realistic goals?"

Have unexpected obstacles occurred that you could not have predicted? As you progress in applying your plan to your life and work, you need to be constantly on the alert for unexpected obstacles or even unintended consequences of what you do. At the time those things happen, you need to develop action plans for overcoming or getting around the obstacles or unintended consequences. In short, always expect the unexpected, and you'll never be surprised.

QUESTIONS TO ANSWER
FOR TAKING CORRECTIVE ACTION

1. Are your targets realistic? How can you adjust performance ranges to get you closer to the desired conclusion? Do you need to set new or different targets?

2. Are your time frames realistic? Do you need to set new or different deadlines?

3. Are expected resources available? If not, why not? What can you do to make them accessible?

4. Have you accounted for obstacles that you could have predicted? If not, what do you need to do to make your environmental scan more accurate?

5. Are obstacles you thought you could overcome insurmountable? If so, what can you do to change direction to get around those obstacles and to achieve more realistic goals?

6. Have unexpected obstacles or unintended consequences occurred that you could not have predicted? If so, how will you manage the obstacles or unintended consequences?

Putting Together the Self–Management Puzzle

Self-Management Exercises

By the end of this section you will be able to facilitate seventeen exercises that will help solve the puzzle of creating wholeness and that will increase people's self-management skills in the six competencies, each of which has a chapter of its own (Chapters 11–15).

1. Wholeness
2. Self-awareness
3. Self-confidence
4. Self-respect/self-esteem
5. Drive
6. Respect for others

Portrait of a Self-Managed Person

The portrait of a self-managed person in Chapter 1 deliberately oversimplifies the image conveyed to facilitate understanding the self-assessments related to self-management. In reality each competency—self-awareness, self-confidence, self-respect/self-esteem, drive, respect for others—is itself a puzzle formed by a set of specific skills. Wholeness reflects the synergy revealed when we put together all the pieces of the puzzle of the portrait of the self-managed person.

SKILLS THAT MAKE PEOPLE COMPETENT

To be competent, according to the 10th Edition of *Merriam Webster's Collegiate Dictionary,* means, in part, to have "requisite or adequate ability or qualities"; to have "the capacity to function or develop in a particular way"—in short, to have skills. *Each self-management competency consists of a complex set of skills that allow a person to function in a particular way.* Developing and fine-tuning those skills is what I mean by putting the pieces of the self-management puzzle together.

The exercises in this section are designed to encourage participants to solve problems or make discoveries about themselves or other people. You'll find a great deal of satisfaction and enjoyment from the workshop itself when you watch the participants satisfy the requirements you set for them. Among the many ways of deliberately creating problems, two in particular require special attention.

1. Sometimes you don't explain the exercise's learning objectives until the end or you provide deliberately vague or ambiguous instructions. You want the participants to work out the steps they have to take to solve the exercise's problems, otherwise they can't learn how to solve a similar problem in real life, which is precisely one of the learning objectives. You want the participants to find out the learning objectives on their own or to work out the details of their instructions by themselves. It goes back to the child learning to ride a bicycle that I described in Chapter 1; unless the child actually rides the bike without training wheels, she never will learn how to ride on her own.

2. Sometimes a person might lack a piece to a puzzle or a bit of information he needs. He needs to find out if anyone else has that piece or bit of information, but the instructions didn't tell him that. This deliberate lack of resources teaches people to get to one place from another the way a turtle does—sticking his neck out.

The exercises in this section highlight each of the competencies of self-management. Each complex exercise involves one or more of the skills that help people put together the puzzle, and every exercise involves skills related to Self-Awareness and Self-Confidence. The section entitled Self-Management Skills Involved lists the skills essential for improving the self-management competency for which the exercises are designed. Exercise 11.1, for example, is designed to increase Self-Awareness. Unless the participants commit to the skills of risk taking, trust, openness, and honesty, they can't self-disclose to others or accept feedback about themselves from other people. They also have to decide what beliefs they hold to be self-evident as opposed to those they feel a need for evidence or require a degree of proof, and what values or attitudes underlie those self-evident truths. Recognizing that values and attitudes often drive beliefs, and not evidence or proof, is necessary for Self-Awareness. A list of skills will appear in all the exercises. Other skills include:

▶ Goal setting, decision making and action planning

▶ Managing ambiguity and available resources

▶ Accepting defeat, learning from mistakes

▶ Dealing with frustration

Skills Related to Self-Awareness

Any one of the exercises will help build Self-Awareness. Each of them requires the participants to focus on both the demands of the exercise and how they react to the activities in it. If they don't stay focused on the exercise's demands, they will miss out on how it and its messages relate to their lives. Time goals force the participants to keep focused while moving at high speed. The mistakes they make add to their storehouse of self-awareness by calling attention to methods they ordinarily (and often unconsciously) use to solve problems or to relate to other people.

These games or exercises are simple enough to be transparent; the participants can easily see the principles or methods involved. Yet, they're complicated enough to force the participants to think about what the moral could possibly be. They also force the participants to practice the self-awareness skills required for looking "inside" at their own thoughts, beliefs, feelings, or emotions to gain a higher degree of self-awareness than they had before they came to class.

Skills Related to Self-Confidence

Just by committing themselves to take part in a self-management game or exercise people take a risk. But a properly designed and managed self-management workshop provides a safe environment for risky games or exercises, especially when the risk involves self-disclosure: revealing what they really think, believe, or feel. For most people self-disclosure is very painful.

Self-management exercises involve personal risk when, through self-disclosure or through doing or saying things spontaneously, they expose their weaknesses or lack of skills and open themselves up to negative feedback (which they often see as *criticism*). When we put ourselves at risk, we express our self-confidence. At the same time, we also threaten our self-confidence by challenging ourselves to stretch out of our comfort zones and risk repeated failure. If we *never* win at, say, computer solitaire, we'll soon stop playing it. If we never win at work or in our lives, we'll quit that too. These games and exercises reinforce self-confidence by ensuring that even losing or failing produces a personal "win"—gaining an insight, learning a new idea, reinforcing a concept, or developing a skill of personal value.

Goal Setting, Decision Making, and Action Planning

In many situations in the seminar, participants will have to choose among one or more outcomes. Choosing from among alternative goals or actions exercises the decision-making skills of self-management, skills that apply in each of the competencies.

Decisions—decisions made or not made—drive the way our lives evolve. We can make educated guesses about probabilities, but every probability carries with it the possibility of being wrong. Participants in these games or exercises have personal learning goals or change goals, and they look for ways through their activities in the games or exercises for meeting them. They won't know which choice is right until after they make it and see how it pans out. They thereby learn through the games or activities themselves: (1) how to make choices, (2) why making them is important, (3) how to accept the consequences that come from making them, and (4) what to do when the choices are mistakes.

Managing Ambiguity and Available Resources

A game or exercise spelled out in vivid detail *blocks* self-discovery. These exercises don't provide the participants with detailed scripts of what to do or how to do it in any given situation, a circumstance that leaves room for the participants to *figure out* some of the details. For example, one person in a game or exercise may have a want or need that she intentionally doesn't explain or doesn't explain very well. The other person working to develop the skill of trying to understand what people want or need has to figure out ways to get the information he needs—without explicit instructions from the facilitator.

In another game or exercise, participants may not have all the resources, for example, pieces of equipment or kinds of information, they need for performing their roles in the activity. They may have to turn to other people to get what they want, even though they weren't specifically instructed to do so.

Participants who resist this level of ambiguity or lack of resources are probably the ones in greatest need of the type of training you're doing. Empathize with their difficulty, but encourage them to stick with it and learn from what they do.

Dealing With Frustration

Ambiguity and a lack of resources, negative conditions that the games and exercise often deliberately create, produce a certain level of frustration. The training games or exercises help participants learn how to deal with frustration, to recognize that they need to manage those things they can grasp or control and accept those things they can't—*or find a way to change the rules.* That's what "thinking outside the box" or "changing the paradigm" means.

Accepting Defeat, Learning From Mistakes

Contrary to the common practice that games or exercises should teach people how to achieve "win-win" solutions to every *interpersonal problem,* you can use these self-management games or exercises to help participants deal with defeat or mistakes as well as with success. None of these games involves competition, but people view making mistakes or failing as "losing," and losing is a part of life. Making mistakes, especially overlooking the obvious, is the most frequent source of people's sense of failure. That an oversight could cost us everything creates the fear that we can never recover from it, which isn't necessarily true. What is true:

We learn more from what doesn't work than we do from what does (because we usually take for granted what does work and move on). We all have to learn how to live with our mistakes and how to use them to our advantage.

These self-management games and exercises help people make mistakes and survive them. Inasmuch as the workshop is a safe place, designed to help people deal with difficult situations, when they do or say something to put off other people, they get helpful feedback. They can even elect to repeat the situation to "get it right." The challenge is to follow through on the changes they discover they need to make.

PARTICIPATION IN EXERCISES

Most people coming to a self-management workshop have self-selected to attend. They engage in the games and exercises with enthusiasm and with a desire to learn more about themselves and how to get more control over their lives or work. They have fun with what they're asked to do and with one another, and laughter during the activity and feedback sessions is often a good sign of eagerness and satisfaction. However, people who have been sent by their organization for remediation and people in great need of the self-management training you're offering don't always feel good about what they're doing.

Participant Resistance

People who didn't self-select often don't understand why they're in the workshop. When they've been sent to the class, they think that something's *wrong* with them that needs *fixing.* One way to encourage these people to participate fully is to reassure them that coming to the class doesn't imply fixing; rather, everyone needs *improvement.* When these people feel they "ain't broke," you can turn around their thinking with the adage: If it ain't broke, make it better.

Another way to help them feel good about being in the class is to enlist their help in *helping* others, especially helping others to feel comfortable giving feedback. Emphasize that feedback is just another person's opinions or feelings; only if you agree with the feedback do you have to do anything about it.

Many people resist games or exercises that involve frustration, awareness, risk taking, ambiguity, failure or defeat, and challenges to their self-confidence. And, people often skip over consciously setting goals and planning their next steps. It's a testament to your skills as a facilitator if you can get everyone on board with the game or exercise.

▶ Create a positive, fun atmosphere. People are more likely to take risks when they're enjoying themselves.

▶ Offer positive reinforcement when someone does or says something to self-disclose or to manage a difficult situation. Some trainers offer simple, tangible rewards, such as a candy bar.

▶ Pay extra attention to anyone who appears to resist an activity. Find out what bothers the person about it and do what you can to allay his or her fears. Focus on the positive outcomes of the activity rather than on the specifics of it.

▶ "Buddy" participants. Sometimes working together with someone he knows and trusts helps a resistant person feel better about the workshop.

▶ When a person resists what she sees as "acting a part," as in a role play or skill practice, as a last resort, let the person come into the activity in an alternative way, for example, to talk about the situation rather than to engage in it. Give her a chance to watch how the game or exercise unfolds and feel comfortable about coming on board to feel the outcomes from total engagement.

▶ Prevent a resisting person from pulling other people into the resistance. If resistance becomes a real issue for the other participants, facilitate a discussion of the goals of the games or activities, the benefits to the participants, and, particularly, the safety of the environment. A cardinal rule of any self-management workshop: What goes on *here,* stays *here;* no one will tell tales out of school.

11

Self-Awareness

By the end of Chapter 11 you will be able to facilitate four exercises that help people become more aware of who they are and what they have to offer other people.

Exercise 11.1. Truths I Hold to Be Self-Evident

Learning Objectives and Outcomes

By the end of this exercise participants will be able to:

▶ List at least five beliefs they hold to be self-evident (i.e., that they accept without proof or reasoning) and explain the values or attitudes that underlies those beliefs.

▶ List at least five or more beliefs about what it takes to ensure their commitment to a group's goal or task.

▶ Separate the intrinsic from the extrinsic values in their lives.

▶ Build on their own intrinsic values to improve self-awareness.

Self-Management Skills Involved

▶ Decision making

▶ Risk taking and trust

▶ Openness, honesty

Requirements

Time: Approximately forty-five to sixty minutes

Materials: Instructions for Truths I Hold to Be Self-Evident handout

                   Truths I Hold to Be Self-Evident worksheet

Preparation: Photocopy the handout and worksheet.

Room Setup: Any arrangement that meets your needs

Lecture Notes

Beliefs that you hold as self-evidently true—that is, not needing evidence or proof to support them—consist of a variety of values or attitudes you may or may not know you've assumed. A value is any belief or feeling you consider to be worthwhile or desirable. For example, "Personal wealth defines success." An attitude is a readiness to act on a value, as in the willingness to do anything to become wealthy.

Most values and attitudes are assumptions for which you have no objective reason to believe are "good," "bad," acceptable," or "unacceptable." Instead, over time, applying these values has worked for you and other people have usually accommodated our need to fulfill them. As with other assumptions, you take them for granted and rarely if ever examine them. "Personal wealth" as a definition of success seems to have a basis in experience, but, the definition is not accepted in some social systems. Other social systems define success in less pecuniary terms.

Some values are related to factors outside of yourself, such as material things, and are called extrinsic values. Many of them may be out of your immediate or direct control, such as the tangible rewards offered by your business. Believing that your business should give tangible rewards for exemplary work and should distribute them equitably is based on extrinsic values.

Some values are related to your own feelings or beliefs about yourself and are called intrinsic values. These are always in your immediate or direct control, such feelings of self-satisfaction. Believing that feeling self-satisfaction for doing exemplary work is at least as important as receiving tangible rewards is based on intrinsic values. One objective of self-management is to live in accordance with your intrinsic values (principles) and to reward yourself by fulfilling the goals that satisfy those values.

Saying that living in accordance with your intrinsic values doesn't mean that extrinsic values are bad or that you should always reject them in favor of intrinsic values. On the contrary, daily existence depends on many extrinsic values, for example, compensation for work. Love for others is a wonderful intrinsic value, but if you never receive love from others (an extrinsic value), you'll become emotionally starved and incapable of loving. Where intrinsic and extrinsic values compete for fulfillment, you need to learn how to harmonize one set of needs or goals with others in your life and in the lives of other people.

[Facilitator: Read instructions aloud after you distribute the handout and worksheet.]

Processing Questions

Ask these questions after the participants have completed their analyses.

1. What about your beliefs and underlying assumptions did you discover?

   Most people recognize for the first time that what they think is self-evidently true is usually based on values and attitudes that they've developed throughout their lives or that have been imposed on them by, for example, the organization in which they work.

2. How did this analysis of your most cherished beliefs help you become more aware of how you form your beliefs?

   Typical answer: "I'll be more likely to examine my values and attitudes before advancing an opinion, and I'll want to know more about other people's values and attitudes. Unless we do that, we could get into disputes we can't resolve."

3. How could the type of analysis you just did help you get more control over your life and work?

   Typical answer: "I'll be more aware of what I believe to be true for no other reason than I want it to be true, and I won't be as disappointed when the rest of the world doesn't agree with me."

INSTRUCTIONS FOR THE TRUTHS I HOLD TO BE SELF-EVIDENT EXERCISE

1. List five or more of your own beliefs about people you think are self-evidently true. For example, "A camel is a horse designed by a committee."

2. List the value(s) expressed by those beliefs. The example assumes that all committees are bad.

3. List five or more of your own beliefs about what it takes to ensure your commitment to a group's goal or task. For example, "To feel committed to the group's goal or task, I need to feel that I and other group members think that I'm doing something that makes a significant contribution to the group rather than just busy work."

4. List the value(s) expressed by those beliefs. The example assumes that I value feedback from the group about the significance of my contribution (otherwise I couldn't know if they think I'm doing something significant).

5. Identify the quality of the values: Intrinsic or extrinsic. For example, getting the group's approval of my contribution is an extrinsic value. Check the appropriate column, E = Extrinsic and I = Intrinsic.

6. With regard to intrinsic values, how do you satisfy them even if you don't satisfy the extrinsic values you want for yourself? List the things you do to guarantee that you fulfill your intrinsic values. For example, assume you value self-satisfaction from your work, and you would also like tangible rewards for doing that work. However, if you work in an organization that can't (or won't) provide those tangible rewards, what do you do to make sure you still feel good about what you're doing?

Truths I Hold to Be Self-Evident

	Beliefs	*Values*		
About other people	1. 2. 3. 4. 5. 6. 7. 8.			
About my commitment	1. 2. 3. 4. 5. 6. 7. 8.		E	I
Steps for fulfilling intrinsic values				

Exercise 11.2. Looking Into the EIAG Glass

Learning Objectives and Outcomes

By the end of this exercise participants will be able to use the EIAG Model to:

▶ Assess their own actions in staged, specific situations.

▶ Make decisions as to why they feel, think, and act as they do in those situations.

▶ Decide on changes they want to make in how they feel, think, and act in such situations.

Reminder: The EIAG Model was described in Chapter 1. The initial letters of <u>E</u>xperience, <u>I</u>nterpretation, <u>A</u>nalysis, and <u>G</u>eneralization form the acronym. Review Chapter 1 before conducting this exercise.

Self-Management Skills Involved

▶ Decision making

▶ Risk taking and trust

▶ Openness, honesty

Requirements

Time: Approximately sixty to ninety minutes

Materials: Instructions for Looking Into the EIAG Glass handout
Reaction Guide worksheet
Story cards
Game cards

Equipment: None, unless a scenario or case you write requires an overhead projector or videotape player/monitor

Preparation: Photocopy each story and each game on separate 5-by-7-inch cards.
Make stacks of twelve cards each (six story cards and six game cards) and shuffle them to make the order in which they are selected random.
Photocopy the handout and worksheet.

Note: Each story card or game card consists of instructions to the individual who gets it to do or say something that will set the tone of the conversation for the group. For example, a *story*, such as "To Save a Life" tells a story designed to evoke specific emotions. The person receiving the card tells the story to which everyone else responds; the discussion then examines how the people reacted and why. On the other hand, a *game* card is designed to interfere with the conversation and create a distraction. The other people will react to the game and discuss their responses.

Room Setup: Small groups of no more than six people

Lecture Notes

Instructions to Participants

Here's an example of taking steps to change inappropriate behavior. Someone interrupts me, and I get angry and say something rude in return. The other person and I get into an argument that involves a lot of name calling. The feedback I get from the group is that by responding rudely, I negatively escalated the situation. I could have responded with something to the effect, "I really do want to hear what you think, but I'd appreciate the chance to finish my thought before you speak. Please." The first step I have to take is to understand why I responded as rudely as the other person. Then I have to figure out steps for managing my feelings in such a situation, so I don't escalate the situation.

On the other hand, let's say I did manage my feelings when I was interrupted and I did say something to the effect, "I really do want to hear what you think, but I'd appreciate the chance to finish my thought before you speak. Please." Since that's a positive and appropriate response, in similar situations, I want to remind myself of how I managed my feelings this time and follow the same steps then as I did now.

[Facilitator: Distribute the exercise instructions and worksheet and then read the instructions aloud.]

Processing Questions

1. How did this exercise help you examine how you react to situations?

   Typical answer: I was able to understand why I react to some situations the way I do and take steps to change my reactions to similar situations.

2. What did you learn about your responses that you didn't realize about yourself before?

   Typical answer: That I tend to jump to conclusions about people without thinking through what happened and why.

3. How would you apply the methods in this exercise to everyday experiences?

   Typical answer: If I feel myself reacting hostilely, I'll stop myself to look at the situation before I respond. Even if I have to ask the other person for a moment to gather my thoughts, I'll do it.

Lecture Notes After the Exercise

Practice examining your reactions during situations in which you feel anger, frustration, stress, anxiety, or depression. Think about what you experienced, what you interpreted that experience to mean to you, and why you felt that way. It can help you manage yourself and the situation more effectively. It's essential, however, that you memorize this rule: "I may not be able to change the world around me, but I can change how I react to it." It's a matter of choice. You can decide how you will act in the future, no matter what your personal history has been, because you have to react in "the here and now" not in "what is dead and gone."

Achieving self-awareness calls for recognizing not only what you think (cognitive aspects of your reactions) but also how you feel (emotional aspects of your reactions). A whole person experiences both cognitive and emotional aspects of life. It's important, therefore, to know what your emotions are, and the methods we've used here will help you identify them. Those methods will also help you manage your emotions. Using these methods to find out why other people react as they do to situations in which you're involved will help you recognize their emotions, help you to empathize with them. By managing your emotions, you encourage them to manage theirs as well, resulting in more positive and productive relationships.

INSTRUCTIONS FOR THE LOOKING INTO THE EIAG GLASS EXERCISE

1. Each of you will take one card from the stack of cards on each table.

2. The cards will give you individual roles to play—that is, to say or do something no one else knows about. Do not reveal your instructions and wait until everyone has reacted to you before you explain you were instructed to say or do whatever it was you said or did.

3. When you're in the role given to you, do not judge or alter the instructions in any way; however, if the instructions call for you to say or do something you cannot say or do, for whatever personal reasons, feel free to ask for a different script.

4. An individual's instructions will be to tell a story or to do something.

5. Everyone else in your group may say or do something in response to what you say or do, but conform to the following steps.
   - As other people say or do things, respond to them as you would in any real life situation.
   - As the situation unfolds, make note of the following items in your Reaction guides.

   Experience: What did the person say or do? (Be specific and descriptive.)

   Interpretation: What was my first reaction? What did I do or say? What did I think? What did I feel?

   Analysis: Did I fully understand what the person said or did? How do I know that I understood? Why did I feel the way I did? Was it justified? If so, what did the person say or do that warranted my reaction? If it wasn't justified, why did I feel that way? Did I act on my first reaction? If not, why not?

   Generalization: Is that the way I always react to a similar situation? If I think I reacted properly or in proportion to the events, what steps can I take to ensure that in similar situations, I repeat the way I responded? If I think I reacted improperly or out of proportion to the events, what can I do to change the way I behaved?

REACTION GUIDE TO LOOKING INTO THE EIAG GLASS

Experience: What did the person say or do? (Specific, descriptive)	
Interpretation: What did I think? Feel?	
Analysis: Did I fully understand? Why did I feel that way? Was it justified? Was it a warranted reaction? If not, why did I feel that way? Do I always react that way?	
Generalization: If I think I reacted properly, what can I do to repeat that response? If improperly, what can I do to change the way I reacted?	

To Catch a Thief. *Tell this story as if you're talking with a clergyman or other confidante.*

I caught my coworker in the act of stealing supplies; paper, pencils, and stuff. She said it was for her children to take to school. I know she doesn't make much money, but she was taking quite a lot of stuff. She said, "Everyone does it, and I can't afford the supplies right now." I don't know what to do. I should report her, but, it's true, everyone does it. I haven't deliberately taken anything, but, you know, I've walked off with a pen or two in my day.

No Good Deed Goes Unpunished. *Tell this story as if talking with any group of people you know; put plenty of amazement into the telling of the situation.*

I was raised that a man never hits a woman, no matter how angry he gets or what she says or does. So, I was in the park the other day—just walking—and I saw a couple in a playground. She was on a swing, and he was pushing her—higher and higher. And she started screaming, "Let me down. Let me down." He just laughed a nasty laugh. They must have been arguing before that because when she finally got control of the swing and jumped off, she started shouting at him and calling him foul names and talking about something else. He got really angry and hauled off and smacked her. I ran over to protect her, and what happened? They *both* turned on me, calling me foul names and chasing me off. They left all lovey-dovey.

Stealing Time. *Tell this story as if you're talking with a group of friends outside of work.*

No, I didn't get time off this afternoon. I took it. My boss is out of town on a fun trip with his family and won't be back for two days. He told me not to try to reach him and that he won't be calling in. So, as soon as he left, I finished up some work I had to do and split too.

Double-dealing Dating. *Tell this story as if you're talking with a coworker.*

You know the clerk in shipping who's been after me to go out with him/her. Well, he/she made an offer I couldn't refuse. He/She had tickets to that monster show—$50 seats. I've been wanting to go to that show ever since I heard it was coming to town, but $100? No way. So, anyway he/she tells me about the tickets, and, well, I didn't come right out with it, but I let him/her know I'd be willing to go. The show was great, the date was what I was afraid of. Dull. Well, I finally got to see that show, gave the clerk a thrill by going with him/her, but there's no way I'd date him/her again.

STORY CARDS (continued)

Sex for the Fun of It. Tell this story as if you're talking with close friends or relatives.

What a weekend! It was great. A mountain retreat. No phones. No TV. We took a case of wine. Stuff to cook on an open fire. And we had some of the greatest sex ever, but I'll probably never see him/her again. Don't want to. I just wanted the fun of the weekend. If he/she does call again, I'll just brush him/her off. Hey! Why not. It was just for fun—at least it was for me.

To Save a Life. Tell this story as you would tell it to any group with whom you're talking.

I was driving through a wooded area the other day when I saw a dog lying on the side of the road. He must have been hit by a car. Just glanced, but hurt bad enough not to be able to walk. I've heard that a hurt dog would bite you if you touch it, but when I approached, slowly, of course, he just whimpered and tried to crawl over to me. When I reached out my hand, also slowly, he licked my fingertips, so I felt pretty safe. Wrapping him in a coat I had in the trunk of the car, I drove him to a vet. The closest one was about thirty minutes out of my way, but I couldn't just let the poor thing die. I don't know what happened to him, but the vet said he had some internal injuries and a broken leg and since his tags were current, she called the owner right away.

GAME CARDS

Sometime in the exercise, get up and say, "I'm going to get another cup of coffee/glass of juice/glass of water/soft drink, does anyone want anything? I'll be glad to bring it back." Not until people react to your behavior should you tell them that's how you were instructed to act.

Whenever it seems appropriate, say, "Damn! My pen's out of ink." Throw it down on the table and take someone else's without asking, even if it means taking the pen out of someone's hand. If you get a pen, write something and put the pen in your pocket or purse, if you have one. Not until people react to your behavior should you tell them that's how you were instructed to act.

When someone tells a story or states an opinion, act angry. Wad some paper and throw it in his/her direction, saying, "I think that's the dumbest thing I've ever heard." Not to your behavior should you tell them that's how you were instructed to act.

After the exercise has gone on for five minutes, push away from the table, cross your arms across your chest and say defiantly, "I'm not going to play this silly game. It's dumb, it's unrealistic, and you're silly and dumb for playing it." Not until people react to your behavior should you tell them that's how you were instructed to act.

GAME CARDS (*continued*)

Take an opportunity to say, "I'm getting a lot out of this workshop, mainly because of the insights I'm getting from discussions with you in this group. I think we're fortunate to be working together, and I hope we can continue helping one another." Not until people react to your statement should you tell them that you were instructed to say that.

All through this part of the exercise, interrupt other people when they're talking. Be loud and rude. Not until someone reacts to your behavior should you tell them that's how you were instructed to act.

Exercise 11.3. Who Am I? An Ice Breaker

Instructor's Notes

I recommend this narrative as the Lecture Notes for a wrap-up of the exercise.

Typically people describe themselves on a relatively superficial level and in terms of roles they play. For example, most people who have children refer to themselves simply as "a parent" rather than say, "I am a parent of a boy and a girl who are the apple of my eye." The first answer says the speaker happens to be a parent, which may seem essential but is really incidental; anyone can be a parent (unless suffering from a physical disability that prevents childbearing or child producing). The second answer identifies the speaker as a parent and explains how she feels about her children.

In business-related examples, a supervisor might say, "I'm a supervisor" rather than describe what he does in that role. A systems analyst may identify herself by title also. And so on. Now, the question remains to be answered, what does all that mean?

When people meet, they're reluctant to tell each other what they know about themselves. While it's important to keep things to ourselves, it's also important to let people see enough of us that they can understand who and what we are and what makes us tick. Unless people disclose their values, attitudes, and feelings, they make it difficult or impossible for other people to understand them or help them satisfy their needs. By disclosing, we prevent conflicts among different people's values, attitudes, and feelings, while ensuring that we can meet our own needs when living and working with other people.

Learning Objectives and Outcomes

By the end of this exercise participants will be able to explain how they present themselves to other people; whether they project:

▶ Positive images or negative images

▶ Peripheral (sometimes accidental) characteristics or traits, such as their job, or essential characteristics or traits that distinguish them as individuals

▶ Everything about themselves that they can or should, or a limited aspect of themselves (hiding much about themselves)

Self-Management Skills Involved

▶ Risk taking, self-disclosure

▶ Openness, honesty

▶ Trust

Requirements

Time:	Approximately forty-five minutes
Materials:	Poster boards (22 inches by 28 inches) sufficient for each participant to receive a poster, markers in different colors, masking tape, and double-sided tape
Equipment:	Polaroid camera and film sufficient for taking one photograph of each participant
Preparation:	Hold the poster boards vertically (portrait), and mark each one with the question Who Am I? centered across the top. Draw a square at the upper left corner large enough to frame a Polaroid picture.
Room Setup:	Whatever fits your needs, preferably round tables with groups of six people

Instructions to Facilitator

1. As each participant enters the room, have an assistant (or if you don't have an assistant, recruit the first participant) stop him or her, take a snapshot of the person, and hand it to the person to use after it develops.

2. Put a stack of posters, a roll of double-sided tape, and a roll of masking tape where people can access them easily.

3. Encourage everyone to be seated quickly anywhere in the room (unless you are doing team building with intact teams and want team members to sit together).

4. Conduct the exercise.

Lecture Notes

Instructions to Participants

1. Everyone take up one poster board and some double-sided tape.

2. Hold your poster board vertically (portrait) and use the double-sided tape to attach your snapshot in the box at the top of the poster board.

3. Make a bulleted list that introduces who you are to other people; list one item per bullet.

4. After writing your list, use masking tape to hang your poster on the wall vertically.

5. Walk around the room and read every poster.

6. Return to your seat.

Processing Questions

1. How does introducing yourself with one word, for example, "father," or a short phrase, for example, "shipping supervisor," help other people understand who you are?

   Typical answer: One word and short phrases don't really help at all because those words can mean a lot of different things to different people, or even if they mean the same thing, they don't say anything about what you think or feel about yourself.

2. What did the exercise tell you about how you and other people present themselves?

   Typical answer: We're somewhat superficial or unwilling to talk about ourselves to other people when we meet them. We don't trust people enough when we first meet them to tell them more about ourselves than the obvious things, like I'm a parent or a supervisor.

3. What can we do to be more open when we first meet other people?

   Typical answer: We need to be more willing to open up to people, to trust them enough to give them some insight into who we are, what we think and what we feel.

Exercise 11.4. Using the JOHARI Window to Improve Self-Awareness

Instructor's Notes

This exercise works best with intact teams or with workshop groups who have been interacting with one another for at least one day during which the participants will have had an opportunity to observe one another's behavior.

Learning Objectives and Outcomes

By the end of this exercise participants will be able to use the JOHARI Window to:

▶ Describe their own behavior as open or closed.

▶ Use giving or receiving feedback to encourage openness in themselves and in others.

▶ Identify what inhibits or facilitates the exchange of feedback.

Self-Management Skills Involved

▶ Risk taking and trust

▶ Decision making

▶ Openness, honesty

▶ Communication, especially giving and receiving feedback

Requirements

Time:	Approximately two and a half hours
Materials:	Flip chart, multicolored markers, masking tape
	Copies of Giving and Getting Feedback handout from Chapter 1 (page 27)
	The JOHARI Window overhead
	JOHARI Window Self-Rating Sheet worksheet
	Sample JOHARI Window Models handout
	Paper and pencils
	Rulers or some other straight edges for drawing vertical and horizontal lines in the JOHARI Window model handout

Equipment: Overhead projector or computer to display JOHARI Window models on screen (optional)

Preparation: Make the overhead.

Photocopy the worksheet and handout.

Room Setup: Round tables each with chairs for five or six people or a setup that allows for face-to-face discussion

Lecture Notes

When people work together, they must confront each other with issues or concerns about how the work is getting done or how they feel about their relationship. Although the word *confrontation* has recently acquired some negative connotations, it means only to deal with some matter face-to-face; therefore, confronting can be friendly or constructive, or it can be angry and destructive. It's not a matter only of *what* you say but also of *how* you say it. When you follow the guidelines for giving and getting feedback, you create an openness that facilitates friendly, constructive confrontation.

[Facilitator: Distribute the Giving and Getting Feedback handout and use it as a guide for talking about feedback and its guidelines.]

One way to improve the openness with which you deal with other people and they deal with you is to examine our willingness to disclose our thoughts and feelings. The JOHARI Window will do just that.

[Facilitator: Put up the JOHARI Window overhead now.]

This model of self-awareness, self-disclosure, and feedback was first developed by two psychologists *Joseph* Luft and *Harry* Ingham. Thus the name JOHARI [pronounced joe-harry] Window. They created the window as a basic communication tool through which you give and receive information about yourself while receiving information about you or other people. You can draw the windowpanes in any shape that reflects your ability to disclose information about yourself or to accept information about yourself from other people. The more you know about yourself and the more other people know about you, the larger the pane called the Arena. Luft and Ingham called this expanding a windowpane. At the same time, the Blind Spot and the Façade get smaller; they called this contracting. I'll explain the expanding, contracting process after we examine the window a little more closely.

Look at the window in two dimensions: self-orientation and group orientation. When you look at the window from left to right or right to left—the direction labeled Self—the windowpanes consist of things a person knows or doesn't know about himself or herself and about other people's perceptions of or feelings toward him or her. For a person to expand this self-orientation dimension, he or she must change the amount of information he or she reveals or knows about other people's feelings.

To get information about other people's feelings, he or she has to ask for and accept feedback. The way the person sees the world expands or contracts to the extent he or she receives useful information about other people and their feedback about him or her.

When you look at the window from top to bottom or bottom to top—the direction labeled Group—the windowpanes consist of things other people know about a person and about his or her perceptions of or feelings toward them, or things that they don't know about him or her. This Group-oriented dimension expands or contracts relative to the amount of useful information a person offers about himself or herself and the feedback he or she gives to other people about how he or she sees or feels about them. This dimension of self-disclosure and of giving feedback is the world in which a person includes other people in his or her world. Therefore, how much a person discloses or how much feedback he or she gives affects how other people's Arenas expand or contract.

The Arena is the public window. Everyone can see into it. The Façade, or Hidden Area, is the windowpane you control, letting people see through it only as much as you're willing to let them. The Blind Spot is a public window to which *only you aren't* privy. Other people can see through it, and unless you ask them to help you look through it too, you never will.

The last windowpane is probably the most important of all and requires the most personal effort to access: The Unknown. You don't have direct access to this information, but neither does anyone else *unless you ask them to observe you closely and give you feedback about what they see or hear.*

It takes a great deal of trust on your part to ask for feedback about how what you say or do and how you say it and do it affects other people. It also takes a great willingness on their part to give that feedback. However, the more feedback they give you, the greater your insight into how you come across to others and the greater the gains for them; both you and they enlarge our respective Arena windowpanes while shrinking your respective Façades. The greater the flow of information from person to person, the greater the insight for everyone regardless of the information's content.

Luft and Ingham, Freudian psychologists, added an appendage to the Unknown in their model that we don't show: The Unconscious. This is the area forever closed to you (and probably to everyone else) unless you undergo intensive, long-term psychotherapy. This workshop is not the place for dealing with The Unconscious.

The panes of the window shift, grow, or shrink relative to the amount of information that passes through them. The amount of information everyone gets and gives increases to the extent that members of your group experience mutual trust and willingness to exchange feedback or to disclose their thoughts and feelings. The less the trust or willingness to be open, the less the information flows, the smaller the Arena pane, the larger the Blind Spot, the larger the Façade, and the larger the Unknown. So, now it's time to complete the JOHARI Window Self-Rating Sheet.

[Facilitator: Distribute the JOHARI Window Self-Rating sheets now.]

Instructions to Participants

1. On your Self-Rating Sheet, the scale from one to nine across the top of the window describes the extent to which you ask for feedback.

2. Think back over your last few group meetings, including the group activities in this workshop, and decide whether or not you were curious enough about how you were perceived by others to ask for feedback from the group members.

3. Find a point on the horizontal scale that describes the extent to which you *actually* asked for feedback during group meetings. Do not rate the number of times you *felt* like asking for feedback but rather the number of times you *actually* asked for it.

4. After you've located a point on the scale, draw a vertical line from that point straight down to the bottom of the window. Use a straight edge.

5. (After steps 3 and 4 are completed. . . .) Now think back to group settings in which you *actually* disclosed information about your thoughts or feelings, whether those thoughts or feelings were about you or about other people. Not the times you *felt* like disclosing your thoughts or feelings but rather the *actual* times you did.

6. Locate a point in the vertical scale, from one to nine, at your left of the window.

7. With a straightedge draw a horizontal line from the point on the left straight across to the right.

8. Mark the upper left pane, *A* (for Arena), the upper right pane *BS* (for Blind Spot), the lower left pane *F* (for Façade), and the lower right pane *U* (for Unknown).

9. Let's interpret these grids together before we do the group activities.

Interpretations

1. The lower you rated your willingness to ask for feedback, the smaller the horizontal dimension of the pane called the Arena. You know less about yourself at this point because you don't know much about how other people see you, regardless of whether you think their perceptions are accurate or feelings justified, that's how you come across to them; their perceptions or feelings are still information about you that you need to know. As a result the pane called the Blind Spot is larger than you would probably like it to be. Seeing yourself as others see you increases your self-awareness.

2. The lower you rated your willingness to give feedback, the smaller the vertical dimension of the Arena, and the larger is the Façade dimension. That also enlarges the Unknown dimension because you know less about yourself than is ideal, and other people know less about you than is best. The result of all this is that your self-awareness suffers and your relationships with other people will suffer as well. For example, when you provide information to the

group, you may see yourself as being helpful; the other people may see you as overwhelming. They may therefore resist your efforts to provide information in the future. You need to know what the other people are thinking or feeling in order to deal with them appropriately.

3. Let's look at four different possible shapes of the JOHARI Window described by training expert Phillip C. Hanson many years ago.[1] Compare your window to these.

[Facilitator: Distribute Sample JOHARI Windows Models handout now.]

▶ *Ideal Window*: The arrows around the Arena are long, suggesting that you're quite trusting, willing to self-disclose, respectful of other people and their opinions, and willing to accept feedback. You encourage a free discussion of all issues, including how people think or feel.

▶ *Interviewer*: The horizontal arrow is long, but the vertical arrow to the right of the Arena is short, suggesting you're willing to accept feedback and self-disclosure from others, but you're not willing to give it. You probably ask a lot of questions but fend off attempts to draw you out.

▶ *Bull-in-the-China-Shop*: The horizontal arrow is short, but the vertical arrow is long, suggesting that you're only too willing to tell other people what you think or feel but you're not open to listening to what they think or feel.

▶ *Turtle*: With both arrows around the Arena short, you've pulled back into a shell and aren't willing to give or to get feedback. Self-disclosure, either your own or other people's, is painful to you.

Instructions to Participants: Group Activity 1– Comparing Windows

1. In your small group discuss the windows you have drawn for yourself. This activity by itself is a part of the self-disclosure process that reduces the size of your Façade while increasing the size of the Arena.

2. Ask for feedback from the group members as to how they see you and ask for their ratings of you in the four windowpanes. Mark their interpretations on your own chart. This activity by itself reduces the size of your Blind Spot while increasing the size of the Arena.

3. Take twenty minutes to complete this part of the exercise.

[Facilitator: Allow an additional ten minutes if needed; don't rush the discussions.]

---

[1] Phillip C. Hanson, "The JOHARI Window: A Model for Soliciting and Giving Feedback," in John E. Jones and J. William Pfeiffer, editors, *1973 Annual Handbook for Group Facilitators* (La Jolla, CA: University Associates, 1973), pp. 114–119.

Instructions to Participants: Group Activity 2—
Inhibiting/Facilitating Feedback

1. In your small group identify what made it easy or difficult in the activity to ask for or to give feedback.

2. Make a two-column chart. On the left, list the inhibiting factors. On the right, list the facilitating factors.

3. What can you do to increase the influence of facilitating factors and reduce the effects of inhibiting factors?

4. You have fifteen minutes to complete this activity.

5. Elect a spokesperson to explain your decisions to the whole class.

Instructor's Notes

Typically, especially when there is more than one small group, the participants come up with comprehensive lists of inhibitors and facilitators. However, the accompanying table provides some possible answers.

Inhibitors	Facilitators
Not knowing one another very well	The safe environment of the workshop
Not trusting one another very much	Understanding what the exercise is supposed to accomplish
Fear that what I say will be used against me	Trusting the people in my group
Fear that what I say will be leaked back on the job	Believing that what I say to this group will stay with it
Embarrassment	Believing that the exercise will help me be more open and honest
Fear of getting negative feedback	Getting good or useful feedback from other people
Fear that I'll be seen as too critical of other people	
Reluctance to say anything bad about other people	

The most important way to reduce the inhibiting factors and increase the facilitating factors is to increase trust levels, which can only come through experience with one another. Openness means not only disclosing information but also accepting that information with a sense of confidentiality; it belongs only to the person who told us and to us. Openness also requires that we be willing to confront one another with our perceptions and feelings without attempting to do one another harm or to *win* a contest.

THE JOHARI WINDOW

	Self	
	Asks for Feedback	
	Things I Know	Things I Don't Know
Things They Know	Arena	Blind Spot
Things They Don't Know	Façade (Hidden Area)	Unknown

Group ◄───►

Self-Disclosure

or

Gives Feedback

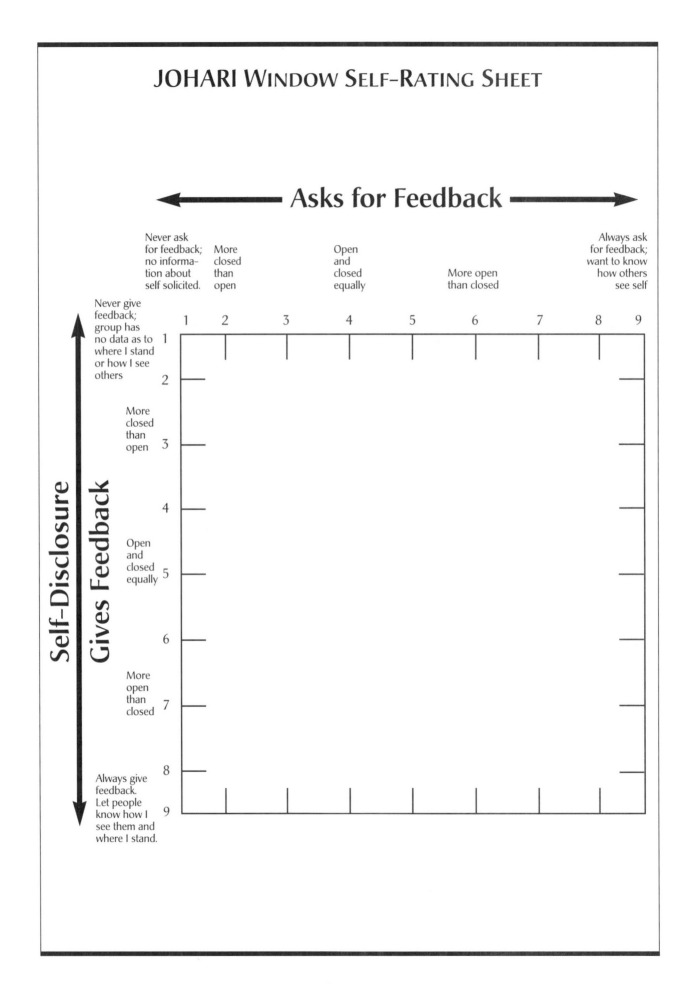

JOHARI Window Self-Rating Sheet

Asks for Feedback ← →

Never ask for feedback; no information about self solicited.

More closed than open

Open and closed equally

More open than closed

Always ask for feedback; want to know how others see self

Self-Disclosure

Gives Feedback

Never give feedback; group has no data as to where I stand or how I see others

More closed than open

Open and closed equally

More open than closed

Always give feedback. Let people know how I see them and where I stand.

1 2 3 4 5 6 7 8 9

1
2
3
4
5
6
7
8
9

Sample JOHARI Window Models

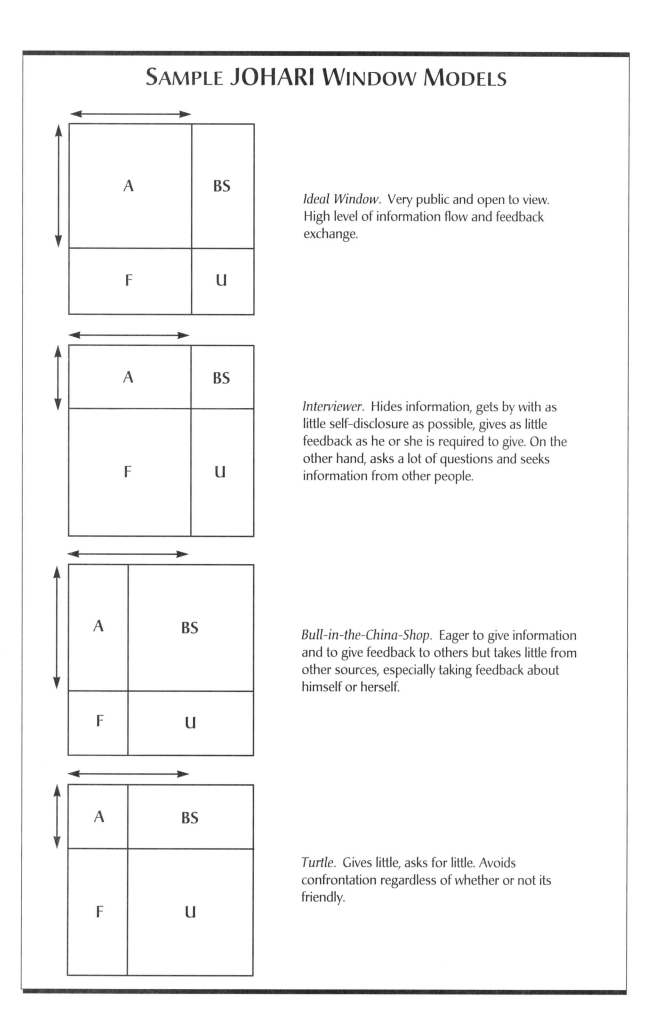

A	**BS**
F	**U**

Ideal Window. Very public and open to view. High level of information flow and feedback exchange.

Interviewer. Hides information, gets by with as little self-disclosure as possible, gives as little feedback as he or she is required to give. On the other hand, asks a lot of questions and seeks information from other people.

Bull-in-the-China-Shop. Eager to give information and to give feedback to others but takes little from other sources, especially taking feedback about himself or herself.

Turtle. Gives little, asks for little. Avoids confrontation regardless of whether or not its friendly.

Follow-Up Activities for Increasing Self-Awareness

Learning Objectives and Outcomes

By doing this activity, participants will take steps to:

▶ Evaluate or assess how other people see them.

▶ Take corrective action when needed.

Self-Management Skills Involved

▶ Evaluating or assessing one's own behavior

▶ Openness to feedback from other people

▶ Openness to making changes in one's behavior

Requirements

Time: Five minutes for instruction plus discussion time

Materials: Instructions for Writing an Action Plan handout
                   Sample Action Plan handout
                   Knowing Yourself Better handout

Preparation: Photocopy the handouts.

Lecture Notes

[Facilitator: Distribute the Instructions for Writing an Action Plan, the Sample Action Plan, and the Knowing Yourself Better handouts.]

What you just did is only a beginning. In order to increase self-awareness, you need to practice the skills involved, which may include changing the way you say and do things. Most importantly, it will include getting feedback from other people as to how what you say or do affects them. If you then agree that their feedback has merit and warrants change, you need to approach that change systematically.

Before you can make a change of any kind, you need to know what present conditions you want to change based on feedback you get from other people: mannerisms when talking, tone of voice, facial expressions, failing to listen to other people, taking control of group activities, and so on. Feedback from other people, as described in the JOHARI Window exercise, is one way to get your "baseline" information. Then you need to set a change goal and develop an action plan for change by following the outline in the handout Instructions for Writing an Action Plan.

In addition to feedback from other people, use the variety of other techniques for getting feedback about how you appear to other people listed in the handout Knowing Yourself Better.

INSTRUCTIONS FOR WRITING AN ACTION PLAN

Before you can make a change of any kind, you need to know what present conditions you want to change based on feedback you get from other people: mannerisms when talking, tone of voice, facial expressions, failing to listen to other people, taking control of group activities, and so on. Feedback from other people, as described in the JOHARI Window exercise, is one way to get your baseline information. You then need to set a change goal and develop an action plan for change by following the outline in this exercise.

Current Conditions: What do I want to change and why do I want to change it?

Change Goal: What should my behavior be like after I have affected a change?

Milestones: How will I measure my progress?

Resources Needed: What will help me make the change? (Include in your planning a list of resources you already have available to you and any you might need that you don't have at this time.)

Barriers: What can get in the way of making the change?

Action Steps: What do I have to do to effect the change?

SAMPLE ACTION PLAN

Current Conditions: What do I want to change and why do I want to change it?

People tell me I appear to be aggressive when I state my opinions. I'm too intense and I don't seem to listen when other people talk. As a result people push back against my ideas. I don't want to give that impression, and I'd rather we didn't struggle over opinions.

Change Goal: What should my behavior be like after I have affected a change?

As soon as possible, I want to present my opinions in a more acceptable fashion by prefacing what I say with phrases like "In my opinion," "I think that," and by asking for feedback from other people about what they think or feel about my opinions.

Milestones: How will I measure my progress?

At meetings I will express my opinions as stated above, and after the meetings, I will ask people to give me feedback as to how I came across to them. When I get feedback that tells me that I'm not as intimidating as I have been, and that I seem more receptive to other people's opinions, I will know I'm making progress.

Resources Needed: What will help me make the change?

(Include in your planning a list of resources you already have available to you and any you might need that you don't have at this time.)
I need a tape recorder with which to record the way I talk when I present an idea. That way I can play it back to hear the words I used and my tone of voice.

Barriers: What can get in the way of making the change?
No one to give me feedback.

Action Steps: What do I have to do to effect the change?

- ▶ Practice using the appropriate phrases.
- ▶ Practice presenting ideas with less intensity.
- ▶ Use my new skills in meetings.
- ▶ Ask for feedback regularly, not just in meetings but also from friends and relatives.

KNOWING YOURSELF BETTER

Some activities people use to become more self-aware are included in this list. You can add any activities you think appropriate. Whatever you do, be sure to extend yourself, get out of your "comfort zone," and take risks to widen your self-awareness.

1. Talk to the "person in the mirror" about any subject. Watch your facial expressions and hand gestures. See yourself as others see you when you talk to them.

2. Record conversations with people (asking their permission, of course, and explaining to them what you're trying to do). Listen to your tone of voice, the words you use, the way you emphasize words, and the pace you use.

3. Ask people for feedback. Explain to them that you're trying to improve your self-awareness and need their help. Take what they say seriously and see what you can do to see and hear yourself as they do.

4. Evaluate your own beliefs, opinions, values, and feelings or emotions. Understand "where you're coming from." Use the EIAG Model at every opportunity to get control over the bases on which you react to other people, make decisions, and choose from among alternative actions.

12

Self-Confidence

B y the end of this chapter you will be able to facilitate two exercises for helping participants to increase their self-confidence by:

▶ Identifying behaviors generally associated with self-confidence and with the lack of it

▶ Recognizing how their own behaviors exhibit self-confidence or the lack of it

▶ Taking steps to build on their strengths and minimize their weaknesses

Typically people talk about "feeling" self-confident, which is an accurate form of self-expression, but self-confidence takes behavioral forms as well. The first of these two exercises calls attention to those behaviors that demonstrate and support the feelings of self-confidence to both the individual and to others observing him or her.

Exercise 12.1. Expressing Self–Confidence Through Assertiveness

Instructor's Notes

This two-part exercise is complex and touches on sensitive personal issues. It works best with an intact team or with workshop groups that have been interacting with one another for at least one day during which the participants will have had an opportunity to build levels of trust. Your expertise with personal behavior styles also will play an important role. However, be careful not to import other behavior style concepts, for example, the DISC model or Myers-Briggs, into this exercise. They describe how a person takes in and processes information in more ways than students will be able to digest in this exercise. Stay focused on the one competency: Self-Confidence.

Learning Objectives and Outcomes

By the end of this exercise participants will be able to:

▶ Identify their own level of self-confidence in a variety of different situations.

▶ Relate feedback from other people abut how self-confident they appear to those people and to their self-perceptions.

▶ Apply an action plan to increase their levels of self-confidence.

Self-Management Skills Involved

▶ Risk taking and trust

▶ Decision making

▶ Openness, honesty

▶ Respect for others

▶ Communication, especially giving and receiving feedback

Requirements

Time:	Three hours or longer
Materials:	Flip chart, multicolored markers, masking tape
	Paper and pencils
	Self-Assessment: How Do I Respond to Situations?
	Scoring and Interpretation Guide
	Behaviors and Feelings Associated with the Levels of Self-Confidence handout

Self-Confidence Behaviors handout

Instructions for Teammate in the Barrel handout

Teammate in the Barrel Scripts

Feedback Guide for Teammate in the Barrel

Sample Observer's Guide for Teammate in the Barrel

Observer's Guide for Teammate in the Barrel

Name tents or name tags for the second part of the exercise

Equipment: Overhead projector or power point (optional) and screen

Preparation: Photocopy the self-assessment and its scoring and interpretation guide, the handouts, and the Teammate in the Barrel scripts, feedback guide, sample observer's guide, and observer's guide; make enough copies of the feedback guide and observer's guide for each person on the team to give feedback and to observe all members of the team.

Make name tents or name tags: Electrical Engineer, Mechanical Engineer, Production Coordinator, Buyer, Observer 1 (and Observer 2 for six-person teams)

Room Setup: Allow for people to talk to one another face to face. Teams should be no more than six people. Best arrangement if available: breakout rooms, with round tables, chairs for five or six people. If breakout rooms are not available, separate the teams as much as possible in the main meeting room.

Lecture Notes Prior to Self-Assessment Activity

[Facilitator: Distribute the self-assessment and its accompanying scoring guide. Then read aloud the following, which includes more information than is on the handout.]

Instructions to Participants. Working by yourself, read the description of each situation. Then consider the possible responses that follow and decide which response is the *closest* to the one you would make. The word "Agree" in the assessment means "I would say this." Put a check mark after the responses *a, b, c,* and *d* in each of these situations: agree completely (column 1), agree under some circumstances (column 2), disagree completely (column 3). You must agree with at least one response (i.e., you cannot disagree completely with all responses).

This is not a test. There are no right or wrong answers. These are ways a person might respond to the situation. Be honest with yourself as to which way you would respond.

When you have finished checking your responses, follow the instructions to the handout for scoring and interpreting the self-test. You have twenty minutes to complete this individual activity.

Lecture Notes Prior to Group Activity

[Facilitator: Distribute the Behaviors and Feelings Associated With the Levels of Self-Confidence handout now.]

The chart in the handout describes behaviors associated with the levels of self-confidence, or the lack of it, as assertive, aggressive, passive, or laissez-faire behavior. "You" refers to anyone whose behavior fits the description. These behaviors and the response to them are the main methods by which people identify another person's level of self-confidence. In this manner, the chart provides us with a behavioral, empirical definition of self-confidence.

As you read this chart, notice that any person might exhibit behaviors in one level or another depending on the situation. A person might behave aggressively in one situation, as when dealing with coworkers, but passively in another, as when dealing with his or her spouse. Different conditions evoke different responses not only from person to person but also from the same person at different times, different places, and under different circumstances. By extension, any individual may feel a high degree of self-confidence in some situations, as when, for example, he or she has expertise in a subject or a skill in a technique, and may feel a low level of self-confidence in others, as when, for example, he or she has little experience in social relationships. As a result of this variation in behaviors, it isn't appropriate to label a *person* as assertive, aggressive, and so forth, but rather only the behavior the person exhibits at any one time.

[Facilitator: Allow time for participants to read the handout and to discuss questions raised.]

Self-Confidence as Assertiveness or as Aggression

[Facilitator: Distribute the Self-Confidence Behaviors handout now.]

Self-confidence can take two different behavioral forms from two different ends of a spectrum: as assertive behavior and as aggressive behavior. Most self-confident behavior typically falls somewhere between the two extremes.

Assertiveness. Assertive behavior leads to honest, mutually respectful, supportive, and creative relationships by assuming these values.

[Facilitator: Read aloud the section of the Self-Confidence Behaviors handout relating to assertiveness.]

When you're assertive, you use "I-Language," which makes it clear that you have taken ownership of your beliefs or feelings. "I think . . ." "I feel . . ." "I wish . . ." "In my opinion . . ." These prefaces say that you're reporting something about yourself, not imposing your beliefs or feelings on anyone else, leaving room for differences of opinions or judgments, and you are open to discussion or dialogue. "I" statements convey the mind, heart, and spirit of assertiveness.

You don't have to be an expert or skilled or the best and the brightest to have self-confidence. Assertiveness when you are standing on unfamiliar ground or have little experience in similar situations isn't necessarily bravado. It comes from the self-confidence found in being secure in yourself and provides a strong basis for rational risk taking.

Aggression.   Aggressive behavior in contrast prevents all of the above. Most aggressive behavior in the workplace reflects an overabundance of self-confidence rather than a lack of it. This behavior may or may not reflect any special knowledge or skill; it usually reflects values and attitudes developed over many years. It's behavior that has worked and has produced results. As wisely said by the old maxim: Any virtue can be carried to extremes, and any virtue carried to extremes can become a vice.

> *[Facilitator: Read aloud the section of the Self-Confidence Behaviors handout relating to aggression.]*

If the feedback people give you says that they see you as aggressive, they mean, in part, that your language gives you away. When aggressive people use "I-Language," it usually emphasizes the selfishness or self-centeredness in their behavior, as when they say things such as "I want . . ." More to the point, "You-Language" marks aggressiveness. "You are . . ." "You did . . ." "You should . . ." "You shouldn't . . ." "You ought to . . ." "You ought not . . ." Control over other people is the endgame. You need to take notice of the way you talk with people before you can get control of the one thing you should or could truly control: yourself.

None of this negates the real possibility that a specific person's aggressiveness has its roots in some past experience of feeling vulnerable, or of not being assertive, or of overreacting to some past negative emotional experience, three experiences that could generate a lack of self-confidence and produce a compensatory reaction. However, few of us have sufficient training to see through a façade of aggression to the hurt person inside. We can deal only with the overbearing behavior as we experience it.

Low Self-Confidence: Passivity or Nonassertiveness

Passive behavior over a relatively extended period of time usually reflects how a person perceives herself (a low level of self-esteem or belief in oneself), which then affects her level of self-confidence, her willingness to take risks or to assert herself. The most common outcome from this lack of self-confidence is sociality in the extreme, which includes being a "yes man." (However, an aggressive person may often use the mask of "yes-man" behavior to manipulate people, a behavior many psychologists label "passive-aggressive.") Another common passive response is withdrawing into a shell. Dishonest, insincere relations result from the first passive pattern, sociality in the extreme. The lack of openness in the second passive pattern, withdrawal, produces relatively few, if any, relationships.

[Facilitator: Read aloud the section of the Self-Confidence Behaviors handout relating to passivity now.]

If you get feedback from people that they hear you use a lot of "You-Language," what they hear is compliant and nonjudgmental language that marks passivity: "You want . . ." "You need . . ." "You wish . . ." To them it seems that what "I" want, need, or wish is not important.

What they'll tell you in their feedback is that they think you don't reveal your needs. It seems to them you fear that they'll take advantage of you. On the other hand, they hear you asking to know about their needs, that it seems that if you don't help satisfy their wishes, they'll not like you.

People might see this kind of passive behavior as a "lose-win" situation in which you, if you exhibit passive behavior, always lose. However, if that's what you think you want or need, then for you *at that moment*, if you have our friendship needs met, or if you're left alone, you will believe and feel that you win too. Over time, passive behavior has been reinforced because it has achieved the results you want. However, to be successful in achieving our goals through passive behavior must be a conscious choice on your part.

Low Self-Confidence: Laissez-Faire or Willingly Giving Up Control

"Being laid back" often characterizes the behavior we call laissez-faire, French for "leave alone" or "do nothing." Laissez-faire behavior repeated over a period of time reflects a low level of self-confidence, even though the person may rationalize his or her actions with, "I trust everyone to do their jobs and do them well." In the extreme, this behavior usually signifies passive behavior, withdrawing from responsibility or accountability.

When exhibited by managers, this style may seem like assertive, democratic, or participative behavior. The difference between laissez-faire and democratic behaviors emerges from the context, especially if the person you need or rely on isn't there for you when you need him. Democratic behavior is participative, and the democrat participates too. Not so the laissez-faire person with low self-confidence, although he is not locked up in a productive shell.

Contrast two different managers' responses to this situation. Top management wants your engineering unit to design a new valve for a pump that has been giving customers problems. A laissez-faire manager would say, "Top management wants you to design the valve" and leave it at that. You flounder from the lack of direction, the project misses its standards or deadline, and the manager lets you take the heat. On the other hand, the democratic or assertive manager would say, "Top management wants us to design the valve. Let's take a look at what that requires." If, then, you don't happen to meet the standards or deadline, the manager tells top management, "My people gave it their best shot but will need more time."

People can spot the laissez-faire quality in our behavior by dishonesty about feelings. They'll hear you say things like "I really want you to succeed," but do nothing to help them when they need help. Insincere about roles, you'll say things you never do.

> *[Facilitator: Read aloud the section of the Self-Confidence Behaviors handout relating to laissez-faire behavior now.]*

If feedback from other people suggests that our behavior is laissez faire, that results from confusion about you and what you want. You probably will use a mix of "I-Language" and "You-Language," which confuses most people; it appears that you have a high level of self-confidence, when in fact you don't. When you say something like, "I think you should take care of this on your own," how should the other person interpret what you mean? It may signal a real desire for the person to take the responsibility away from you, if you should have at least a share in that responsibility. Many managers push responsibility off on to other people even though, in the end, they are responsible for anything their work unit does.

"You're competent and capable" may signal your concern that you aren't. "Do what you want or what you think right" may signal your inability or reluctance to make a decision. You *seem* to care about the other person, but, in fact, you are really protecting yourself. If anything the other person decides or does should backfire or fail, you're likely to say, "I had nothing to do with it. It was all your idea."

If you're getting feedback that your behavior is anything like we've described, you need to make a serious effort to turn it around. You need to set goals that will lead you to take responsibility for what happens around, to make accountable for your own actions. One way you can begin to do that is to monitor what you say to people that you will do and then be sure to do that. Another way is to ensure that what you say to people is sincere, that you truly believe what you say.

Lecture Notes Prior to the Teammate in the Barrel Group Activity

Instructions to Participants.   In this portion of the exercise, you will all participate in one way or another within your team here in the workshop. Here are the scenario and the instructions.

> *[Facilitator: Distribute Instructions for Teammate in the Barrel handout now. Then read the instructions aloud and answer questions about the exercise.]*

Facilitator's Notes

1. Distribute exercise materials.

2. Send teams to their breakout rooms (if available) or have them assemble in different parts of the main meeting room.

3. Take each team member aside before the exercise begins for special coaching on how to create pressures on the teammate in the barrel.
Examples:

— Tell the Electrical Engineer to shout or pound the table when accusing the person of slacking off, do anything within reason to be aggressive.

— Coach the Mechanical Engineer to be pleasant to the teammate in the barrel but to get between people and the teammate in the barrel. At the same time, he or she should not be rude or offensive to anyone.

— Tell the Buyer to physically pull back from the group, sitting a foot or two outside the team's circle, not to offer any opinions or solutions to problems, but to offer disparaging remarks about everyone.

— Coach the Production Controller to be very rude and judgmental, disparaging everything everyone else has to say.

Processing Questions After Both Parts of the Exercise

1. How close did your scores come to the perceptions other people had of how you handled the situation when you were in the barrel?

Typical answer: There were many differences.

2. What do you think accounts for the gaps in opinions?

Typical answer: I don't see myself the way other people see me, and I think I handle pressure situations better than I do.

3. If you are not satisfied with the results of your self-test or the feedback from the exercise, and think you have room for improvement, what steps should you take immediately to achieve better results in the future?

There are no typical answers here; people respond in terms of the results they received in their feedback.

SELF-ASSESSMENT: HOW DO I RESPOND TO SITUATIONS?

Instructions: Put a check mark in one of the columns after each response. Column 1 = agree completely. Column 2 = agree under some circumstances. Column 3 = disagree completely.

Situation and Possible Responses	*1*	*2*	*3*
1. Your office mate has spoken very little lately and only about trivia.			
a. You say, "I'm worried about you. Everything okay?"			
b. You say nothing, thinking he will work out the concern for himself.			
c. You say, "Something's bothering you. You always clam up whenever you should speak up."			
d. You say, "It seems like something's bothering you. If we talk about it, we might be able to work it out together."			
2. A coworker has asked you to cover for her twice this week when she has left early. If implicated, you could lose your job, as well as she can for lying.			
a. You say, "What can I do to help you?"			
b. You say nothing because it's no skin off your nose if she gets caught, as long as you're not implicated.			
c. You say, "I'm tired of your taking advantage of me. It's your problem, not mine."			
d. You say, "Look. I don't mind helping you out when you need it, but only when it's right. I can get in trouble for this, too, and I don't want to risk my job."			
3. A customer is very angry and has been shouting at you about how the machine you sold him has broken down twice this past quarter.			
a. You say, "I know how bad this is for you. I've talked to the engineers 'til I'm blue in the face. They keep promising me they'll fix it."			
b. You say, "Sure, I know it's bad, but I'm sure you and our engineers can get things back on track."			
c. You say, "Okay. Okay. It's tough on all of us. I'll get it fixed."			
d. You say, "I understand how frustrating and expensive this has been for you. Our engineers are working on the problem and we should have it fixed soon. In the meantime, what can my company do to make up for the inconvenience?"			
4. You receive two or three vendor calls a day. One salesperson is particularly obnoxious about setting an appointment even though you've told her repeatedly that your company doesn't need her products right now.			
a. You say, "Just keep calling. Eventually we may need your products."			

(continues)

Situation and Possible Responses	1	2	3

  b. You thank her for calling but refuse to set an appointment. She'll eventually give up.

  c. You say, "I've told you time and again, don't call me, I'll call you."

  d. You say, "As I've said, we're not in the market just now. I will call you when we need your products. I'll keep my word, and I'd like you to stop calling now."

5. You and your boss have been discussing your work during the annual appraisal interview. You think you deserve a significant raise, but you don't know how your boss will take it if you ask for one.

  a. You say, "I don't know what you can do, but if you can see to it, I'd like a better raise than last year."

  b. You say, "I know I can trust you to do right by me."

  c. You say, "I've worked hard and I want a significant raise, or I might have to find higher pay elsewhere."

  d. You say, "We both know that I've produced excellent results, and I think we need to discuss what we think those results are worth to the company."

6. One of your employees has been coming in late this week, causing problems for his coworkers. It's now Thursday, and he is late again.

  a. You say, "Can you get here on time, please?"

  b. You say, "You've been late every day this week. Please work it out so you can get here on time."

  c. You say, "You're late again. Once more and I'll put you on discipline report."

  d. You say, "I'm concerned about your being late every day and how it affects everyone else. Let's talk about what's going on and see what we can do about it."

7. One of your coworkers has "hit on you" twice this week. You know this person's married but separated. You like working with the person, but you'd rather not have a social relationship. The coworker asks you to go out tonight.

  a. You say, "I'm sorry, but I have other plans."

  b. You say, "You're separated, I know, but you'll find someone you really love."

  c. You say, "Stop it! Or I'll report you for harassing me."

  d. You say, "Look. I understand that you're going through a rough time, but I'm feeling very uncomfortable with this. I think you're a great person, and we really work well together, but I'd like to keep our relationship strictly professional. Please back off and stop asking me out."

Situation and Possible Responses	1	2	3

8. The team leader has called a meeting for a day you planned to spend with an important client, the only day she'll be available for a month. You know you're needed at the meeting, but you also need to spend that time with the client.

    a. You say, "I'll see if we can reschedule the appointment."

    b. You say, "You probably can run the meeting without me."

    c. You say, "That's a bad day for me. Reschedule it."

    d. You say, "That's the day I'm supposed to meet with Ms. Smith. I understand that I need to be at the meeting, but I also have to take advantage of this only opportunity to be with her. Could we please reschedule the meeting for either the day before or the day after?"

9. At a team meeting, one person keeps interrupting you (and other people).

    a. You say nothing rather than have a confrontation.

    b. You say nothing, thinking that eventually he'll stop it.

    c. You say, "Stop interrupting me, dammit."

    d. You say, "I'm getting really angry. I would like to finish my thought and then give you a chance to respond or speak your piece. Okay?"

10. An employee reporting to you has an important project deadline coming up within a week. She's highly skilled and very competent. On the other hand, the success of this project means a great deal to you and to the company, as well as to her.

    a. You say, "How are things going?"

    b. You say nothing, She'll do just fine.

    c. You say, "Look. The deadline's on top of us. What have you been doing?"

    d. You say, "I have great confidence in your ability to get this job done, but we both know how important this project is, so you can't fault me for being anxious. I'd like to know what's happening. Please bring me up to date."

11. You have set aside time from 4:00 P.M. to 5:00 P.M. to clean up details and odds and ends. You look forward to the peace and quiet for getting these things done. A coworker e-mails you: "I need to see you today. 4:00."

    a. You e-mail back: "Okay."

    b. You do nothing. Maybe he'll get the hint.

    c. You e-mail back: "Bad time."

    d. You e-mail back: "That's not a good time for me. How about 3:00 or tomorrow, first thing in the morning?"

(continues)

Situation and Possible Responses	1	2	3
12. You are interviewing for a job, and the manager suggests that you go to dinner together as a couple. You don't want to do it, but you want the job.			
a. You say, "I'm tied up tonight, but thanks for asking."			
b. You say nothing and hope the manager gets the hint.			
c. You say, "I could report you for making an unwanted advance."			
d. You say, "I would like the job, and I'm highly qualified for it, but I don't think it's a good idea that we go to dinner together. Perhaps my friend/spouse and I can join you and your spouse or significant other for dinner."			
13. At a party, your spouse/significant other criticizes your clothing in front of friends and coworkers. This really embarrasses you.			
a. You say, "Hey! She ought to know. She's got much better taste than I do."			
b. You say nothing, thinking that other people will just shrug it off.			
c. You say, "Hey! She ought to know. she buys this junk for me."			
d. You say, "I guess I can improve my wardrobe. We should talk about this later, maybe shop together in the future and come to an agreement on what I should wear."			
14. Your recently divorced assistant has confided in you that she's sleeping with a man in your department. She says that the two of them are in love and that he'll divorce his wife for her. You know that he has had these flings with other people before, and you're afraid she'll get hurt.			
a. You say, "I'm glad you found someone to love and to love you. Keep me posted."			
b. You say, "I'm sure things will work out for you one way or another."			
c. You say, "Don't be a sap. He messes around all the time."			
d. You say, "I'm sure you're very taken with him, and that he feels strongly for you, but I think you might think very carefully about what you're getting into—keep a realistic outlook about the relationship, about him, and about yourself. If you ever need someone to talk to, I'm here for you."			
15. You're writing an important proposal, but you don't have all the information you need. You know your boss has it, but he gets antagonistic with people who come to him when he thinks they should be on top of everything. And he thinks you should be on top of this.			
a. You say nothing to him and ask his administrative assistant to get the information for you.			
b. You say nothing and hope somehow to find the information on your own.			
c. You say, "I have to have this information, or you'll have to find someone else to write this proposal."			
d. You say, "I have everything I need for this proposal except the one piece of information I think only you have. With it, we'll have a slam-bang proposition for the company."			

SCORING AND INTERPRETATION GUIDE

Give yourself two points for each *d* answer with which you agree completely (column 1), one point for each answer with which you might agree sometimes (column 2), two points each time you disagree completely with answers *a*, *b*, or *c* (column 3). Total the scores for each answer: *a, b, c, d*.

Responses to *d* are assertive responses, which suggest self-confidence. The total score to response *d* indicates a degree of assertiveness and self-confidence.

Score	*Interpretation*
60	You're an exceptional person, very assertive and extremely self-confident.
50–59	You're above average in assertiveness and self-confidence.
40–49	You're reasonably assertive and self-confident.
30–39	You're about average in assertiveness and self-confidence.
20–29	You're below average in assertiveness and self-confidence.
below 20	You should carefully study how to become more assertive and raise your level of self-confidence.

Responses *a*, *b*, and *c* are, respectively, passive, laissez-faire, and aggressive. Agreement under some circumstances (column 2) with these three responses suggests one of the following:

▶ You are likely to fall back on this behavior when you're under pressure.

▶ You can't decide on your proper course of action in those circumstances.

▶ That the better part of valor is to do as the response suggests.

Regardless of the reason, none of the three responses is assertive or reflects a great deal of self-confidence. A score of 15 or more for responses *a*, *b*, and *c* demonstrates a certain lack of self-confidence that you may want to beef up by coming to grips with your reasons for not choosing the assertive response.

Disagreeing completely with *d*, especially when viewed in relation to the responses with which you did agree in some way, also suggests a certain lack of self-confidence. Contrarily, complete disagreement with responses *a*, *b*, and *c*, especially if you agree completely with response *d*, strengthens your opinion concerning your positive assertiveness and self-confidence.

Mark your scores with an *X* on the appropriate places. For example, if you scored very high on assertiveness, for example, 50, place an *X* on the horizontal axis far to the left of the vertical axis. If you scored very low on Laissez-faire, place an *X* on the vertical axis close to the junction of the vertical and horizontal axes. Do the same for Passive and for Aggressive.

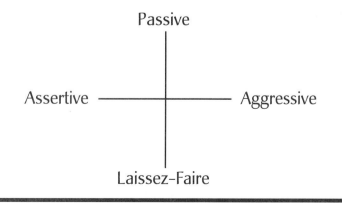

BEHAVIORS AND FEELINGS ASSOCIATED WITH THE LEVELS OF SELF-CONFIDENCE

Behavior Type	Behavior Characteristics	Feelings in Situations	Other People's Feelings in Response
Assertive	▶ Strong eye contact ▶ High self-esteem ▶ Self-expressive ▶ Honest about feelings, rights ▶ Good listening skills ▶ Supportive and helpful	▶ Self-respect ▶ Confident	▶ Respect for "you" ▶ Comfortable with "you" ▶ Valued, respected by "you" ▶ In control of their own lives
Aggressive	▶ Strong eye contact ▶ Self-absorbed, self-esteem out of proportion to reality ▶ Honest about feelings, rights but demanding ▶ Closed to others' feelings, opinions ▶ Poor listening skills	▶ Self-righteous ▶ Superior ▶ Judgmental	▶ Hurt, humiliated by "you" ▶ Angry with, resentful, vengeful toward "you" ▶ Angry with self for seeming weak ▶ Powerless
Passive	▶ Little or no eye contact ▶ Self-denigrating, self-denying ▶ Withdrawn ▶ Nonconfrontational ▶ Good listening skills ▶ Goes overboard to please	▶ Eager to please, while doing without or injuring "yourself" ▶ Self-satisfaction ▶ Relieved ▶ Sometimes resentful, bitter	▶ Irritation, disgust with "you" ▶ Sometimes pity for "you"
Laissez-faire (sometimes a disguise for Passive)	▶ Detached ▶ Cold ▶ Emotionally dishonest and not direct or expressive ▶ Good listening skills ▶ Often nonsupportive or not helpful	▶ Above the fray ▶ Self-satisfied ▶ Relieved	▶ Confused about "you" and "your" opinions or feelings ▶ Often anger and disgust with "you" ▶ In control but without direction or checks and balances ▶ Guilt for wanting more direction

SELF-CONFIDENCE BEHAVIORS

SELF-CONFIDENCE AS ASSERTIVENESS OR AS AGGRESSIVENESS

Assertiveness

▶ Results: Honest, mutually respectful, supportive, and creative relationships

▶ Values
  – I am a worthwhile person who respects myself, and I believe I'm due appropriate respect from others.
  – I am in control of myself and secure in myself.
  – I have rights, which include the right to assert those rights.
  – It is important that I should and that I can express my feelings toward other people.
  – It is important that other people should know that I'm sensitive to their needs and that I expect them to be sensitive to mine.
  – Confrontation can be positive, nonjudgmental, and constructive.

▶ Assertiveness is marked by "I" language.
  – Reporting something about yourself
  – Not imposing your beliefs or feelings on anyone else
  – Leaving room for differences of opinions or judgments
  – Open to discussion or dialogue

▶ Self-confidence found in "being secure in yourself" provides a strong basis for rational risk taking.

Aggressiveness

▶ Result: Control

▶ Values
  – I am a worthwhile person who respects myself and feels I'm due more respect from others than I'm willing to give.
  – I am in control of myself, secure in myself, and I have a right to control other people.
  – I have rights that other people do not have.
  – I need not express my true feelings toward other people and I don't need to know theirs toward me.
  – It is important that other people be sensitive to my needs but I don't need to be sensitive to theirs.
  – Confrontation must always have a positive result for me regardless of how other people come out.

▶ "I-Language" usually self-oriented: "I want . . ."

▶ "You-Language"
  – Judgmental
  – Harsh
  – Demanding
  – Emotional

(continues)

LOW SELF-CONFIDENCE

Passivity or Nonassertiveness

▶ Results: Sociality in the extreme, for example, being a "yes man," withdrawal, dishonest, insincere relations, no or relatively few relationships

▶ Values
  - Safety first.
  - Asserting my rights is dangerous to my safety.
  - Friendship is better than meeting my real needs.

▶ "You" language, compliant and nonjudgmental

Laissez-Faire or Willingly Giving Up Control

▶ Results: Withdrawing from responsibility or accountability, dishonesty about feelings and insincerity about roles, few relationships other than tenuous friendships

▶ Values
  - Safety first.
  - People misjudge my value to them; they don't need me as much as they think they do.
  - People don't really want me to work with them or to manage things or processes; they're better off without me.
  - I don't need to take control of anything except meeting my own needs or fulfilling my interests.
  - Mix of "I-Language" and "You-Language" depends on context to understand.

INSTRUCTIONS FOR TEAMMATE IN THE BARREL

CONDUCTING THE EXERCISE

1. You are members of a cross-functional team charged with designing a prototype of a revolutionary chemical processing machine your company will produce and sell.

2. Each person on the team has a technical or administrative role, identified by a name tent or name badge. It doesn't matter if you don't have skill or knowledge in what you're scripted to do with regard to the team's project. What you say or do is more important than your technical skill or knowledge.

3. You are in a meeting called to discuss the fact that the project on which your team is working is behind schedule, and the work produced so far has not been altogether satisfactory.

4. Each of you on the team has a skill and a responsibility, which are provided in the scripts each of you will receive.

5. Each of you also has instructions as to how to act during this meeting. In addition to having a functional role on the team about which everyone will know, you will have a script that you do not share with anyone else.

6. The meeting is scheduled to take ten minutes, during which time one person will be the focus of attention. He or she will be the "teammate in the barrel." Each person will take a turn at dealing with a situation on your team.

7. The teammate in the barrel will have the same skills and responsibilities as scripted, for example, those of Mechanical Engineer, but, since things will happen that will deliberately create distracting pressures, the question to which he or she will respond during the turn is "How do I handle what is going on here?" When you're in the barrel, be yourself, respond as you would in the real world. Don't play a role. Your teammates will be evaluating what you do and how you do it.

8. No one is the *team leader*, or has managerial status or power. No one person has that role in a self-managed team, yet everyone does.

9. One person (two people on six-person teams) will be the Observer, but the Observer will also take a turn in the barrel. He or she will trade roles with the Buyer, and the Buyer will be the Observer at that time. Elect the Observer(s) now.

10. The other people will have a handout they will use for evaluating the behavior of the person dealing with the situation immediately after the round ends.

11. After each person has had a turn, the group discusses one another's behavior in response to the group's actions. They tell each person in turn how they evaluated the behavior (assertive, aggressive, passive, or laissez-faire) and explain:

    — This is what I thought was effective and why.

    — This is what I thought was ineffective and why.

    — This is what I suggest you might do differently in a similar situation and why.

12. You will also need a scribe/timekeeper, to call time when ten minutes are up, and to write and report on the conclusions and insights from this exercise your team draws. Elect that person now.

(continues)

13. Before beginning, read the script you received; it should fit with the title you have. Make sure you keep the details to yourself.

14. When a round is over, take a five-minute breather, but hold on to your feedback until everyone has had a turn in the barrel.

DISCUSSING THE EXERCISE AFTER EVERYONE HAS HAD A TURN IN THE BARREL

1. After everyone has had a turn in the barrel, everyone on the team discusses his or her impressions of each person's responses when he or she was in the barrel. Each person on the team will give the Observer's Guide materials to that person at that time.

2. Each person compares where on the grid people place their X marks with where he or she scored in his or her assessment of his or her assertiveness/self-confidence in the individual exercise.

Teammate in the Barrel Scripts

Person 1: Electrical Engineer

These instructions are to be followed only when you are role playing. When you are the person dealing with the situation, you will have the title, but you will be yourself at all times.

Your job is to design the wiring scheme in the equipment the team is responsible for producing. You think that the person in the barrel is not doing his/her job well enough (whatever that job is). Be aggressive, somewhat abusive. When the meeting begins, you be the first to speak up and accuse the person of slacking off. Ad lib anything you wish to create pressure for the person in the barrel. Always be aggressive but vary your approach from one situation to another to keep everyone off balance.

Person 2: Mechanical Engineer

These instructions are to be followed only when you are role playing. When you are the person dealing with the situation, you will have the title, but you will be yourself at all times.

Your job is to design the structure and the mechanical functions of the machine. Your company doesn't manufacture the parts. Rather a buyer purchases parts from suppliers. Be passive, extremely friendly. Act intimidated by the Electrical Engineer. You think that the person in the barrel is not doing his/her job well, but keep that to yourself, and when anyone accuses the person of not doing his/her job well, defend the person however you can. Ad lib anything you wish to create pressure for the person in the barrel; for example, getting in the person's way by interrupting him or her to come to his or her defense. (Interruptions and otherwise getting in the way are very frustrating no matter how well intentioned). Always be passive but vary your approach from one situation to another to keep everyone off balance.

(continues)

Person 3: Buyer

These instructions are to be followed only when you are role playing. When you are the person dealing with the situation, you have the title, but you will be yourself at all times.

Your job is to take the specs provided by the Engineers and the Production Controller and buy the parts and equipment necessary for assembling the machine they design. You don't know anything about engineering and rely completely on what they have asked you to purchase. You admire these other people, but you are a bit intimidated by them as well. Be laissez-faire in your approach to the entire group and project, saying things such as, "You people work it out and let me know what you want from me." You don't know who is responsible (if any one person is), so you don't want to get into it with anyone, but you want to make sure that no one thinks it's you. Ad lib anything you wish to create pressure for the person in the barrel. Always be laissez-faire but vary your approach from one situation to another to keep everyone off balance.

Person 4: Production Controller

These instructions are to be followed only when you are role playing. When you are the person dealing with the situation, you will have the title, but you will be yourself at all times.

Your job is to oversee the production of the prototype from the plans drawn by the engineers, using the parts and equipment purchased by the buyer. You think the engineers don't know what they're doing, and you let them know it every chance you get. Be aggressive, hostile. Verbally bully everyone, as well as the person in the barrel, to create pressure for him or her. Always be aggressive but vary your approach from one situation to another to keep everyone off balance.

Person 5: Observer (and Person 6)

Sit outside the immediate circle of the team, using the Observer's Guide for evaluating the behavior of the person handling the situation, and only that person. Everyone else is playing a role they've been assigned. When it's your turn to handle the situation, trade places at the table with whomever is playing the Buyer. However, do not assume his/her behavioral assignment. Just be yourself.

As the Buyer, your job is to take the specs provided by the Engineers and the Production Controller and buy the parts and equipment necessary for assembling the machine they design. You don't know anything about engineering and rely completely on what they have asked you to purchase.

FEEDBACK GUIDE FOR TEAMMATE IN THE BARREL

INSTRUCTIONS

After the ten-minute turn is over, write brief comments in the spaces provided to give feedback to the teammate in the barrel. Write legibly because you will give this paper to the person after you have discussed his or her behavior at the end of the exercise.

Teammate in the Barrel's Name _____

This is what I thought was effective and why.

This is what I thought was ineffective and why.

This is what I suggest you might do differently in a similar situation and why.

SAMPLE OBSERVER'S GUIDE
FOR TEAMMATE IN THE BARREL

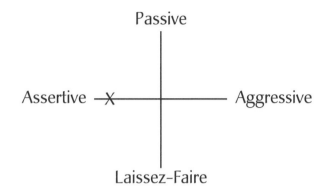

Explanation

1. I said you exhibited *fairly assertive* behavior because when the *Electrical Engineer called you lazy and incompetent, you remained calm and asked him to refrain from name calling but to point out what specifically you did wrong.*

2. I think *staying calm* was effective.

3. I think *not asking the Buyer to participate* was ineffective.

4. I think in the future you might try *asking people like the Buyer to accept more responsibility for what is going on.*

OBSERVER'S GUIDE FOR TEAMMATE IN THE BARREL

INSTRUCTIONS

For each person in the barrel, and for only that person, observe and evaluate his/her behavior, that is, Assertive, Aggressive, Passive, or Laissez-faire. Place an X on the axis (axes) at the point that reflects the degree to which the person exhibited the behavior(s). For example, if you think the person was very aggressive, place an X at a point in the horizontal axis far away from the vertical axis. If you think the person was aggressive with one person and passive with others, place an X on each of the axes. Close to the intersection of the axes means "not very." Far from the intersection means "very." Then explain your decisions. See the Sample Observer's Guide.

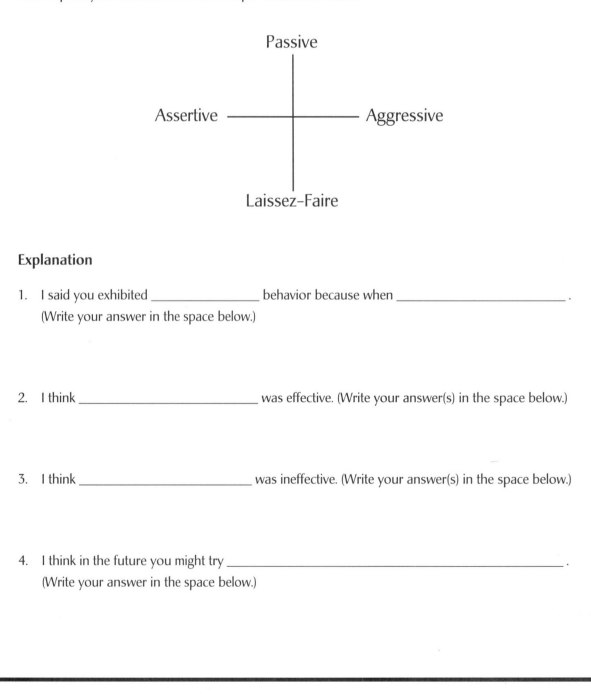

Explanation

1. I said you exhibited _____ behavior because when _____ .
   (Write your answer in the space below.)

2. I think _____ was effective. (Write your answer(s) in the space below.)

3. I think _____ was ineffective. (Write your answer(s) in the space below.)

4. I think in the future you might try _____ .
   (Write your answer in the space below.)

Exercise 12.2. Managing the Challenges to My Self-Confidence

Instructor's Notes

This exercise is divided into four parts: two individual activities and two group activities. Because it may be too long to use in a short workshop, I have added Exercise 12.3, Building Self-Confidence, as a *alternative* to Exercise 12.2.

Note: This exercise works best with an intact team or with workshop groups that have been interacting with one another for at least one day during which the participants will have had an opportunity to build levels of trust.

Learning Objectives and Outcomes

By the end of this exercise participants will be able to:

▶ Identify the variety of different challenges (needs to change) that affect their self-confidence negatively.

▶ Take feedback from other people as to the strengths they see and suggestions for change.

▶ Apply an action plan to increase their levels of self-confidence.

Self-Management Skills Involved

▶ Risk taking and trust
▶ Decision making
▶ Openness, honesty
▶ Respect for others
▶ Communication, especially giving and receiving feedback

Requirements

Time:	Approximately ninety minutes
Materials:	Flip chart, multicolored markers, masking tape
	Instructions for Strengths, Challenges, and Barriers Chart handout
	Strengths, Challenges, and Barriers Chart worksheet
	Instructions for Self-Confidence Action Planner handout
	Sample Self-Confidence Action Planner
	Self-Confidence Action Planner worksheet

Preparation: Photocopy the handouts, worksheet, and sample.

Room Setup: Allow for people to talk to one another face to face. Teams should be no more than six people.

Lecture Notes

Self-confidence is learned behavior, usually expressed as assertiveness. You build self-confidence by recognizing your strengths, acknowledging what about yourself you cannot change, and confronting the challenges to your self-confidence. The more you feel secure in yourself and your ability to manage your strengths and use them for meeting your challenges head on, the greater will be your self-confidence. As with anything else in self-management, increasing self-confidence takes planning.

[Facilitator: Distribute Instructions for Strengths, Challenges, and Barriers Chart handout and Strengths, Challenges, and Barriers Chart worksheet now.]

The first part of this exercise asks you to identify your strengths, to make a list of qualities or characteristics you think are effective in helping you manage your life. A strength may be as simple as "I am an adult," as important as, "I believe I have rights to my beliefs, values, and opinions," or as sophisticated as "I have a desire to succeed in what I do." Strengths are the source of self-confidence, and the basis on which you can manage the changes you need to make.

However, you may not be as aware of all your strengths as you think you are. In fact, people typically underplay their strengths, shortchange themselves with respect to their rights, and deny themselves the ability to satisfy their needs or wants. You need feedback from other people that helps you see yourself through their eyes. Getting feedback about your strengths should be quite an eye-opener for you.

Second, the exercise will also ask you to make a list of all the qualities or characteristics that they think get in the way of your self-confidence but about which you can do *nothing*. Let's say, you think your height works against you, and you wish you could be taller. Short of surgically replacing bones in your legs, you can't do anything about that. Or, say you think your gender works against you, and you wish you could be the other gender. Again, short of surgery, you can't do anything about that, either. When you can do nothing about realities, you have to accept them and work around them.

Third, the exercise asks you to list the challenges to your self-confidence, the things in your life or about yourself you would like to change and that you can change. For example, if you can change them, you might feel more self-confident. In fact, changing those things will in themselves be acts of building self-confidence. However, as in any other planning situation, you must look for the obstacles or barriers that can stand in your way.

One example of a challenge is "My inability to assert myself with my boss when I know he's wrong." If I want to change that, a barrier that could get in the way of doing something about this is "my boss's temper and my fear of confrontation." I might not be able to do anything about my boss's temper, but I can do something about my fear of confrontation. So, what do I have to do for myself to overcome that barrier?

The first step would be to set a goal for overcoming the barrier. What's the target for change? For example, I might say, "By the end of the week, I will present a short report to my boss on the subject on which I disagree and in which I build a strong case." Building a strong case is one objective toward that end, and writing the report is the second objective. Confidence in my case contributes to confidence in myself, and putting it in writing reinforces that confidence. The only thing left to do is to accept the responsibility to make that presentation.

[Facilitator: Distribute the Instructions for Self-Confidence Action Planner handout, the Sample Self-Confidence Action Planner, and the Self-Confidence Action Planner worksheet now.]

Many people find that the lack of a plan is the enemy of action, and the lack of action is the enemy of a plan. Completing an action plan to face up to our challenges boosts our self-confidence. Not all plans work to their fullest, but at least we know what we might or could do. We have a place from which to start.

We have to consider the resources at our disposal to help us overcome our challenges. We begin with the strengths we can exert in meeting this challenge. We identify the resources we need for overcoming our challenges but do not have, such as a willingness to confront other people. The lack of a resource is also a barrier. If we don't think about the resources we need or the barriers we need to overcome, our plan can't help us prevent obstacles from barring our efforts.

Not every challenge in life has equal importance with every other challenge. In fact, some challenges may not have enough payoff to make it worthwhile to attack them now. If, for example, the disagreement with my boss is over a trivial matter, such as who cleans the coffee pot in the evening, would risking a confrontation over that be as beneficial as dealing with a major sales campaign with which I disagree. We have to decide which of our challenges will provide us sufficient payoff and which will not.

Talking with other people can help us rise to our challenge. If others think our plan is a good one, their positive feedback boosts our self-confidence. If people think we can do other things to rise to our challenge, and we accept their suggestions, their support gives a charge to our self-confidence. The whole feedback process tends to lift people's feelings about themselves.

Instructions for Strengths, Challenges, and Barriers Chart

INDIVIDUAL ACTIVITY 1

On your own, complete the Strength, Challenges, and Barriers Chart. When writing your lists, be as honest with yourself as you can, and be specific.

► **Strengths:** In the upper left box, list the qualities or characteristics you think most support your self-confidence.

► **What I Can't Change:** In the upper right box, list the qualities or characteristics you think get in the way of your self-confidence but about which you can do nothing (short of drastic measures, such as surgery).

► **Challenges:** In the lower left box, list the challenges, the qualities or characteristics you think get in the way of your self-confidence but about which you can do something.

► **Barriers to Change:** In the lower right box, list the obstacles that would make change difficult or could even prevent you from making the changes you want.

► You have twenty minutes to complete this individual activity.

GROUP FEEDBACK FOR ACTIVITY 1

Instructions

1. After everyone completes his or her chart, each person will take a turn reading his or her *strengths*.

2. As each person reads his or her list, the teammates give him or her feedback about what he or she said, or provide input about strengths they see that the individual might not have listed.

STRENGTHS, CHALLENGES, AND BARRIERS CHART

Strengths

Example:

My determination; I don't give up

What I Can't Change

Example:

My height; I'm too short

Challenges

Example:

My inability to assert myself with my boss when I know he's wrong

Barriers to Change

Example:

My boss's temper and my fear of confrontation

Instructions for Self-Confidence Action Planner

INDIVIDUAL ACTIVITY 2

1. In the margin of your Strengths, Challenges, and Barriers Chart, alongside the Challenges box, rank the challenges as to importance and immediacy (priority). The most important/immediate = 1.

2. There can be no duplication of ratings.

3. Answer the questions on the second page of the handout (Discussion Questions) to evaluate how those challenges affect you and your self-confidence.

4. Use the Self-Confidence Action Planner to design an action plan; follow the instructions and use the sample as a guide.

5. You have twenty minutes to complete this activity.

GROUP FEEDBACK FOR ACTIVITY

1. After everyone completes ranking his or her challenges and setting up action plans, each person takes a turn reading his or her plan to the team.

2. Everyone gives feedback using this format:
   - I think your plan should be effective.
   - This is what I think will be effective.
   - This is what I think will not be effective.
   - This is what I suggest you try.

3. Add useful suggestions from other people to your plan.

4. You have thirty minutes to complete this group feedback activity.

DISCUSSION QUESTIONS FOR THE SELF-CONFIDENCE ACTION PLANNER

1. How did you decide that the challenge you have numbered one has the highest priority? Explain your feelings about the fact that this is number one, especially how the challenge affects your self-confidence.

2. How did you decide that the challenge you have numbered two has the next highest priority? Explain your feelings about this, especially how the challenge affects your self-confidence.

Sample Self-Confidence Action Planner

CHALLENGE

▶ Change Goal:

By the end of the week, I will present a short report to my boss on the subject on which I disagree and in which I build a strong case.

▶ Milestones:

1. Build a strong case.

2. Write the report.

3. Accept the responsibility to make the presentation.

▶ Resources Needed (both available and not available) that will help me make the change:

1. Sales reports for last year at this time

2. Data concerning market changes this year

3. Spreadsheet

▶ Barriers (What can get in the way of making the change): Data concerning market changes this year may not be up to the minute. Therefore, provide most recent data available.

▶ Action Steps (What I have to do to effect the change):

1. Gather the data.

2. Enter data into spreadsheets.

3. Develop the report.

4. Pass to my colleague for review.

5. Make changes if necessary.

6. Practice the presentation with my colleague and get feedback.

7. Make an appointment with the chief.

8. Make the presentation.

SELF-CONFIDENCE ACTION PLANNER

INSTRUCTIONS

Use your Strengths, Challenges, and Barriers Chart to identify challenges you want to overcome. Using the sample as a model, write the targets for change (for overcoming your challenges), milestones you have to reach for making the change, the resources you need, the barriers you may encounter while making the change, and what action steps you have to take. *Use this format not only in the workshop but also as a follow-up guide to change outside the workshop.*

Challenge 1:

▶ Change Goal:

▶ Milestones:

▶ Resources Needed (both available and not available):

▶ Barriers:

▶ Action Steps:

Challenge 2:

▶ Change Goal:

▶ Milestones:

▶ Resources Needed (both available and not available):

▶ Barriers:

▶ Action Steps:

How have designing these plans and discussing them with my teammates affected my self-confidence?

Exercise 12.3. Building Self-Confidence Follow-Up Activity

Instructor's Notes

In a short workshop, instead of having the participants work through the detailed and long Exercise 12.3, Managing the Challenges to My Self-Confidence, use this follow-up activity as a way for participants to increase their self-confidence on their own.

Learning Objectives and Outcomes

By doing these activities participants will take steps to:

▶ Identify and reinforce their strengths.

▶ Identify areas in which they need to improve in order to increase self-confidence.

▶ Get feedback from other people about their perceptions of the participants' self-confidence.

▶ Use the EIAG Model for changing areas in need of improvement and making wanted changes.

Self-Management Skills Involved

▶ Risk taking and trust

▶ Decision making

▶ Openness, honesty

▶ Respect for others

▶ Communication, especially giving and receiving feedback

Requirements:

Time:	Thirty minutes to prepare participants for the take-home assignment
Materials:	Instructions for Building Self-Confidence handout
	The EIAG Model overhead
Equipment:	Overhead projector and screen
Preparation:	Photocopy the handout.
	Make the overhead.
Room Setup:	Any classroom arrangement

Lecture Notes

[Facilitator: Distribute the Instructions for Building Self-Confidence handout now. If you have not read Chapter 1 and the explanation of the EIAG Model, read it now or review it if you need to.]

People do a variety of things to increase their self-confidence. Most commonly they find other people they trust and who are willing to help them by giving them feedback. This includes what I call "the person in the mirror"—your reflection of yourself. Get feedback from watching yourself talk to the mirror: your facial expressions, your hand gestures. Do the same assessment by listening to yourself talking on a tape recording. Feedback isn't criticism, it's information about how we appear to other people that we can use to make effective behavior changes that increase self-confidence.

[Facilitator: If you haven't provided the participants with the EIAG Model before, do so now. USE the EIAG Model overhead.]

Another effective device is an assessment method called EIAG. The acronym stands for:

▶ Experience

▶ Interpretation

▶ Analysis

▶ Generalization

When you undergo an experience that leaves you unsettled as to what you said or did, how you said it or did it, you assess what happened. Start by describing the experience to yourself as objectively as possible. This describes *what* happened. For example, "My colleague said I failed to support her during her presentation."

Then interpret that experience by asking yourself how you felt about it. This describes how you feel about that kind of experience and is likely to reflect your values or your attitudes when something like that happens. "When she said that, I became angry."

Next, analyze what happened by answering "Why?" questions. Determining why you feel as you do helps explain your values or attitudes. "I get angry when someone accuses me of something I don't think I did."

Finally, generalize to decide on how to make a change in how you react under such circumstances. You might say, for example, "In the future, before I get angry, I will ask what I did to lead the person to think I was unsupportive."

[Facilitator: Read Instructions for Building Self-Confidence aloud.]

INSTRUCTIONS FOR THE BUILDING SELF-CONFIDENCE FOLLOW-UP ACTIVITY EXERCISE

Some activities people use to become more self-confident are included in this list. Add any activities you think appropriate. Whatever you do, be sure to extend yourself by reaching for new goals, new ways of doing things; get out of your "comfort zone" and take risks to widen your self-awareness.

1. Make a list of everything you've ever done about which you are very proud, searching back into your earliest memory and working up to the present. Tell someone (your spouse or significant other) what you're doing and why, and ask that person to let you read the list to him or her and to explain why you're proud of each item. You could also ask the person to tell you things he or she felt proud that you did or said. Find ways to engage in similar activities from now on.

2. Talk to the "person in the mirror" about any subject. Watch your facial expressions and hand gestures. See yourself as others see you when you talk to them. Assess whether what you see projects self-confidence: for example, strong eye contact, smiling as you speak, hand gestures that emphasize your main points, and so forth.

3. Record conversations with people (asking their permission, of course, and explaining to them what you're trying to do). Listen to your own tone of voice, the words you use, the way you emphasize words, and the pace you use when speaking. Assess whether you think what you hear projects self-confidence: for example, a firm, quiet tone of voice, emphasis on words that communicate your meaning, words that communicate your feelings or emotions, conviction, and so forth.

4. Ask people for feedback. Explain to them that you're trying to improve your self-confidence and need their help. Take what they say seriously and see what you can do to see and hear yourself as they do.

5. Evaluate your own beliefs, opinions, values, and feelings or emotions. Understand where you're coming from. After an unsettling or difficult situation, stop to reflect on what you said or did by using the EIAG Model. Determine on what basis you react to other people, make decisions about why you say or do things, and choose from among alternative actions you might take to change those reactions.

6. Volunteer to make an oral presentation at a later date; develop it, rehearse it carefully, and deliver it with confidence.

7. During a meeting speak up when you disagree with someone (and it is worthwhile to do so). Express your opinions or feelings with conviction.

8. When talking with people in authority exhibit self-confidence. Here are some examples: hold your head up, make eye contact, shake hands firmly, feel free to politely disagree (if appropriate), and express your opinions or feelings with conviction. Ask other people to give you feedback as to what you do to detract from appearing self-confident and add things to your list.

9. Take on an activity totally different from anything you've ever done before: for example, wall climbing, sky diving, scuba diving—anything that involves an element of risk or stamina about which you can feel a proud sense of accomplishment.

THE EIAG MODEL

▲ Experience

Describe the Experience objectively: *what* happened.

"My colleague said I failed to support her during her presentation."

▲ Interpretation

Describe how you felt about it.

"When she said that, I became angry."

▲ Analysis

Answer "Why?" questions.

"I get angry when someone accuses me of something I don't think I did."

▲ Generalization

Decide on how to change under such circumstances.

"In the future, before I get angry, I will ask what I did to lead the person to think I was unsupportive."

13

Self–Esteem/Self–Respect

By the end of this chapter, you will be able to facilitate three exercises for helping the participants increase their self-esteem/self-respect by:

▶ Identifying behaviors generally associated with self-esteem/self-respect

▶ Recognizing how their own behaviors exhibit self-esteem/self-respect

▶ Taking steps for building on their strengths and improving their self-esteem/self-respect

Exercise 13.1. What I Like and Don't Like About Myself

Instructor's Notes

This two-part exercise works best with an intact team or with workshop groups that have been interacting with one another for at least one day during which the participants will have had an opportunity to build levels of trust.

Learning Objectives and Outcomes

By the end of this exercise participants will be able to:

▶   Identify the perceptions and feelings that indicate their level of self-esteem/self-respect.

▶   Relate feedback from other people about how they appear to those people.

▶   Apply an action plan to increasing their levels of self-esteem/self-respect.

▶   Build self-esteem/self respect.

Self-Management Skills Involved

▶   Risk taking and trust

▶   Decision making

▶   Openness, honesty

▶   Communication, especially giving and receiving feedback

Requirements

Time:	Approximately one hour
Materials:	Flip chart, multicolored markers, masking tape
	Paper and pencils
	Instructions for What I Like and Don't Like About Myself handout
	What I Like and Don't Like About Myself worksheet
	Interpretation Guide for What I Like and Don't Like About Myself
Preparation:	Photocopy the handout, worksheet, and interpretation guide.
Room Setup:	Allow for people to talk to one another face to face. Teams should be no more than four to six people.

Lecture Notes

Self-esteem and self-respect, which in the context of self-management are synonymous, are feelings about ourselves that are exhibited in behaviors, such as when we accept negative feedback or admit mistakes we make. What constitutes self-esteem/self-respect varies from person to person, and from time to time for each person. Experiences, skills, knowledge, aptitudes, interest, group membership, our own responses to everything, all these things affect how we feel about ourselves.

Frequently, as adults, we still remain dependent on other people's perceptions and feelings about us to maintain our sense of importance or worth. How others react to us makes us feel good or bad about ourselves.

Low self-esteem/self-respect comes from many different sources. Self-esteem and self-respect can be affected by negative childhood experiences, a lack of positive reinforcement throughout our growing years, being deprived of love and affection, a lack of caring on the part of significant others, our physical, intellectual, or psychological limitations, and our own failures.

Feelings about ourselves can also change with time and experience. High levels of self-esteem/self-respect can be lowered by bad experiences. Low levels can be raised by good experiences or by deliberate exercise. In the end, however, how we feel about ourselves depends on us.

The only person who really matters to me is me. We can't please everyone, and we shouldn't even try. We can please ourselves, and that means defining who we are and deciding whether or not that's who we want to be.

[Facilitator: Distribute the instructions, worksheet, and interpretation guide for What I Like and Don't Like About Myself now. Read the instructions aloud.]

Instructions to Participants: Individual Exercise

This exercise will help you identify the perceptions and feelings that indicate your level of self-esteem/self-respect.

1. In the handout What I Like and Don't Like About Myself worksheet, put a check mark at the number of each item with which you *agree*. It is most likely that if you check an item in the one column, you will not check its contrary or opposite in the other column. For example, if you check "I feel optimistic about my future," you won't check "I usually feel pessimistic."
2. Add up to three items you think should be included on the lists.
3. Rate each item you checked on a scale from one to five, where five means the most to you with regard to how you feel about yourself. For example, if you rate the item "I believe in myself as a person" as a five, you are saying that belief in yourself contributes to your feelings of self-esteem/self-respect. If you rate the item "I usually feel pessimistic" as a five, you are saying that your feelings of pessimism contributes to your *lack* of self-esteem/self-respect.
4. Total the ratings in each column.
5. Read the interpretations that follow the tables.
6. You have thirty minutes to complete this individual activity.

Instructions to Participants: Group Activity

1. As a group, discuss the items in both lists of the table.
2. Explain why you think the items in the first column that you rated with five are so important or so valuable.
3. Explain why you think the items in the second column that you rated with a five are so unimportant.

4. Elect a scribe/reporter.

5. As a group, define self-esteem/self-respect.

6. List three or more insights or conclusions that you, as a group, have drawn from this exercise.

7. There are no right or wrong answers to anything in this exercise.

8. You have thirty minutes to complete this group feedback activity.

INSTRUCTIONS FOR THE
WHAT I LIKE AND DON'T LIKE
ABOUT MYSELF EXERCISE

1. Put a check mark at the number of each item with which you *agree*. It is most likely that if you check an item in the one column, you will not check its contrary or opposite in the other column.

2. Add up to three items you think should be included on the lists.

3. Rate each item you checked on a scale from one to five, where five means the most to you with regard to how you feel about yourself.

4. Total the ratings in each column.

5. Read the interpretations that follow the tables.

6. You have thirty minutes to complete this individual activity.

WHAT I LIKE AND DON'T LIKE ABOUT MYSELF

What I Like About Myself	Rate	*What I Don't Like About Myself*	Rate
1. I believe in myself as a person.		1. I frequently doubt myself.	
2. I have a realistic perception of my place and roles in the world.		2. I don't know where I fit in the world.	
3. I feel optimistic about my future.		3. I usually feel pessimistic.	
4. I feel capable of meeting the challenges in my life.		4. I feel overwhelmed by the challenges in my life.	
5. I know what it is about myself I don't like and can change.		5. I know why I don't get ahead like other people.	
6. I accept what it is about myself I don't like and can't change.		6. I resent many of my own physical and personality traits.	
7. I take pride in what makes me unique or different from others.		7. I try not to stand out from other people or be different.	
8. I take pride in having value to other people.		8. I try not to do much to call attention to myself.	
9. I feel good about myself even when I make mistakes or fail.		9. I get very angry with myself when I make mistakes or fail.	
10. I enjoy working with other people who treat me as an equal.		10. I don't feel that I'm an equal to the people with whom I work.	
11. I am patient with people who don't know me or my abilities.		11. I get angry with people when they question me or my abilities.	
12. I look for the good in other people.		12. I have bad feelings about people.	
13. I respect people for who they are even if I don't like what they do.		13. I get angry with people easily, even if they don't affect me.	
14. I feel successful in my present work or career.		14. I feel like I'm a failure in my present work or career.	
15. I can do whatever I want to do as long as I put my mind to it.		15. I'm physically and emotionally unable to do what I want to do.	
16. I accept and appreciate compliments.		16. I don't like being complimented; it makes me uncomfortable.	
17. I feel comfortable with public speaking or talking in a group.		17. I don't like speaking in public or in a group.	
18. Although not boastful, I enjoy telling people about my successes.		18. I feel uncomfortable talking about my successes.	
19. I am not afraid to admit mistakes or failures to other people.		19. I blame something or someone else for my mistakes or failures.	
20. I am not afraid to take responsibility for what I do wrong.		20. I try to hide my mistakes or failures from other people.	

What I Like About Myself	Rate	What I Don't Like About Myself	Rate
21. I take rational or reasonable risks.		21. I don't like taking risks.	
22. I feel comfortable in leadership roles.		22. I try to shirk from taking leadership roles.	
23. I don't mind making decisions for myself.		23. Making decisions for myself is very difficult.	
24. I don't mind making decisions for a group.		24. I don't want to make decisions for a group.	
25. I feel comfortable making decisions with a group and conceding my own point of view when appropriate.		25. I usually concede my own point of view when I work with a group to make decisions.	
26. I listen well to other people.		26. My mind wanders when people speak.	
27. People show me respect.		27. I don't think people respect me.	
28. People trust me.		28. I don't think people trust me.	
29. I don't mind disagreeing with people on controversial issues.		29. I won't disagree with people on controversial issues.	
30. I feel physically fit.		30. I don't feel physically fit.	
31. I feel emotionally fit.		31. I don't feel emotionally fit.	
32. I feel I give as much time and effort to my interests outside of work as I do to my work.		32. I don't give as much time and effort to my interests outside of work as I do to my work.	
33. I think I have a pleasant and attractive appearance.		33. I don't think I have a pleasant and attractive appearance.	
34. I think I look good in the clothing I wear.		34. I don't think I look good in the clothing I wear.	
35. I think other people find me attractive and appealing.		35. I think other people find me unattractive and unappealing.	
36. I like to be around people.		36. I don't like to be around people.	
37. I think people like to be around me.		37. I don't think people like to be around me.	
38. I feel comfortable when I'm alone.		38. I don't like being alone.	
39. I have many interests.		39. I don't have many interests.	
40. I enjoy everything I do.		40. Everything I do takes an effort.	
41. I deserve respect from others.		41. I expect no respect from others.	
42. I feel the equal of anyone.		42. I feel humbled by other people.	
43. _____		43. _____	
44. _____		44. _____	
45. _____		45. _____	
Total Score		Total Score	

INTERPRETATION GUIDE FOR WHAT I LIKE AND DON'T LIKE ABOUT MYSELF

	What I Like	*What I Don't Like*
Extremely high level of self-esteem/self-respect	210–225 (or more)	Below 98
High level of self-esteem/self-respect	170–209	98–118
Moderately high level of self-esteem/self-respect	140–169	119–139
Moderately low level of self-esteem/self-respect	119–139	140–169
Low level of self-esteem/self-respect	98–118	170–209
Extremely low level of self-esteem/self-respect	Below 98	210–225 (or more)

Exercise 13.2. What I Fear in Social Situations

Instructor's Notes

Fear contributes to lowering self-esteem/self-respect, and fears showed up in Exercise 13.1 in such checklist items as "I don't like speaking in public or in a group." The causes of fears are too numerous to mention and probably out of place unless the exercise is led by a clinical psychologist.

Since the issues in this exercise may be very sensitive, people may not want to explore too far beyond concerns such as "fear of public speaking." Don't push anyone to go deeper than he or she wants to go. Explain that the exercise in the workshop is practice for what the participants can do on their own, for themselves, as follow-up to the workshop.

Note also that this exercise works best with an intact team or with workshop groups that have been interacting with one another for at least one day during which the participants will have had an opportunity to build levels of trust.

Learning Objectives and Outcomes

By the end of this exercise participants will be able to:

▶ Identify some of the fears that contribute to lowering their self-esteem/self-respect.

▶ Identify areas in need of change to eliminate or reduce the negative effects of fear on their self-esteem/self-respect.

▶ Take feedback from other people as to the strengths others see in them and suggestions for change.

▶ Create and apply an action plan to increasing their levels of self-esteem/self-respect.

Self-Management Skills Involved

▶ Risk taking and trust

▶ Decision making

▶ Openness, honesty

▶ Respect for others

▶ Communication, especially giving and receiving feedback

Requirements

Time:	Approximately ninety minutes
Materials:	Attack on My Fears worksheet
	Sample Self-Esteem/Self-Respect Action Planner
	Self-Esteem/Self-Respect Action Planner worksheet
Preparation:	Photocopy the worksheets and sample.
Room Setup:	Allow for people to talk to one another face to face. Teams should be no more than four people.

Lecture Notes

Fear is a strange emotion, with both upsides and downsides. Sometimes fear generates flight, other times it generates fight. What frightens some people exhilarates others. Fear causes a loss of self-esteem and self-confidence, and a low level of self-esteem and self-confidence causes fear. As degrees along a continuum from ordinary fears at one end to cowardice at the other, fears can further our life's plans or destroy them. How fears affect us and how we manage them determines our ability to succeed.

A life without ordinary fears would be very dangerous and short. Fears keep people from taking totally irrational risks with their own and other people's lives. They prevent crime, they prevent accidents, and they prevent people from killing themselves. That's the upside of ordinary fears. But, obviously, since crimes, accidents, and suicides happen, fear isn't a limiting factor in everyone's life.

Ordinary fears are therefore a virtue, but any virtue carried to extremes can become a vice. The downsides of fears are that they pop up at the wrong time, at the wrong place, or for the wrong reason—and that they can incapacitate us. In social situations, they can ruin our career, our family, and friendships.

[Facilitator: Distribute Attack on My Fears worksheet now and read aloud the following instructions.]

Instructions to Participants: Individual Activity

This exercise is designed to help you identify your social fears and find ways to manage them

1. In the Attack on My Fears handout, identify what three things in social situations you fear most. For example, you might write, "Afraid of speaking up at a meeting."

2. After identifying a fear, and before listing another one, briefly explain what you think would happen in that situation. To follow through on the example, you might write, "I might say something everyone thinks is stupid."

3. After explaining what you think will happen in that situation, explain why you feel that way. Pertaining to the example, you might say, "I think I have the least expertise in the group."

4. You have twenty minutes to complete this activity.

5. When you're finished, you will have a baseline of information you can use for developing an action plan for managing those fears.

Instructions to Participants: Group Activity

1. Elect a timekeeper/scribe who will keep the group on schedule, who will take notes at the end of the exercise, and who will report to the class what the team learned from the exercise.

2. After participants have finished describing their three most significant fears, each person in the group will take a turn explaining the fear he or she thinks is most important to manage. For example, say someone listed "I fear speaking up in the group" as her first fear and the third one as "I fear being questioned about what I know," and she thinks the third one is more debilitating and more threatening to her career than the first one, discuss that fear with the group.

3. Discussions should focus not on the fear itself, but rather on why the person feels that way and what everyone thinks he or she can do to overcome the fear. Related to the example again, say the person claims she is afraid people will find out that she isn't as expert as the others in the group. In this case, you might talk about (1) what the person does feel expert about that can contribute to or influence the group, and (2) what the person can do to let other people know about it.

4. Help the person identify a well-designed action plan, like the one in the Sample Action Planner, for dealing with that fear.

5. After all team members have had a chance to talk about their most important fears, discuss what the team learned from this activity, three or more insights your scribe will write on a flip chart and present to the class.

ATTACK ON MY FEARS

What I Fear	What I Think Will Happen	Why I Feel This Way

SAMPLE SELF-ESTEEM/SELF-RESPECT ACTION PLANNER

Most Important Fear: *Fear of speaking in a group*

Change Goal: By the end of one month, I will express at least one opinion in every weekly meeting.

Milestones:

1. Speak up at the first meeting after this workshop and ask for feedback from people who know what I'm trying to accomplish. I expect to feel very tense at this meeting.

2. Speak up at the second meeting and ask for feedback from people who know what I'm trying to accomplish. I should feel more comfortable this time.

3. Speak up at the third meeting and get my feedback from visual or verbal cues. I should feel even more comfortable now than I did in the previous meeting.

4. Speak up at the fourth meeting and get my feedback from visual or verbal cues. I should be very relaxed by now.

Resources Needed (both available and not available): Appropriate information around which to form opinions.

Barriers: My own fear.

Action Steps:

1. Talk with my office mate about what I'm attempting to do to overcome my fear of speaking up in the group.

2. Attend the first meeting after the workshop and sit next to my office mate.

3. I may have to force myself to speak up, and no matter how I present my opinion, press on until I'm through doing it.

How has designing this plan and discussing it with my teammates affected my self-esteem/ self-respect?

At the moment, I still feel queasy about what I intend to do, but talking it over with other people and hearing that they too have some problems expressing themselves in a group has helped me feel better about myself. They think I can do it, and that encourages me to think I can also.

Self-Esteem/Self-Respect Action Planner

Most Important Fear: _____

▶ Change Goal:

▶ Milestones:

▶ Resources Needed (both available and not available):

▶ Barriers:

▶ Action Steps:

How has designing this plan and discussing it with my teammates affected my self-esteem/
self-respect?

As a follow-up activity complete this action planner for the two other fears you identified earlier.
Use extra paper and follow the same format you used for your most important fear.

Exercise 13.3. What Makes Me *Me*

Instructor's Notes

Most people don't like to brag, but as they say in Texas, "Everyone has braggin' rights." Additionally, most people have difficulty accepting compliments. They get this "Aw shucks" look on their faces or dismiss the compliment with, "It's nothing, really." This exercise is designed to help students accept their positive qualities and to accept compliments from others, both of which help to build self-esteem/self-respect.

This exercise works best with an intact team or with workshop groups that have been interacting with one another for at least one day during which the participants will have had an opportunity to build levels of trust.

Learning Objectives and Outcomes

By the end of this exercise participants will be able to:

▶ Identify some of the personal qualities that contribute to their self-esteem/self-respect.

▶ Take feedback from other people as to the strengths they see.

Self-Management Skills Involved

▶ Decision making

▶ Trust

▶ Communication, especially giving and receiving feedback

Requirements

Time: Approximately forty-five minutes

Materials: Paper and pencils
Flip chart and multicolored markers

Room Setup: Allow for people to talk to one another face to face. Teams should be no more than six people.

Lecture Notes

Something Oprah Winfrey, TV and movie personality, said fits nicely with our theme. "The more you praise and celebrate your life, the more there is in life to celebrate. The more you complain, the more you find fault, the more misery and fault you will have to find."[1]

People often fail to celebrate what is good and admirable about themselves. They also tend to throw away compliments.

Someone says to a woman, "That's a beautiful dress you're wearing." And she's likely to answer, "This old thing?"

Someone might tell a person, "I think your presentation to the Executive Committee was great." He is likely to answer, "Well, I had a lot of help from my assistant."

People find it difficult just to say thank you or to acknowledge the compliments. Those civilities seem trivial, but they're not. They reflect a form of modesty that may or not be genuine. Thank you and acknowledgment, on the other hand, express what we really feel when we're complimented—pleased that we've been recognized for something good or admirable in ourselves.

Failure to recognize what is good and admirable in ourselves breeds an ongoing attack on what is in fact good and admirable. Everyone has, as they say in Texas, "Braggin' rights."

That doesn't mean that we should go about bragging to everyone about everything we do, but we should take the time to brag most of all to ourselves. When the opportunity presents itself, we should also make the most of compliments we receive. A simple "Thank you, I'm glad you noticed" makes the other person feel good, too.

We base our life's success on the backs of little successes. We build our overall strength on the backs of smaller strengths. Out of this self-acknowledgment, we build our self-esteem/self-respect.

Instructions to Participants: Individual Activity

1. Make a list of positive statements about some personal characteristic, trait, or skill that you think represents you in the best possible light. Brag a little. Don't use words such as "I think I am . . ." or "I feel I can . . ."

2. Use sentences that begin with "I am . . ." and "I can . . ." For example, you might say, "I feel good about the fact that I'm open to other people's opinions." Or, "I am very creative in my work."

3. Write as many of these sentences as you can in five minutes.

---

[1]In *Quotations from Women on Life,* Rosalie Maggio, compiler (Paramus, N.J.: Prentice-Hall, 1997) 64.

Instructions to Participants: Group Activity

1. Each person gets a turn at reading his or her list.
2. Anyone in the group may add anything complimentary he or she thinks the person may have left out.
3. After all team members have discussed their lists, elect someone to write the outcomes of the next discussion.
4. As a group, identify three or more things you learned from this exercise.

Follow-Up Activities for Increasing Self-Esteem/Self-Respect

Instructor's Notes

Provide the participants with this opportunity after they have completed either Exercise 13.1 or 13.2 or both.

Learning Objectives and Outcomes

By doing these activities participants will take steps to:

▶ Identify and reinforce their strengths.

▶ Practice expressing their self-esteem/self-respect.

Self-Management Skills Involved

▶ Risk taking and trust

▶ Decision making

▶ Openness, honesty

▶ Communication, especially giving feedback in a variety of ways

Requirements

Time:	Thirty minutes to prepare participants for the take-home assignment
Materials:	Instructions for Follow-Up Activities for Building Self-Esteem/Self-Respect handout
Preparation:	Photocopy the handouts.
Room Setup:	None

Lecture Notes

[Facilitator: Distribute Instructions for Follow-Up Activities for Building Self-Esteem/Self-Respect now.]

Sometimes, when we feel lowest about ourselves, when our self-esteem/self-respect is in the dumpster, it helps to read inspirational books and quotes. However, as with anything else that people tout as a quick fix for a problem, beware of the glib and easy solutions. Read these books, but, in the words of writer Etty Hillesum, "Life cannot be captured in a few axioms . . . for life is full of endless nuances and cannot be captured in just a few formulae."[2]

Reading inspirational books can help us to encourage self-esteem/self-respect, especially if they provide us with ideas that we can convert into a personal motto, a thought that we can use as a banner that reflects who we are or what we want to accomplish in our lives.

[Facilitator: Read aloud Instructions for Follow-Up Activities for Building Self-Esteem/Self-Respect now.]

---

[2]Etty Hillesum in *Quotations from Women on Life,* Rosalie Maggio, compiler (Paramus, N.J.: Prentice-Hall, 1997) 32.

INSTRUCTIONS FOR FOLLOW-UP ACTIVITIES FOR INCREASING SELF-ESTEEM/SELF-RESPECT

1. Adopt a motto that encourages your self-esteem/self-respect. Adapt it into the first person to make it yours. Examples:

   – "Let me dare to be myself, for I do that better than anyone else can." Adapted from a quote by American author Shirley Brigg.

   – "What I truly and earnestly aspire *to be,* that in some sense I *am.*" Adapted from a quote by American author Anna Jameson.

   – "The happiest people don't necessarily have the best of everything; they just *make* the best of everything." Anonymous, in *Leadership . . . with a human touch.*

   – "I should not be afraid of life. I will believe that life is worth living and my belief will create the fact." Adapted from a quote by American psychologist/philosopher William James.

   – "It is impossible for me to be cheated by anyone but myself." Adapted from a quote by American essayist/poet Ralph Waldo Emerson.

   – "I am what I believe." Adapted from a quote by Russian author Anton Chekhov.

   – "To thine own self be true." William Shakespeare in *Hamlet.*

2. Make a conscious effort to improve your physical poise. Stand in a front of a full-length mirror every day and study your posture, the way you hold your head, how you look in your clothing. Stand erect with good but relaxed posture, head up, shoulders back, arms at your sides, hands open or fingers only slightly curled. Smile at what you see.

3. Walk with a full stride, don't shuffle. Maintain the physical appearance described in item 2. Smile at how you feel.

4. Talk with yourself in the privacy of your own room. Self-talk about what you feel good about or admire in yourself will help you fulfill this quote from Anna Jameson: "The mere aspiration, by changing the frame of the mind, for the moment realizes itself."

5. Use visualization to *see* yourself in situations in which you ordinarily feel fear. See yourself conducting yourself well and admirably. Rehearse what you have to say before meetings or in making a presentation and feel comfortable with it. Then get directly involved in those situations.

6. Ask other people for advice on what to do and what to say in situations in which you feel fear.

7. Accept compliments graciously, thanking and acknowledging the person who gave the compliment.

8. An important don't: Don't internalize other people's negative impressions of you. Remember that they only report on what they personally think, feel, or believe. They may be wrong about you. If they give you feedback you feel or believe is appropriate and useful, remember they only deal with what they see or hear. You can change that if you wish, but you can't and shouldn't change who you are; that is your business, no one else's.

14

Drive

By the end of this chapter, you will be able to facilitate three exercises that will help the participants find the sources of energy within themselves that they need to become self-managed.

Exercise 14.1. The Wellness Factor

Learning Objective and Outcome

By the end of this exercise participants will be able to identify ways of maintaining their physical fitness.

Self-Management Skills Involved

▶ Decision making
▶ Listening to suggestions from other people

Requirements

Time: Approximately sixty minutes

Materials: Paper and pencils

Flip chart and multicolored markers

Instructions for Compiling Fitness Profiles handout

Preparation: Photocopy the handout.

Room Setup: Allow for people to talk to one another face to face. Teams should be no more than six people.

Lecture Notes

"Energy is beauty—a Ferrari with an empty tank doesn't run."[1] The American designer Elsa Peretti sums up the idea of drive with that one statement. And you can think of energy in several forms, especially as physical energy, emotional energy, and creative energy. Self-managed people derive their drive from all three forms of energy.

Physical energy is the gas in the tank. Benjamin Franklin's homily, "Early to bed, early to rise, makes [a person] healthy, wealthy, and wise," offers good advice. A good night's sleep, an appropriate method for relaxing in the middle of a stressful situation, a regularly scheduled time-out from the rigors of the day, week, month, or year—all these renew your energy. Likewise, a well-balanced diet with proper nutrition keeps the body going strong. Feeling alive is as important as being alive.

Emotional energy comes from having a passion for life, for our careers, for our families, and for the world around us. It's our ambition our resolution to succeed. Self-management is in itself a passion for life. It strengthens our willingness to constantly stretch beyond ourselves in the present in order to realize a satisfying future.

Creative energy expresses the physical and emotional zeal with which we manage our lives. Doing something differently. Doing something new. Exploring the unknown. Taking rational risks. Facing the future enthusiastically, with the desire to create change, not merely to manage it. The future is what we create, not something that happens to us.

Drive is the fuel that turns us into a Ferrari.

Instructions to Participants

List your own suggestions for staying physically and emotionally fit: fitness profiles. After you complete your fitness profiles, listen to one another's suggestions, adding

---

[1]Elsa Peretti (1940–), quoted in *Quotable Business: Over 2,500 Funny, Irreverent, and Insightful Quotations About Corporate Life,* Louis E. Boone, compiler (New York: Random House, 1992), 132.

their suggestions to yours where you might have missed something you now think will in fact help enhance your fitness profiles.

After discussing your profiles for fifteen minutes, rate yourself on a scale of one to five, where one means never do and five means always do, as to how much of yours and other people's suggestions you *actually practice.* Some people discover that they rarely follow their own advice, frequently rating their own suggestions less than five. They also find that they do things to enhance their own fitness without even realizing it, when they rate other people's suggestions from three to five.

In the final part of the exercise, each team will list the three most important suggestions for enhancing physical fitness and three most important suggestions for enhancing emotional fitness. The outcome will be a list of suggestions all of you consider to be the most valuable methods for enhancing your drive toward success.

[Facilitator: Distribute Instructions for Compiling Fitness Profiles now.]

INSTRUCTIONS FOR COMPILING FITNESS PROFILES

1. Make two lists: (1) suggestions for staying physically fit, and (2) suggestions for staying emotionally fit.

2. Take five minutes to complete these lists.

3. In your group, take fifteen minutes to exchange suggestions, adding new or different ideas other people offer to your own list.

4. After everyone has offered his or her suggestions, on a scale of one to five, where five is the suggestion you always follow and one means never follow, compare how well you follow these suggestions with the fitness profiles.

5. Elect a scribe.

6. As a group, list the three most important activities for maintaining physical fitness and the three most important activities for maintaining emotional fitness.

7. Take ten minutes to complete this activity.

Exercise 14.2. Making Use of Your Creative Energy, Part 1

Instructor's Notes

This is a two-part exercise: an individual activity and a large group activity. The exercises themselves are traditional training games that some people in your workshops will have done before. The processing questions after the activities are more important than the activities themselves; however, treat the activities seriously and encourage participants to think of them as challenging and difficult.

Learning Objectives and Outcomes

By the end of this exercise participants will:

▶ Be able to take new approaches to old problems.
▶ Have discovered the importance of looking into their own minds to solve problems.
▶ Have seen the value of group effort in solving problems.

Self-Management Skills Involved

▶ Creative decision making
▶ Communication

Requirements

Time:	Approximately ten minutes (including processing questions)
Materials:	Nine Dots worksheet
	Solution 1: Nine Dots With Four Lines overhead
	Solution 2: Nine Dots With Three Lines overhead
	Paper and pencils
	Flip chart and multicolored markers
Equipment:	Overhead projector and screen
Preparation:	Photocopy the Nine Dots worksheet.
	Make overheads of solutions 1 and 2.
Room Setup:	Allow for people to talk face to face. Teams should be no more than six people.

Lecture Notes

[Facilitator: Distribute the Nine Dots worksheet and then read aloud the following instructions.]

Instructions to Participants: Individual Activity[2]

1. There are nine dots on the handout.
2. When I tell you to start, without lifting your pen or pencil from your paper, connect all nine dots with four straight lines. Wait until I tell you to start.
3. Who has seen or done this puzzle before?
4. [If people raise their hands, and several probably will . . .] Since you've already practiced this using four straight lines, your job is to connect the dots with three straight lines, and you, too, may not lift your pen or pencil from your paper. Wait until I tell you to start.
5. You have five minutes to complete this activity.

[Facilitator: You may extend the time for this activity if participants need it. After participants have completed the activity, put up the overheads showing solutions 1 and 2.]

Processing Questions

1. What were some of the problems you had in solving this puzzle?

   Typical answer: I couldn't see anything other than nine dots, when I tried to connect them, I kept coming back to a rectangle.

2. What did it take to solve the puzzle?

   Typical answer: Looking at the nine dots as independent of one another and connecting them in new or different ways.

3. How does this puzzle reflect situations in ordinary life?

   Typical answer: I often see things one way, the way I'm most accustomed to seeing them.

4. How can we connect the dots with just one stroke?

   Typical answers: Use a wide paint brush or fold the paper so that the dots are partially superimposed on one another.

Lecture Notes: Wrap-Up

The only way to put the lie to the expression "There's nothing new under the sun" is to look at old things or situations in novel ways. That is probably the most important lesson of this activity and the following one.

---

[2] Adapted from *More Games Trainers Play*, Edward E. Scannell and John W. Newstrom, editors (New York: McGraw Hill, 1983) 229–231.

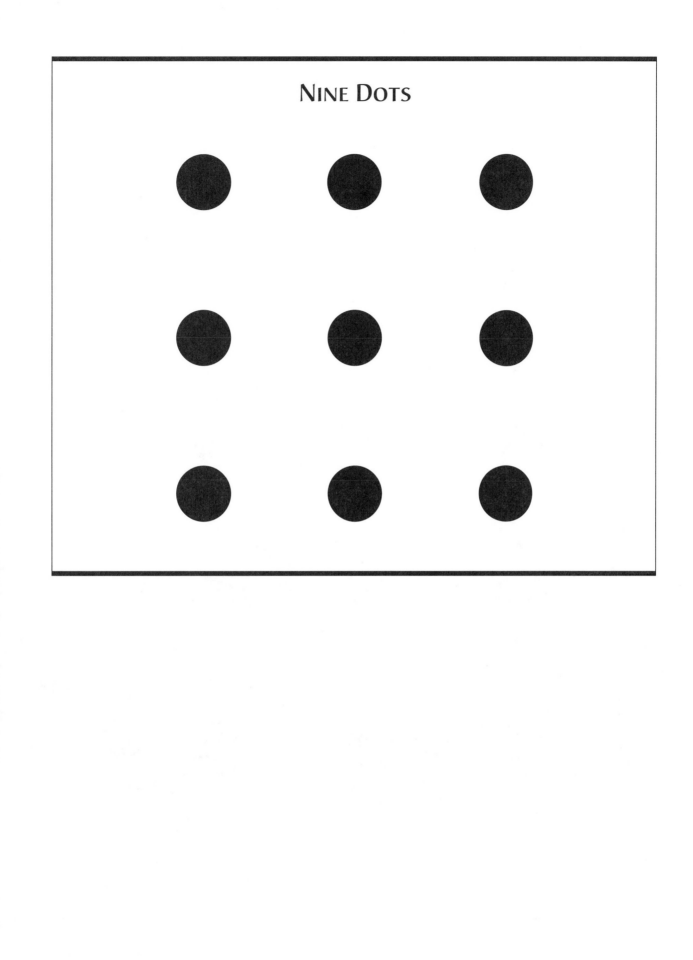

Solution 1: Nine Dots With Four Lines

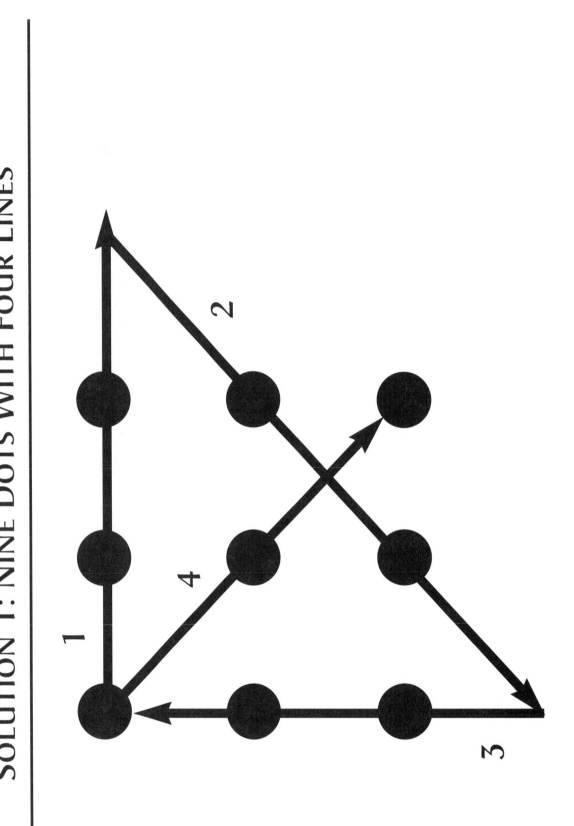

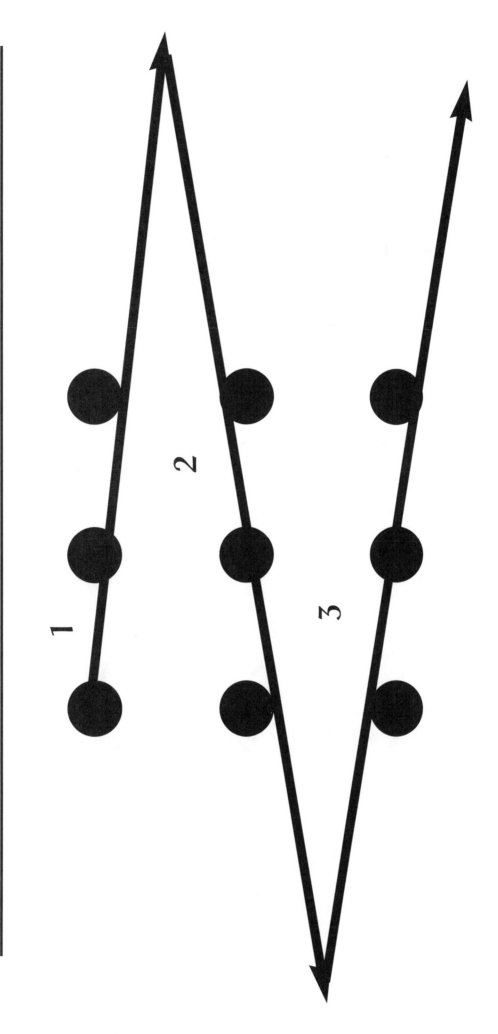

Exercise 14.3. Making Use of Your Creative Energy, Part 2

Instructor's Notes

In this exercise, students recognize that brainstorming in a group increases the energy for creativity. They play off each others' ideas and in some cases compete with one another for "the most creative" idea. Some people feel intimidated by the group and say nothing, fearing that people will laugh at their ideas or shoot them down. Some people feel they have nothing to contribute, everyone else's ideas are better than theirs. The purpose of the exercise is to show people how to draw on one another's opinions or ideas to take novel approaches to old experiences and that in a group anyone's ideas or opinions are as good as anyone else's.

Learning Objectives and Outcomes

By the end of this exercise participants will be able to:

▶ Explain the value of looking at old things in new ways or in ways not originally intended.

▶ Identify the ways working together as a group encourages creativity.

▶ Identify barriers to being creative, especially in a group.

▶ Identify methods for overcoming those barriers.

Self-Management Skills Involved

▶ Creativity

▶ Willingness to listen to other people

▶ Willingness to express one's opinion to other people

Requirements

Time:	Approximately fifteen minutes
Materials:	One empty coffee can
	Flip chart and multicolored markers
Preparation:	Acquire an empty coffee can.
Room Setup:	Whatever arrangement meets your needs: classroom, theater, or groups of six

[Facilitator: Set the coffee can on a table visible to everyone. As in any large group discussion, some people will not make a contribution; make note of these people as the activity progresses and call on them to make at least one contribution.]

Lecture Notes

Instructions to Participants

1. Take five minutes to brainstorm possible uses of an empty coffee can, except as a coffee can.
2. Just call out the ideas as they come to mind and don't stop to evaluate them.
3. Everyone must make at least one suggestion.
4. I need two volunteers to write the answers as people call them out.

[Facilitator: If no one volunteers, you act as scribe but pay careful attention to who is not contributing.]

Processing Questions

1. How did working in a large group encourage creativity?

   Typical answer: I felt energized by everyone shouting out ideas without stopping to evaluate them.

2. What were some of the barriers to making suggestions? (If anyone didn't contribute, see if you can draw out the person [people] to answer this question.)

   Typical answers might include time pressure, size of the group, someone else blurting out my suggestion before I could, better ideas than mine were already expressed, I was afraid people would laugh at my suggestion, and so forth.

3. What can you do to minimize the effects of those factors on your creativity?

   Typical answer: Recognize that in a group anyone's ideas or opinions are just as good as anyone else's.

4. What did you learn from this activity?

   Typical answer: The importance of looking at things from more than one perspective.

Lecture Notes: Wrap-Up

Creativity is often seen as a personal virtue. However, sometimes in a group, you can enhance individual creativity. Even under time constraints, new or novel ways of looking at old things can be generated and some may be really exciting or useful. Today, more so than historically, creativity for solving problems comes from teamwork rather than from isolation.

Exercise 14.4. Managing Emotions

Instructor's Notes

During the exercise, circulate around the tables to ensure that everyone is following the instructions, but do not intervene unless the group is off track. Process the activity by discussing the results of the activity reported by the groups.

Learning Objectives and Outcomes

By the end of this exercise participants will be able to:

▶ Apply the practice of recognizing their own emotions to everyday events.

▶ Describe steps for managing their own emotions.

Self-Management Skills Involved

▶ Openness and honesty

▶ Communication

Requirements

Time:	Approximately sixty minutes
Materials:	Emotional Intelligence Summary handout
	Instructions for Managing Emotions Exercise handout
	Experience Cards (one set of twenty-five 3-by-5-inch cards for each group of five)
	Flip charts and multicolored markers
Preparation:	Photocopy the handouts.
	Make twenty-five Experience Cards from the list provided (one set of twenty-five 3-by-5-inch cards for each group of five) by writing or printing one experience on each card. You may photocopy the twenty-five experiences presented here, or you may create your own Experience Cards if you wish by summarizing emotionally charged events in your own life or in the lives of people you know.
Room Setup:	Teams of no more than five people at round tables or other arrangement where participants can face one another

Lecture Notes

Cicero, the Roman commentator, said that "[People resolve] many more problems by hate, love, lust, rage, sorrow, joy, hope, fear, illusion, or some similar emotion, than by reason or authority or any legal standards, or legal precedents, or law."[3] In short, according to Cicero, even though people do make rational decisions, they more frequently make decisions on the basis of emotions.

Cicero therefore agreed with thinkers who argue that we arrive at conclusions or make decisions that lead to action through *both* emotion and reason, or more likely through either emotion or reason. Which decisions are better? Emotional ones or rational ones? Ancients like Plato argued that reason must take control of emotions. Moderns like Sigmund Freud, on the other hand, called reason, especially in the form of conscience, a constraint on our lives that "makes cowards of us all." And some people can be a slave to either emotions or reason. Regardless of the basis on which we make our decisions, emotions can either enhance or inhibit drive. It falls upon self-managed people to manage how their emotions affect the energy with which they attack the challenges of their lives.

Moderation in all things, an ancient Greek virtue, serves the self-managed person well, but it is only one aspect of the self-management of emotions. Self-managed people apply the intelligence of *informed* emotions to a life in which neither reason nor emotions rule. Instead, both reason and emotions get their fair share of fulfillment. Therefore, we have to focus on tools that prevent emotional extremes from enslaving our lives. We have to develop tools that help us avoid extremes by tempering reason with emotions and managing emotions through intelligence.

Many contemporary thinkers agree that rational decisions are as dependent on feelings or emotions as they are on thought. What makes sense to us satisfies an emotional need. Feelings give direction and meaning to our thoughts. They help us sort through ideas and opinions to find those most meaningful to us, and the ideas we find most meaningful or useful are those that fit with how we feel about or view the world (our *paradigms*).

Thought, on the other hand, can prevent extremes of emotion from blocking creativity and innovation. When we stop to think about our feelings concerning events or ideas, we can get past the subjectivity inherent in emotions to a more objective perception to what has happened or the ideas we hear or read. Thought and feelings or emotions can therefore work together, and only in the extremes do they conflict.

[Facilitator: Distribute Emotional Intelligence Summary handout now.]

The seven basic or universal emotions are anger, fear, happiness, love, surprise, disgust, and sadness. They each have their own function in managing our survival and suiting us for social life. However, when, for example, anger becomes rage or fear becomes cowardice our emotions do themselves, and us, in. Five guidelines help us to develop emotional self-management.

---

[3] Marcus Tullius Cicero, *De Oratore,* ii, 178. Quoted in *The Great Thoughts,* George Seldes, compiler (New York: Ballantine Books, 1985), 80.

1. Self-managed people use self-awareness to recognize their feelings as they happen and do not let them get out of control. They look at what is happening or has immediately just happened and analyze their feelings toward those events. They ask questions such as, "What did I feel? Why did I feel that way? What results did my feelings produce? If the results were undesirable, what can I do to prevent those feelings from disrupting my life and my relationships in the future?"

2. Moderation actually means *appropriateness.* Self-managed people feel and express their emotions appropriately. Anger, for example, frequently disrupts a person's life or relationships. One way to decide how to react is to compare whatever is happening to the worst possible thing that could happen. Unless what occurred is in fact the worst possible thing that could happen, we have a basis for moderating our feelings. Letting emotions get out of hand not only produces bad feelings from others toward us, they produce bad feelings about ourselves in the form of shame or guilt. By feeling and expressing our emotions appropriately, we can bounce back from uncomfortable emotions and deal with the circumstances around them more effectively.

3. As in all other aspects of self-management, using rational thought to set goals and to develop action plans helps to structure our emotional life and to short circuit impulsive actions. Our goals and plans give us a basis for deciding what's important to us. Our emotions marshal our energies toward accomplishing our priorities. Those achievements then provide the reason to celebrate, whereas not achieving those goals provides a reason for feeling sad.

4. Recognizing, being sensitive to, and understanding other people's feelings and emotions—*empathizing*—makes it possible for us to accept them as individuals while dealing with what they say or do. Empathy is essential for respecting others. Unless we recognize other people's feelings for what they are and empathize with what the people experience, we react to the expressions of their feelings rather than manage our own feelings, and self-management requires that we manage our own feelings.

5. Self-management and respect for others also implies that we manage relationships. Self-managed people find ways to evoke positive emotions in others even under circumstances that are less than ideal or positive. Let's take, for example, too many errors in work produced or missed deadlines; they usually provoke negative emotions. Venting unmanaged anger or bad feelings evokes anger or bad feelings from the other person. Self-managed people manage the relationship by expressing their anger in a circumstance like this through the productive use of words and tone of voice. A firm "These errors are unacceptable, and I know you can do better" gets more good accomplished than does shouting or name calling.

The activity that follows will help participants identify (not measure) their emotional self-management and provide opportunities to engage in emotional learning.

Facilitator's Instructions

Photocopy or otherwise reproduce each item of the Experience Cards (a, b, c, d, and e) on twenty-five separate 3-by-5-inch cards, one item per card. Make enough copies to distribute all twenty-five cards to each group in your workshop. If you separate your workshop students into four small groups, you will need four sets of twenty-five cards.

After you have created the number of sets required, separate the cards into stacks of like items, that is, *a*'s with the *a*'s, *b*'s with the *b*'s, *c*'s with the *c*'s, *d*'s with the *d*'s, and *e*'s with the *e*'s. Keeping each stack separate, shuffle the cards to change their order. Place each stack face down. Mark the back of the top card of each stack TOP CARD and bind each stack with a rubber band.

Place all twenty-five cards (*a*'s, *b*'s, *c*'s, *d*'s, *e*'s) in an envelope. If you have four groups, you should have four envelopes with twenty-five cards in each envelope. Distribute one envelope to each group along with the Instructions for Managing Emotions Exercise.

EMOTIONAL INTELLIGENCE SUMMARY

SEVEN BASIC OR UNIVERSAL EMOTIONS

1. Anger

2. Fear

3. Happiness

4. Love

5. Surprise

6. Disgust

7. Sadness

FIVE GUIDELINES FOR DEVELOPING EMOTIONAL SELF-MANAGEMENT

1. Self-managed people use self-awareness to recognize their feelings as they happen and do not let them get out of control.

2. Self-managed people feel and express their emotions appropriately.

3. Self-managed people use rational thought to set goals and develop action plans for structuring their emotional lives and for short circuiting impulsive actions.

4. Self-managed people recognize, are sensitive to, and understand other people's feelings and emotions—they *empathize*—which makes it possible for them to accept others as individuals while dealing with what they say or do.

5. Self-managed people manage relationships, finding ways to evoke positive emotions in others even under circumstances that are less than ideal or positive.

Instructions for the Managing Emotions Exercise

1. Each group has been given twenty-five cards in an envelope, divided into stacks of five, each of which is bound with a rubber band; the top card in each stack says TOP CARD.

2. Remove the cards from the envelope and remove the rubber bands without turning over any card.

3. Place each of set of five cards face down, with the TOP CARD at the top, to form five stacks.

4. Each person draws one card from any one stack, at random.

5. Read the card as if it really does pertain to you and react to what it says. Speak in the present tense. For example, you might read a card statement aloud that says, "Your boss assigns you a task without providing any resources," and you say, "I'm furious. It's very unfair for him to do that." That would be your immediate (first) emotional reaction and your immediate (first) rational thought about the card's information. Do *not* think about your reactions (what you feel or think) to the card's statement until you evaluate it.

6. After you read the card, assess your *immediate* emotional and intellectual reactions to what the card says by answering the following questions.
   - What was your immediate (first) emotional reaction to the card's information?
   - What was your immediate (first) rational thought about the card's information?
   - Why did you react as you did in both circumstances?
   - How effective or ineffective do you think your reactions were?
   - What are the consequences of those reactions under most circumstances?
   - Have you reacted like that before? Under what circumstances?
   - Why do you think you react that way?
   - If you think your reactions were ineffective, what can you do to improve on your ability to manage your emotions?

7. For five minutes, discuss your answers with your teammates, who will then answer these questions.
   - How effective or ineffective do you think the person's reactions were?
   - What are the consequences of such reactions under most circumstances?
   - If you think the person's reactions were ineffective, what can he or she do to improve on his or her ability to manage emotions?

8. After each person has had a turn, repeat the activity, and this time each person will draw a card from a different stack than the one from which he or she drew in the first round.

9. Elect a timekeeper and a scribe.

10. After everyone has had two turns, as a group, list three or more things you have learned from the activity.

11. Each team will report to the whole group, and we will discuss what you've learned.

Experience Cards

a. As you're preparing to leave for the office, you see your four–year-old boy trip and spill his milk into your open briefcase and on a report you have to deliver first thing this morning.

b. One of your coworkers gets angry when you come to work late and complains loudly that she has had to handle three customer calls for you.

c. You are queued up next at the department's copier to make one copy of one page and have been waiting quite awhile. The man behind you says, "I have only one page from which to make one copy, can I get ahead of you?"

d. Your supplier has sent you defective parts for the second time in a week.

e. Your 14-year-old dog, whom you brought home as a puppy, died last night, and you had the County Animal Shelter take her body away for disposal.

a. Your sister, with whom you're very close but haven't seen in five years, calls you to tell you she will visit you over the next three-day holiday. She may stay a few days longer than that.

b. While you're at lunch, your boss leaves you a voice mail that he wants to see you, but he doesn't leave an explanation or set a time.

c. An employee who deals with the public comes to work with a day old beard and appearing disheveled. When you approach him, you can tell that he hasn't showered or washed his shirt.

a. Your office mates remember it's your birthday and they decorate the office and throw you a surprise party.

b. Your boss has just given you an important assignment that you don't think you're prepared to complete.

d. Your mentor, the senior manager who has taught you just about everything you know about your job and how to get about in the corporate structure, died this morning.

e. A vendor whom you've trusted has actually been cheating you for the last year.

EXPERIENCE CARDS *(continued)*

e. The manager of another department, during the meeting of your cross–functional team, disagrees with your point of view. She says, "I know why we can't agree. On the Myers–Briggs Personality Profile, you're an ENTJ and I'm an INSJ." You have no idea what's she's talking about and doubt that she does either.

a. You've been expecting a five or six percent raise and a small bonus. Your boss tells you you will be lucky to get a 3 percent raise and not to expect a bonus.

c. You've been on vacation, and, believing in participative man–agement, you left no one in charge. However, on your return this morning you find the department in total disarray, work undone, deadlines missed, complaints piled up.

d. A coworker suffers from manic–depression, and like others with this illness, when she feels good, she goes off her med–ication. However, that backfires, and she now comes into the office screaming at you and challenging you to fight her over an attack she only imagined.

d. Your boss calls you into her office and tells you that a new round of layoffs will begin in two weeks and that you're one of the people who will be let go.

e. You have applied for a promotion to a vacancy created when your boss announced his retirement. The company decided to replace him with someone from the outside with less experience than you.

b. A police sergeant calls to tell you that your 16–year-old son has been arrested for shoplifting.

c. Your child calls you from school and tells you he fell and cut himself badly.

Experience Cards (*continued*)

a. Your boss announces his retirement and, without telling you first, also announces that you are her replacement.

b. Your boss, the owner of a family owned company, tells you that he is laying off 25 percent of the workforce, but you aren't among the people he's letting go. Instead, he's cutting your salary by 32 percent.

c. You've been working late, and when you get to the parking garage only a few cars are still there. A few seconds after you step out of the elevator, the power goes out and you're standing in pitch darkness.

d. The young man you hired six months ago tells you he has been living with another man and they have both been diagnosed with HIV.

e. Your company has experienced cash shortages, and you've been accused of stealing the money, a charge you know isn't true.

Follow-Up Activities for Increasing Drive

Learning Objectives and Outcomes

By doing this activity, participants will take steps to:

▶ Increase or improve their energy levels and drive.

▶ Take corrective action when needed.

Self-Management Skills Involved

▶ Evaluating or assessing one's own behavior

▶ Openness to making changes in one's behavior

Requirements

Time: Thirty minutes to prepare participants for take-home activity

Materials: Instructions for Follow-Up Activities for Increasing Drive handout

Preparation: Photocopy the handout.

Room Setup: None

Lecture Notes

Drive requires refueling and constant maintenance, like a fine automobile. Therefore, we can always maintain our drive or energies if we work at it. The handout, Instructions for Follow-Up Activities for Increasing Drive, provides you with a list of things you can do to keep your engine running and purring.

[Facilitator: Distribute Instructions for Follow-Up Activities for Increasing Drive.]

INSTRUCTIONS FOR FOLLOW-UP ACTIVITIES FOR INCREASING DRIVE

1. Adopt a motto that encourages energizing yourself. Examples:
   - "All things are possible until they are proved impossible—and even the impossible may only be so, as of now." Pearl S. Buck
   - "It is necessary to try to surpass one's self always; this occupation ought to last as long as life." Christina, Queen of Sweden
   - "We must have a passion in life." Poet George Sand
   - "To be what we are, and to become what we are capable of becoming, is the only end of life." Scottish author Robert Louis Stevenson
   - "Always bear in mind that your own resolution to succeed is more important than any other one thing." Abraham Lincoln
   - "You can't have a better tomorrow if you are thinking about yesterday all the time." American inventor Charles F. Kettering

2. Get a decent night's sleep, every night. Sleep experts say the best sleep begins before midnight. Most people require from seven to eight hours each night. Some people can get along with less. Avoid sleeping more. Avoid those who say, "I get by with only three or four hours. So can you." They can, but you may not be able to; try it and see for yourself.

3. Rest during the day when you can. However, rest is not a substitute for sleep. Most people's body rhythms call for a nap at midday. *Siesta* is not just a quaint custom. Since most people work in an office or a factory during the day, this may not be possible for everyone.

4. Eat a balanced diet. Avoid fad diets. However, some health food energy products may work for you, even if they are nothing more than placebos. Those effects are better than none.

5. Avoid carbohydrates (bread, potatoes, cake, donuts, rice, etc.) during the day. They'll make you sleepy.

6. Exercise. Find the best time of day for you to do aerobic exercise. Some people find that early morning exercise drains them, others find noon exercise programs exhausting, and other people find evening exercise makes sleep difficult. Experiment to find what works for you.

7. Plan. Set goals, design action plans, put yourself on a course to achieve your goals.

8. Avoid emotional extremes. Know yourself. Learn what circumstances evoke intense feelings, and learn how to moderate your reactions to avoid needlessly draining yourself of needed energy.

9. Find ways to have fun. Celebrate the victories at work. Harmonize work, family, friends, and enjoy your family and friends and social activities.

10. Demonstrate your vitality to others, and others will become "infected."

15

Respect for Others

B y the end of this chapter, you will be able to facilitate five exercises that encourage and develop respect for other people's thoughts, beliefs, values, and feelings.

Exercise 15.1. Reading Feelings and Emotions: A Nonverbal Exercise

Instructor's Notes

In this exercise, each participant selects a controversial topic out of a stack of thirty topic cards and talks about it for from two to five minutes, while one other person listens and watches how the speaker expresses his or her feelings or emotions. The pair doesn't debate or argue the topic. Rather, the participants give each other feedback about what they heard or saw during the exercise. The listener gives feedback to the speaker about what he or she experienced, the speaker evaluates the accuracy of the feedback, and the speaker gives feedback about how he or she perceived the listener's reactions to what the speaker said.

This exercise works best with a relatively small class, and the workshop should be limited to no more than twenty people (ten pairs). Do what you can to have an even number of people in the class if you have more than twenty people. It is difficult to do this exercise in triads.

The thirty controversial discussion topics, although sensitive, only on rare occasions have provoked more than a heated presentation by the speaker, inasmuch as the listener is instructed not to argue the point of view the speaker expresses. If an argument does break out, remind the offending pair that debate isn't the purpose of the exercise. In fact, a debate demonstrates that someone doesn't respect another person's right to his or her opinions and feelings.

Likewise, only on rare occasions has someone wished not to express himself or herself on a topic. Encourage openness but expect that some people might hold back their true feelings ("sandbag") when talking about a given topic. By telling the participants that they can draw up to three cards to find a topic on which they're willing to speak, you'll encourage them to greater openness.

The listener could, and probably will, recognize that his or her partner sandbagged feelings. He or she should be encouraged to say something such as, "I heard what you said, but I think you really didn't express your true feelings about this." That's part of reading feelings or emotions.

Everyone receives Instructions for the Reading Feelings and Emotions Exercise, and the Interpretation Guide. When you distribute the handouts, read the instructions aloud because they are complex. The participants will need to refer to them during the exercise.

Learning Objectives and Outcomes

By the end of this exercise participants will be able to:

▶ Recognize common nonverbal or quasi-verbal expressions of emotion in tones or quality of voice, facial expressions, and body language or gestures.

▶ Mirror feelings or emotions and ask for confirmation of the interpretations.

Self-Management Skills Involved

▶ Awareness of other people's self-expression
▶ Openness and honesty
▶ Communication

Requirements

Time:	Approximately thirty to forty-five minutes
Materials:	The Gap Between Us overhead
	Instructions for the Reading Feelings and Emotions Exercise handout

Interpretation Guide handout

Controversial Discussion Topics cards

Flip chart and markers

Equipment: Overhead projector and screen

Preparation: Read the list of controversial discussion topics.

If you feel uncomfortable with any of the topics in your workshop, replace it with one with which you are more comfortable. The new topic should evoke feelings or emotions.

Prepare The Gap Between Us overhead.

Photocopy the handout and the interpretation guide.

Print out or photocopy the thirty controversial discussion topics, one topic per 3-by-5-inch card. Prepare enough sets to give each pair of participants a complete set of thirty cards.

Divide the class into pairs and separate the pairs far enough apart so that they don't interfere with one another.

Room Setup: Any way that is appropriate to your session that will allow you to divide the group into pairs

Lecture Notes

People don't always use words to tell us what they think or feel. Rather, they frequently communicate to us through facial expressions, tone or quality of voice, and body language or gestures. Respect for others includes truly listening to what they say, not only with their words but also with quasi-verbal and nonverbal cues many people miss.

Words, verbal expressions, denote the content of what a person thinks and can refer to feelings or emotions, as when someone says, "I'm angry." On the other hand, nonverbals such as facial expressions, body language or gestures, and quasi-verbals such as tone or quality of voice, convey feelings or emotions, even if the words don't explicitly identify them.

Self-managed people show respect for the person speaking by listening carefully to voice tones and quality and by paying attention to everything the other person is doing as he or she speaks. They know that communication involves two levels of activity and work to ensure that the communication process is complete. The two levels of activity are:

1. Content and feelings or emotions expressed by the speaker (intent)
2. Content and feelings or emotions understood by the listener (interpretation)

When someone speaks, he or she intends to convey two different kinds of meaning: the content of the message spoken, and the feelings or emotions that accompany the content. On the other hand, when we listen to that person speak, we might hear only the content (for example, "The shirt is blue.") while missing the emotional loading that the speaker intends, if, for example, the speaker doesn't like blue shirts. The result is a gap in communication between us and the speaker that could, if the matter is serious, lead to a disagreement, perhaps even a conflict.

Self-managed people try to distinguish between content and feelings in order to fully understand what the other person intends to communicate. That closes a gap between what a speaker intends or means and how we interpret what he or she said.

[Facilitator: Put up The Gap Between Us overhead now.]

A gap always exists between people when they try to communicate. What we intend or mean and what the person understands or interprets us to mean can never be exactly the same. To narrow the gap between people is the purpose of improving the way in which we communicate, that is, the way in which we tell people what we think or feel and the way in which we listen to people. Giving and receiving feedback serves to narrow that gap.

In fact, the effective use of feedback closes that gap more than anything else can. The most effective form of feedback is to paraphrase what the person has said and mirror the feelings as well. Suppose I'm talking about raising the age of retirement to seventy, in order to protect the Social Security fund. You hear me say, "I think the idea's stupid" while I shake my head in apparent disbelief. You could paraphrase that and mirror my feelings by saying, "You don't like the plan to raise the retirement age, do you?" That's fairly obvious, but you get the message.

[Facilitator: An alternative is to ask someone to make a comment about some controversial issue and you demonstrate or model the process by paraphrasing and mirroring it. Then have other people do the same thing.]

Self-managed people are sensitive to other people's feelings and recognize that everyone has an equal right to have them. Statements such as, "Now, don't be angry" are patronizing at best. The more often you practice the suggestions in Reading Feelings and Emotions, the more adept at sensing feelings you will become.

[Facilitator: Distribute the Instructions for the Reading Feelings and Emotions Exercise handout, the Interpretation Guide, and the sets of discussion cards now. Read the instructions aloud because they are complex. The participants will need to refer to them during the exercise.]

THE GAP BETWEEN US

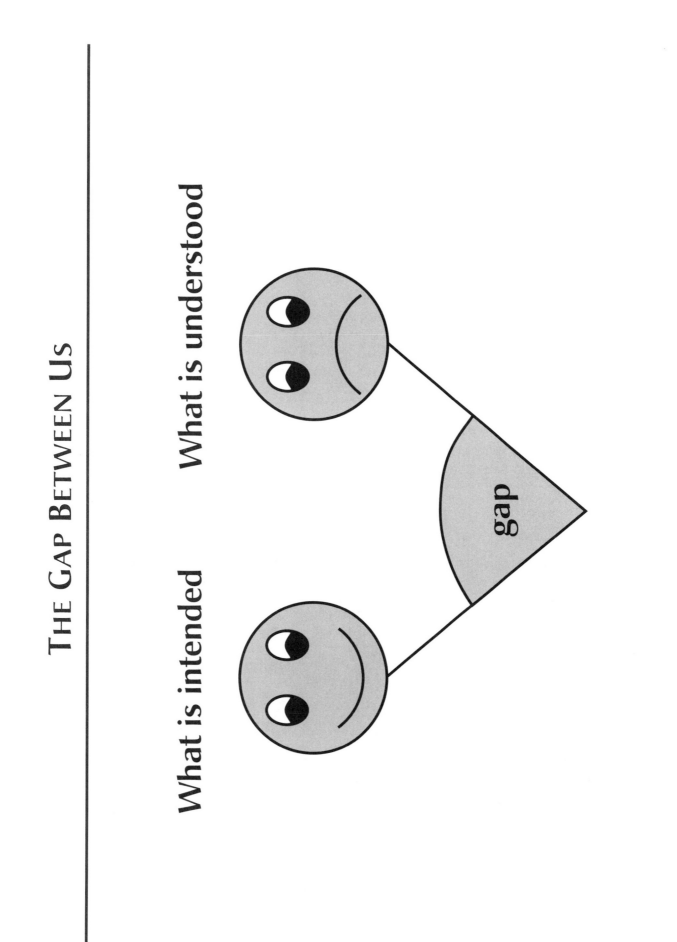

What is intended

What is understood

gap

INSTRUCTIONS FOR THE
READING FEELINGS AND EMOTIONS EXERCISE

WHAT TO WATCH FOR TO SENSE FEELINGS

▶ Watch people's faces, especially their eyes, when they're talking. Anger, fear, happiness, love, surprise, disgust, and sadness are universal emotions and few people can hide those feelings from their faces. Common facial aspects of emotion include redness when angry, grimaces when frightened or disgusted, smiles or grins (eyes "lit up") when happy or when feeling affection, fullness of lips and softness of expression when feeling love, wide eyes when surprised, and droopy lids and tears when sad.

▶ Listen to the tone or qualities in people's voices. The universal emotions also show up in what we call quasi-verbal expressions. When a person reacts to what you've said or done, you can usually tell from a tone of voice the emotion and its intensity. Common expressions include loudness when angry, quavering when frightened, high laughter when happy, softness or cooing when expressing affection or love, high-pitched squealing when surprised, guttural sounds when disgusted, and lack of energy when sad.

▶ Watch people's body posture or gestures. However, some postures or gestures don't always mean what some textbooks say they do; like Sigmund Freud said, sometimes a cigar is really just a cigar. When a person folds her arms across her chest, she may be angry and closed down, or she may just be comfortable sitting that way. Common gestures include pointing or shaking a fist when angry, hands up and pushing outward or covering the face when frightened, fidgeting (difficulty sitting or standing still) when happy, reaching outward when expressing affection or love, startle response when surprised, backing away when disgusted, and listlessness when sad.

▶ Ask people for their feelings as well as for their thoughts. Inasmuch as interpreting other people's behavior is an inexact exercise, don't rely on your own judgment. Test your perception. "It seems you're angry about that. Am I right?" Although awkward, that kind of feedback, called "Mirroring," and the request for confirmation prevent escalating tensions or pouring cold water on good feelings. If the other person isn't angry, but you think he or she is, you may say or do something that will in fact get an angry response. If the person happens to frown for some unknown reason but actually feels good about what is going on at the moment, your response to a mistakenly perceived anger could sour the other person's response to you.

LOGISTICS

1. On my signal everyone will get up and move about the room, talking to people you don't know as well as you might know others in the room.

2. Talk only to one person at a time rather than in small groups.

3. After two or three minutes, on my next signal, the pairs of people talking with one another at that moment will work together during the exercise.

4. Move apart from other pairs so you don't interfere with others' discussions.

5. Take a deck of thirty Controversial Discussion Topic Cards and follow the instructions in the next four sections of this handout.

EXPRESSING YOUR OPINION

1. In your turn, holding the deck face down, draw one card from anywhere in the deck. That's the topic you will be asked to talk about.

2. If you feel too uncomfortable to talk about that topic, put the card at the bottom of the deck, and draw another card from anywhere else in the deck. You may do that only twice.

3. If you draw a third card with which you are uncomfortable, do not tell your partner of your discomfort with it. It will be his or her job to identify that discomfort through nonverbal means.

4. You will have from two to five uninterrupted minutes to express your own viewpoint concerning that topic with the intent to be as persuasive as you can be.

READING FEELINGS

1. As the person is expressing his/her opinion and feelings, the listener watches and listens for:
    - Facial expressions
    - Body posture and gestures
    - Tone or quality of voice

2. The listener should use the Interpretation Guide for noting the emotions or feelings expressed by these nonverbal or quasi-verbal behaviors.

3. At the same time, the speaker should be watching for the following in the listener's nonverbal responses:
    - Facial expressions
    - Body posture and gestures

LISTENER'S FEEDBACK

1. The listener tells the speaker what feelings or emotions he/she observed and in what way. For example, if the speaker seems angry, the listener can say something to the effect, "I thought you were angry about . . . because your face reddened while you were talking and you punched your fist into your hand."

2. If the listener thinks the speaker didn't express his or her real feelings or emotions, the listener should bring up the subject. "I heard what you said, but I think you really didn't express your true feelings about this." That's part of reading feelings or emotions.

3. *Do not debate the point of view.* Regardless of whether you agree or disagree with what the speaker said, the object of this exercise is to understand not to make a point.

4. Follow your notes from your Interpretation Guide that you completed as the speaker talked.

5. After you make a statement about the speaker's feelings, ask, "Is that right?" or some similar question to confirm whether you understood correctly.

6. The speaker will answer only either yes or no.

7. The listener will write the response in front of each interpretation.

8. After the listener is finished, the two of you discuss the listener's accuracy; if accuracy is low, you will discuss what he/she could do to improve it. The speaker might tell the listener something like, "When I was talking about soft money the parties raise, I not only thought it was not a good idea, I also spoke angrily about it, and I don't think you realized how strongly I felt about it. I suggest you pay more attention to how people say things as well as to what they say."

(continues)

SPEAKER'S FEEDBACK

1. After discussing the listener's feedback, the speaker gives his/her impression of the listener's responses. *Do not judge the listener's response as "good" or "bad," "right," or "wrong."* Rather, judge it as accurate or inaccurate.

2. Since you, the speaker, aren't taking notes, your comments will be somewhat general; however, be as specific as you can be. For example, you might say something such as, "When I said . . . I thought you were pleased with what I said and agreed with me because you nodded your head in agreement. Was I right?"

3. Discuss the listener's accuracy and, if necessary, what he/she can do to improve it.

4. You have a total of fifteen minutes for the whole discussion, including the original five minutes.

5. After this discussion reverse roles and repeat the instructions.

INTERPRETATION GUIDE

INSTRUCTIONS

Use the three categories below for jotting notes that describe your interpretation of what the person is feeling as he or she speaks. Mark the item or items in the checklists that best describe what you experienced. Write cue words, as in the example in each category.

1. Facial Expression

   Example of a note: IRS audits, angry, face reddened describing his own.

   Smiled

   Frowned

   Bit lower lip

   Flushed (reddened)

   Narrowed eyes

   Pursed lips

   Other _____

2. Body Language, Gestures

   Example of a note: Rights protection for homosexuals, saddened, shrugged when talking about cities that have rejected equal rights ordinances.

   Shook head

   Nodded head

   Shrugged

   Waved hands

   Crossed arms

   Pointed

   Pounded fist in hand

   Other _____

(continues)

3. Tone or Quality of Voice

   Example of a note: NAFTA, happy, lighthearted voice when talking about benefits to company.

   Happy, lighthearted

   Raised voice, happily

   Raised voice, angrily

   Lowered voice, conspiratorially

   Lowered voice, angrily

   Other _____

Controversial Discussion Topics

Protection of rights based on sexual preference

Equal rights for women

Abortion, Pro Choice

Abortion, Pro Life

CONTROVERSIAL DISCUSSION TOPICS (*continued*)

Health management organizations (HMOs)

Flat tax plans

Affirmative action

Universal health care

Controversial Discussion Topics (*continued*)

Capital punishment

Premarital and extramarital sex

Legalization of marijuana for medical purposes

Legalization of drugs as a way of managing drug-related crime

Use of the military for peacekeeping operations

Use of the military for humanitarian aid

Powers of Independent Counsels

Election finance reform

International space station

AIDS

Disarmament

Nuclear arms destruction

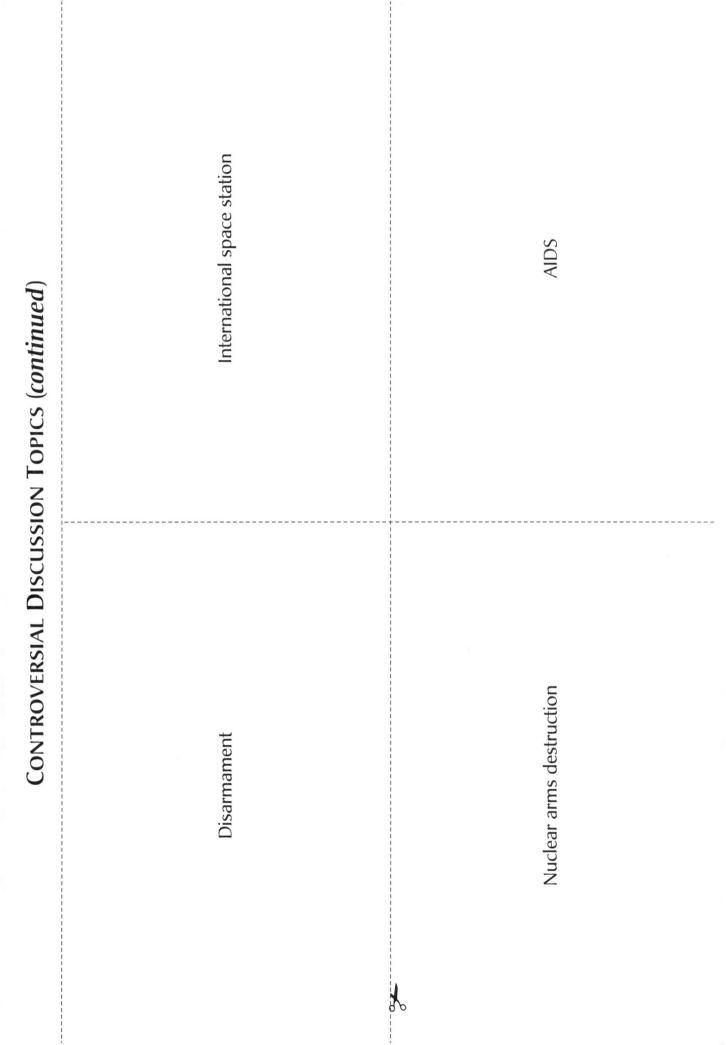

Controversial Discussion Topics (*continued*)

Free trade

Unions and collective bargaining

The right of homosexuals to adopt children

International aid for companies in financial straits

Controversial Discussion Topics (*continued*)

Income tax reform

Needle exchanges for drug users

American companies sending work overseas

Social Security reform

CONTROVERSIAL DISCUSSION TOPICS (*continued*)

Prayer in schools

Sex education in the schools

Exercise 15.2. Listening for Content, Listening for Feelings

Instructor's Notes

Whereas Exercise 15.1 is very complex, requiring participants to listen for cues from tone or quality of voice and to watch for cues from facial expressions, body language, or gestures, Exercise 15.2 is simpler in one respect and more difficult in another respect.

It's simpler insofar as the participants have to listen to the words and how the words are expressed, whereas in the previous exercise, they had to interpret many more cues. It's more difficult, insofar as you're asking them to make interpretations based solely on words and how they're expressed, which is what people have to do when they converse on the telephone or listen to the radio.

In this exercise each participant selects a controversial topic out of a stack of thirty topic cards and talks about it for from two to five minutes, while another person listens to the words and how the speaker verbally or quasi-verbally expresses his or her feelings or emotions. The pair doesn't debate or argue the topic. Rather, the participants give each other feedback about what they heard while the other person was speaking. The listener gives feedback to the speaker about what he or she experienced, the speaker evaluates the accuracy of the feedback, and the speaker gives feedback about how he or she perceived the listener's reactions to what the speaker said.

This exercise works best with a relatively small class, and the workshop should be limited to no more than twenty people (ten pairs). Do what you can to have an even number of people in the class if you have more than twenty people. It is difficult to do this exercise in triads.

The thirty controversial discussion topics, although sensitive, only on rare occasions have provoked more than a heated presentation by the speaker because the listener is instructed not to argue the point of view expressed. If an argument does break out, remind the offending pair that debate isn't the purpose of the exercise. In fact, a debate demonstrates that someone doesn't respect another person's right to his or her opinions and feelings.

Likewise, only on rare occasions has someone wished not to express himself or herself on a topic. Encourage openness but expect that people might hold back their true feelings ("sandbag") about a given topic. By telling the group that they can draw up to three cards to find a topic on which they're willing to speak, you'll encourage them to greater openness.

On the other hand, the listener could recognize that his or her partner sandbagged feelings. He or she should be encouraged to say something such as, "I heard what you said, but I think you really didn't express your true feelings about this." That's part of listening for content and for feelings.

Learning Objectives and Outcomes

By the end of this exercise participants will be able to:

► Distinguish between content and feeling when other people are talking by listening for verbal and quasi-verbal cues.

► Give feedback that acknowledges both content and feelings.

Self-Management Skills Involved

► Awareness of other people's feelings

► Openness and honesty

► Communication

Requirements

Time:	Approximately sixty minutes
Materials:	Instructions for Listening for Content, Listening for Feelings Exercise handout
	Interpretation Guide handout
	Controversial Discussion Topics cards from Exercise 15.1
	The Gap Between Us overhead from Exercise 15.1
	Flip chart and markers
Equipment:	Overhead projector and screen
Preparation:	Read the list of controversial discussion topics.
	If you feel uncomfortable with any topic in your workshop, replace it with one with which you are more comfortable but that should evoke feelings or emotions.
	Photocopy the handout and the interpretation guide.
	Print out or photocopy thirty controversial discussion topics from Exercise 15.1, one topic per 3-by-5-inch card. Prepare enough sets to give each pair of participants a complete set of thirty cards.
	Divide the class into pairs and separate the pairs far enough apart so that they don't interfere with one another.
Room Setup:	Any way that is appropriate to your session that will allow you to divide the group into pairs. Seat each pair shoulder to shoulder, facing in opposite directions.

Lecture Notes

When computerized voice mail answers our call, it gives us information and instructions in a monotone, and we can't tell if the voice is happy or angry that we called. After it puts us on impersonal, terminal hold, we curse it and slam down the handset. So much for interpersonal communication with a computer.

> *[Facilitator: As an alternative to the lecture, ask and discuss: What are the differences between computerized voice mail and a person answering the phone?]*

When people, rather than machines, talk, they communicate two messages at the same time: what they think and what they feel. We call the first the content message, and the second the feeling message—or, simply, content and feeling. The content is conveyed by the words themselves. "This object is blue." Said in a straightforward manner, matter-of-fact, that's merely the objective description of a thing's color.

Now say the same thing, but emphasize different words. "This object is *blue.*" This time, because of the emphasis, the sentence conveys two messages. One, the object is blue, and two, surprise, or anger, or happiness—depending on the context. Whatever it conveys, it's letting us know about a feeling concerning the object's color.

> *[Facilitator: As an alternative to the lecture, ask and discuss: What does that emphasis convey?]*

Feelings are spoken by what we call quasi verbals, as well as by words. In fact, along with nonverbals, quasi verbals make up most of our communication. Nonverbals also include facial expressions, body language and gestures, but we're concerned in this exercise with *only* the feelings or emotions conveyed by words, tone of voice, and qualities of voice. When we're conversing on the telephone or listening to the radio, only the vocals convey the feelings or emotions.

The words we choose may convey a feeling. For example, "That object's an ugly shade of blue" not only says the object is blue, it tells you I don't like it as clearly as if I had said, "I don't like that shade of blue."

Tone or quality of voice can tell you how I feel. I can express the same feeling by saying "That object's blue" with a tone of disgust in my voice.

Or, I can tell you how I feel with a noise. "That object's blue. Ugh!"

> *[Facilitator: If you have used Exercise 15.1 in this workshop, you can omit this part of the lecture or use the following adaptation.]*

Self-managed people show respect for the person speaking by listening carefully and paying attention to how the other person is talking. They know that communication involves two levels of activity and work to ensure that the communication process is complete. The two levels of activity are:

1. Content and feelings or emotions expressed by the speaker (intent)
2. Content and feelings or emotions understood by the listener (interpretation)

When someone speaks, he or she intends to convey two different kinds of meaning: the content of the message spoken, and the feelings or emotions that accompany the content. On the other hand, when we listen to that person speak, we might hear only the content (for example, "The shirt is blue.") while missing the emotional loading that the speaker intends, if, for example, the speaker doesn't like blue shirts. The result is a gap in communication between us and the speaker that could, if the matter is serious, lead to a disagreement, perhaps even a conflict.

Self-managed people try to distinguish between contents and feelings in order to fully understand what the other person intends to communicate. That closes a gap between what a speaker intends or means and how we interpret what he or she said.

[Facilitator: Put up The Gap Between Us overhead (page 273) now.]

A gap always exists between people when they try to communicate. What we intend or mean and what the person understands or interprets us to mean can never be exactly the same. To narrow the gap between people is the purpose of improving the way in which we communicate, that is, the way in which we tell people what we think or feel and the way in which we listen to people. Giving and receiving feedback serves to narrow that gap.

In fact, the effective use of feedback closes that gap more than anything else can. Paraphrasing content and mirroring feelings or emotions are the most effective forms of feedback. Suppose I'm talking about raising the age of retirement to seventy as a way to protect the Social Security fund. You hear me say, "I think the idea's stupid." You could paraphrase the content and, by responding to my tone of voice, mirror my feelings by saying, "You don't like the plan to raise the retirement age, do you?" That's fairly obvious, but you get the message.

[Facilitator: Ask someone to make a comment about some controversial issue and you demonstrate or model the process by paraphrasing and mirroring it. Then have other people do the same thing.]

Instructions to Participants

In this exercise you will practice reading people's feelings from what they say. The process is popularly called active listening. It acknowledges the other person, acknowledges that what he or she has said is important to you, and demonstrates that you are in fact listening.

[Facilitator: Distribute the Instructions for the Listening for Content, Listening for Feeling Exercise handout and the Interpretation Guide now. Read the instructions aloud because they are complex. The participants will need to refer to them during the exercise. Then distribute the sets of discussion cards. Use the deck of cards from Exercise 15.1.]

Instructions for the Listening for Content, Listening for Feelings Exercise

ACTIVE LISTENING

1. Clear your mind as well as your environment of distractions by putting away notepads, books, or other materials you may have with you.

2. Concentrate on what the person is saying, not on how you'll respond to it.

3. Ask questions for clarification, such as "What did you mean by that?"

4. By paraphrasing what the person said, you ensure that you understand the content properly. Then ask a confirming question.

5. By telling the other person the feelings you perceive, you're mirroring or reflecting back to the person those feelings. Acknowledge and mirror or reflect the feelings you think the person is expressing, and ask a confirming question.

LOGISTICS

1. On my signal everyone will get up and move about the room talking to people you don't know as well as you might know others in the room.

2. Talk only to one person at a time rather than in small groups.

3. After two or three minutes, on my next signal, the pairs of people talking with each other at that moment will work together during the exercise.

4. Move apart from other pairs in order that you do not interfere with others' discussions.

5. Place your chairs next to each other but turn them in opposite directions, sitting shoulder to shoulder. This way you can hear each other talk, but you can't see visual communication cues.

6. Take a deck of thirty Controversial Discussion Topic cards and follow the instructions in the next four sections of this handout.

EXPRESSING YOUR OPINION

1. In your turn, holding the deck face down, draw one card from anywhere in the deck. That's the topic you will be asked to talk about.

2. If you feel too uncomfortable to talk about that topic, put the card at the bottom of the deck, and draw another card from anywhere else in the deck. You may do that only twice.

3. If you draw a third card with which you are uncomfortable, do not tell your partner of your discomfort with it. It will be his or her job to identify that discomfort through nonverbal means.

4. You will have up to five uninterrupted minutes to express your own viewpoint concerning that topic with the intent of being as persuasive as you can be.

READING FEELINGS

1. As the person is expressing his or her opinion and feelings, the listener listens for:
   - The words that convey feelings rather than information
   - Quasi-verbal sounds, such as "Ugh," that convey feelings
   - Tone or quality of voice, such as speaking louder

(continues)

2. The listener may make any verbal or quasi-verbal response at any time, even interrupting the speaker if necessary.

3. The listener should use the Interpretation Guide for noting the emotions or feelings expressed by these nonverbal or quasi-verbal behaviors.

4. At the same time, the speaker should be listening for the following in the listener's responses or questions:

   – The words that convey feelings rather than information

   – Quasi-verbal sounds, such as "Ugh," that convey feelings

   – Tone or quality of voice, such as speaking louder

LISTENER'S FEEDBACK

1. The listener summarizes the speaker's point of view by paraphrasing the content of what the speaker said. Ask for confirmation, "Is that right?"

2. The speaker answers *only* either yes or no.

3. The listener tells the speaker what feelings or emotions he/she observed and in what way. For example, if the speaker seemed angry, say something to the effect, "I thought you were angry about . . . because your voice grew louder while you were talking." *Do not debate the point of view.*

4. Read from your Interpretation Guide.

5. After each statement, ask, "Is that right?" or some similar question.

6. The speaker answers *only* either yes or no.

7. The listener will write the speaker's response in front of each interpretation.

8. After the listener is finished, the two of you discuss the listener's accuracy of both content and feeling; if accuracy is low, you will discuss what he or she could do to improve it.

SPEAKER'S FEEDBACK

1. After discussing the listener's feedback, the speaker gives his or her impression of the listener's responses. *Do not judge the listener's response as "good" or "bad, "right," or "wrong."* Rather, evaluate the accuracy of the response.

2. Since you, the speaker, aren't taking notes, your comments will be somewhat general; however, be as specific as you can be. For example, you might say something such as, "When I said . . . I thought you were pleased with what I said and agreed with me because you said 'Uh huh' several times. Was I right?"

3. Discuss the listener's accuracy and if necessary what he or she can do to improve it.

4. You have a total of fifteen minutes for the whole discussion.

5. After this discussion reverse roles and repeat the instructions.

INTERPRETATION GUIDE

INSTRUCTIONS

Use the three categories below to mark the items in the checklist or to write a list that reflects what you experienced, and for jotting notes that describe your interpretations of what the person is feeling as he or she speaks. Write cue words, as in the example in each category.

1. Tone or Quality of Voice

   Examples of notes: IRS audits, angry, voice loud when describing his own.

   Happy

   Angry

   Surprised

   Disinterested

   Amused

   Other _____

2. Words Used

   Example of notes: Rights protection for homosexuals, disgusted, refers to homosexuality as a sin.

3. Quasi-Verbal Sounds

   Example: NAFTA, happy, answered "Uh huh!" when asked if he liked it.

Exercise 15.3. Preventing Disagreements From Becoming Conflicts

Instructor's Notes

This exercise requires that two people talk to each other about an interpersonal relations problem and then get feedback from other people in their immediate group about what they did or said and how effective or ineffective they were in resolving the disagreement.

1. Divide the group into teams of no more than six people.
2. Divide each team into pairs in which each person will have a problem to solve. If one team has an odd number of people, one person will work on two problems.
3. Distribute an Observer's Guide to each person.
4. Distribute envelopes of all the problem scripts to each team.
5. Distribute instructions to each person.
6. Provide the explanation before the exercise.
7. Discuss the conclusions drawn by the teams.

Learning Objectives and Outcomes

By the end of this exercise participants will be able to:

▶ Use active listening for preventing disagreements from becoming conflicts.
▶ Use problem-solving methods for using disagreements as opportunities for creative problem solving.

Self-Management Skills Involved

▶ Listening skills
▶ Openness and honesty
▶ Problem-solving skills

Requirements

Time: Approximately ninety minutes

Materials: Instructions for Preventing Disagreements From Becoming Conflicts handout

Preventing Conflict Skill Practice Situation Cards

Observer's Guide handout

Preparation: Photocopy the handouts.

Photocopy each pair of situation scripts on separate cards and place each pair in a separate envelope. Make enough copies so each team has all the Skill Practice scripts.

Photocopy enough observer's guides to allow all participants to get feedback from their teammates.

Room Setup: Up to six people at round tables or other face-to-face arrangement

Lecture Notes

If necessity is the mother of invention, disagreement is its father. In other words, disagreements are good opportunities for creative problem solving. On the other hand, disagreements also breed conflict, situations in which at least one person believes that his right to satisfy his needs or interests is being trampled. Self-managed people recognize that everyone has the right to satisfy his or her needs or interests; they also recognize when conflict situations might arise out of disagreements. They then take appropriate steps to prevent people from trampling on their needs or interests and from trampling on anyone else's.

Self-awareness is essential to preventing conflict. Self-managed people must know and fully understand their own positions and interests. They must also know, understand, and respect other people's positions and interests as well, and the only way to do that is through effective communication, especially through effective listening (also know as active listening).

With active listening we acknowledge the other person, we acknowledge that what he or she has said is important to us, and we demonstrate that we are in fact listening.

[Facilitator: Distribute the Instructions for Preventing Disagreements From Becoming Conflicts now and read aloud the following instructions.]

Instructions to Participants

Here's what you do as a listener:

1. Clear your mind as well as your environment of distractions by removing papers, books, or other materials from the table.
2. Concentrate on what the person is saying, not on how you'll respond to it.
3. Ask questions for clarification, such as "What did you mean by that?"
4. Acknowledge and paraphrase what the person says to ensure that you understand it properly. For example, you could say, "If I understand you, you think that affirmative action hasn't worked at all." Then ask a confirming question, such as, "Is that right?"

5. Acknowledge and mirror or reflect the feelings you think the person is expressing. For example, you could say, "From your tone of voice, it seems that you're angry about the effects of affirmative action." Then ask a confirming question, such as, "Do I understand how you feel?"

By using this process, you narrow the communication gap that always exists between two people.

[Facilitator: If you haven't discussed "The Gap" in Exercises 15.1 and 15.2, refer to the discussion in Exercise 15.1 and present it here.]

It's the gap in understanding between people that leads to conflict. The less people know about and understand each other, the more likely they will escalate disagreement into conflict. Only when you narrow the gap, can you then engage in problem solving.

In this exercise, you will attempt to resolve disagreements by engaging in problem-solving activities. Resolving disagreements and problem solving, as a form of negotiation, include these three steps:

1. *Identify the real problem.* First, identify the indicators or symptoms of the problem, giving each person a chance to air his or her position and interests. Before anything else constructive can happen, each person, in turn, answers: "What do I want, why do I want it, what makes me think I'm not getting it, and what do I feel about the situation?" Only then can you trace indicators or symptoms to their causes. Each person explains: "This is what I think prevents me from satisfying my needs or interests."

2. *Resolve the disagreement.* Before a mutually satisfactory solution can be found, each person must answer: "What do I think I have to have in order to satisfy my need or interest." Then you can identify the points on which you both can agree. Each person has to understand the other person's point of view and look for ways in which each overlaps the other. You also have to discuss differences between your suggested solutions. Each person has to understand the other person's point of view and look for ways in which each diverges from the other. Then you can use the points of agreement to discuss ways of getting past the differences. Together you find ways of satisfying each other's needs or interests, which may involve designing another solution that mutually satisfies them both.

3. *Design an action plan for making sure the resolution to the disagreement does in fact satisfy both people's needs and interests.* Together you design an action plan for satisfying your mutual needs and interests. The plan should include steps for monitoring what happens and ensuring that both of you do in fact satisfy your needs and interests.

Here's the rub. Both parties must want to work with each other to arrive at a solution satisfactory to both. Respect for others, then, is essential for preventing disruption in your life.

When you get your situation cards, you will read them to yourselves and not tell anyone else what your script tells you to do or say.

[Facilitator: Distribute the situation scripts and Observer's Guide handout now.]

INSTRUCTIONS FOR THE PREVENTING DISAGREEMENTS FROM BECOMING CONFLICTS EXERCISE

ACTIVE LISTENING

1. Clear your mind as well as your environment of distractions by removing papers, books, or other materials from the table.

2. Concentrate on what the person is saying, not on how you'll respond to it.

3. Ask questions for clarification, such as "What did you mean by that?"

4. Acknowledge and paraphrase what the person says to ensure that you understand it properly.

5. Acknowledge and mirror or reflect the feelings you think the person is expressing.

THREE STEPS FOR RESOLVING DISAGREEMENTS

1. *Identify the real problem.* First, identify the indicators or symptoms of the problem, giving each person a chance to air his or her position and interests. Each person explains what he or she thinks prevents him or her from satisfying his or her needs or interests by answering:

   - What do I want?

   - Why do I want it?

   - What makes me think I'm not getting it?

   - What do I feel about the situation?

   - What do I think prevents me from satisfying my needs or interests?

2. *Resolve the disagreement.*

   Each person must answer: "What do I think I have to have in order to satisfy my need or interests?"
   - Identify the points on which you both can agree.
   - Understand the other person's point of view.
   - Look for ways in which each point of view overlaps the other.
   - Discuss differences between your suggested solutions.
   - Use the points of agreement to discuss ways of getting past the differences.
   - Find ways to help satisfy each other's needs or interests.

3. *Design an action plan for making sure the resolution to the disagreement does in fact satisfy both people's needs and interests.*
   - Include steps for monitoring what happens.
   - Ensure that each party does in fact satisfy his or her needs and interests.

LOGISTICS

In this exercise, you will do the following:

1. [If participants are not already grouped in teams . . .] Form teams of no more than six people.

2. Pair up with another person on your team.

3. Each person will have a turn. If your team has an odd number of people, choose one person to help the last person to practice.

4. Elect a timekeeper and a backup timekeeper from a different pair. When the timekeeper is involved in his or her skills practice, the backup timekeeper will manage the clock.

5. Each pair takes one envelope, and without reading either script, distributes the pages between you at random.

INSTRUCTIONS FOR THE PRACTICE PAIR

1. Each pair will have two minutes in which to read their own scripts silently; do not share your script with anyone.

2. Each person is responsible for doing or saying what the situation in the script calls for.
   - This is not a role play. It is a skill practice in which you are practicing resolving a disagreement. Talk with your partner as if you are both in a real situation.
   - Be yourself at all times. How would *you* handle the situation if it actually happened to you?

3. When the timekeeper says begin, the person whose script says to begin the conversation will start.

4. In the ten minutes available to you, your job is to practice trying to resolve the disagreement without creating a conflict.

5. You may not reach a final solution before your timekeeper says ten minutes are up, but that's all right. It's the practice, not the solution that counts.

6. After the ten-minute practice is over, each person tells the other how he or she felt about the conversation.
   - What did you [do] [say] that you thought was effective and what made it effective?
   - What did you [do] [say] that you thought was ineffective and what made it ineffective?
   - What would you [do] [say] differently when managing disagreements?
   - What did your partner [do] [say] that you thought was effective and what made it effective?
   - What did your partner [do] [say] that you thought was ineffective and what made it ineffective?
   - What would you suggest your partner [do] [say] differently when managing disagreements?

INSTRUCTIONS FOR THE TEAM MEMBERS WHEN THEY ARE NOT PRACTICING: THE OBSERVERS

1. The remainder of team acts as observers.

2. Using the Observer's Guide, take notes about the way in which the practice pair conducted the discussion. For example, the first row of the Observer's Guide refers to the requirement that the person with the problem identify indicators of symptoms of the problem. Consider, as an observer, whether or not each person did explain his or her interests in the cell under that person's name, write a few words to remind yourself of what the person did in fact say.

3. After the practice pair explains how they felt about the conversation, each observer will tell the practice pair what they observed, using the Observer's Guide to remain themselves of what happened.

4. After giving specific feedback to each person, summarize by suggesting ways for each person to become more effective when managing disagreements.

INSTRUCTIONS FOR DISCUSSING THE EXERCISE

1. When everyone has practiced, elect a scribe to take notes on the flip chart.

2. As a team, list three or more things you learned from this exercise about how to manage disagreements.

Observer's Guide

INSTRUCTIONS

Complete this guide for each pair practicing. Write their names in the spaces provided. Give specific feedback, for example, "I thought you could have expressed with a little more conviction when you said 'I should complete the project, I thought you were throwing your responsibility on to me.'" Explain why you thought the behavior was effective or ineffective, and then make a suggestion for doing or saying something differently when managing disagreements.

Each row refers to a specific step in the process of resolving a disagreement, which we discussed before the exercise began. In each cell after the identified behavior, write a note to yourself about the way in which each person acted in that step.

Observer's Guide

Behavior	Name _____	Name _____
Identified indicators or symptoms of the problem; each person explained his/her position and interests.		
Identified the real problem by tracing indicators or symptoms to their causes.		
Discussed what each person thinks is necessary for resolving the disagreement.		
Identified points in their solutions on which each person agreed.		
Discussed differences between each person's suggested solutions.		
Used points of agreement to discuss ways of getting past the differences.		
Designed an action plan that satisfies both people's needs and interests.		
Discussed ways of executing and monitoring the plan.		

Preventing Conflict Skill Practice Situation Cards

Administering to the Conferee

Conferee's Situation

You have a back problem and cannot sit in a straight-backed chair for more than ten minutes without suffering excruciating pain. At a two-day conference, you request a special chair, the only one of its kind in the conference center. Since it has wheels, it can be rolled from the main meeting room to breakout rooms when you need to engage in small group discussion. The breakout rooms are one floor above the main meeting room. The conference administrator has told your boss that he/she refuses to move the chair from place to place. Your boss has told you that the conference administrator is angry with you. You start the conversation.

Administering to the Conferee

Administrator's Situation

As the conference administrator, you are responsible for seeing to each conferee's needs. You understand that the conferee needs the special chair because of her bad back, but there's no way you will take responsibility for seeing that it gets moved from room to room. You don't have the time, and it's just not your job. That's what you told the person's boss.

To Pay or Not to Pay

Client

You have a consultant that regularly works in your office. He comes from a neighboring state and has hotel bills and other per diem charges you have agreed to pay. For several years, the company had the consultant's hotel direct bill room and meal charges, but the company suddenly changed its policy, but no one sent the consultant a written statement of the change. You told the consultant during a meeting, but he forgot. He has just arrived for your next work session with this group assembled.

To Pay or Not to Pay

Consultant

You have worked for this company for several years, and over the years, it has always paid your hotel charges by direct billing. However, the company has changed its policy and the hotel put the charges on your credit card. When you checked out, you were preoccupied and didn't realize you were signing for a very large bill. On the way home, you tried to use the card and were told that your charge was rejected because you were over the credit limit. You don't remember ever being told about the policy change, and you're angry with your contact at the company. During this visit, in front of many uninvolved people, let him/her know how angry you are about this. You start the conversation.

Just in Time

Supplier

Your customer usually gives you a work-week from order date to delivery date if you don't have a sufficient finished goods inventory for immediate delivery. He/she calls you and tells you he/she needs more parts than you have on hand by tomorrow. You have only two-thirds of what he/she needs, and you can't meet the deadline with the remaining one-third of the order.

A Matter of Style

Sales Manager

R&D has been working on a new product for nearly a year, one that your customers know about and want—yesterday. They know about it because you and your sales people have told them. You've seen the design, you've seen the prototype, and you think it's been sufficiently tested. You want the product in six weeks because you've told your largest customer that it will be ready then. You start the conversation with the R&D manager.

Just in Time

Manufacturer

You have used a supplier for a number of years, and you have recently talked your boss out of shopping around for a different vendor. Your company has received a very large, lucrative rush order from a new customer. The customer's delivery date is now upon you, and you're out of the necessary part to finish the order. You need the parts by tomorrow. You go to your supplier for help and you start the conversation.

A Matter of Style

R&D Manager

You work on a cross-functional team that involves manufacturing, marketing, and sales, as well as your department, R&D. The sales manager insists that the new product on which you're working be available in six weeks. Neither you nor the manufacturing manager believe that's possible. The prototype needs additional testing, the appropriate part of the plant has to be retooled, and the processors have to be trained on how to assemble the product. Time is on your side because the company's doing very well without the product and no one in upper management has demanded that the development process be rushed.

PREVENTING CONFLICT SKILL PRACTICE SITUATION CARDS (*continued*)

Soothing Feelings

Consultant's Boss

You had committed your consulting company to prepare a grant proposal for a not-for-profit social agency to submit to a U.S. government department. You assigned some of your best people to the project, but they said that the agency wasn't qualified for the grant. They said data for the grant unless the proposal misled the grantor to qualify them. You looked at the team's results but decided to go ahead anyway, writing the proposal yourself, without skewing the data. You told the client-agency the proposal had a good chance for success, which the agency's executive director took to be a guarantee. After the grant request was denied, he refused to pay for services rendered. You want your team leader to work things out with the executive director of the agency. You start the conversation.

Fix It

Manager

Your team leader has been complaining for a month that something's wrong with the processing equipment because too much product is rejected and now defects are coming back from customers. You don't agree that equipment failure is the cause of the problem. The plant's maintenance team doesn't know what's wrong. You think the operators are not doing their jobs properly, and you hold the team leader responsible for their failure. You also think it would be far too expensive to have the machine engineers come in to look at the problem because the warranty period is over.

Soothing Feelings

Consultant

The owner of your company, your boss, committed the company to writing a grant proposal for a nonprofit agency to submit to the U.S. government. Your company's team of proposal writers, which you head, came together and, after studying the grant requirements, concluded that the agency would not qualify for the grant unless the proposal misled the grantor about its capabilities. The team collected the appropriate data and gave it to your company's owner. He rejected the team's conclusions and wrote the grant proposal himself, promising the executive director of the client-agency that the proposal had a good chance for success. However, the client-agency not only lost out on the grant, they chastised by the grantor for giving the government misleading information. The executive director of the agency is furious and refuses to pay your company for services rendered. Since you are the original team leader, your boss wants you to smooth it out and to get the agency to pay up.

Fix It

Team Leader

For over a month, you've been asking your manager to have the vendor's engineers come in and look at the processing equipment your team uses. The rate of product rejection is much too high. You've been all over the problem with the operators again and again. Now product is coming back from the customers at a higher rate than ever. The plant's maintenance team doesn't know what's wrong. Your manager has said that the warranty period on the equipment is over, and it would cost too much to get the vendor's engineers in to look at it. Besides, he has said, he doesn't think the equipment's the problem, and he holds you responsible for the team's failure. You start the conversation.

Exercise 15.4. Acceptance/Affirmation

Instructor's Notes

This exercise is designed to help the participants communicate without making value judgments about what another person says, to accept people at face value without judging their worth, and to understand that they think or feel rather than to dispute or argue with them.

Learning Objectives and Outcomes

By the end of this exercise participants will be able to:

▶ Listen nonjudgmentally to another person with the objective of learning more about him or her.

▶ Paraphrase what the other person is saying to ensure understanding.

▶ Ask for clarification of something they do not understand.

▶ Ask for elaboration when they want or need more information.

▶ Ask for feelings behind statements to fully understand the other person's point of view.

Self-Management Skills Involved

▶ Openness and honesty

▶ Self-disclosure

▶ Communication, especially listening skills

Requirements

Time:	Approximately ninety minutes
Materials:	Instructions for Acceptance/Affirmation Exercise handout
	Self-Disclosure Statements handout
	Flip chart and multicolored markers
Preparation:	Photocopy the handouts.
Room Setup:	Any arrangement that allows pairs of people to face each other

Lecture Notes

"Getting to know you." That one phrase from Oscar Hammerstein's song lyrics from *The King and I* sums up the entire basis for respect for others. The more we know about a person, the more we understand what he thinks or feels—and why he thinks or feels as he does. To get to know someone means to listen to and watch that person without forming value judgments about her. It means affirming and accepting the person without reservation, affirming and accepting her as another human being even if we don't approve of what the person says or does.

Nothing requires us to like everything that a person does, or to like a person as we would a friend. "I don't like what you've done" says something much different than "I don't accept you as a person." When we get to know someone, it's easier to accept him because we understand why he acts the way he does. When we know what life experiences the person has had, we have a better understanding of his current actions. This is as important in the workplace as it is in the home.

> *[Facilitator: Ask participants to explain the differences between the two statements: "I don't like what you've done" and "I don't accept you as a person." Discuss the implications of the two statements for preventing conflict.]*

Sometimes, when someone does something of which we don't approve, we find it difficult to respect that person. But, just like members of a family, we can't always pick the people with whom we have to work. We have to find a way to get around our feelings in order to get our job done and to work closely with coworkers, no matter what. One way to do that is, again, to accept the offender as a person, no matter what she says or does. That, too, requires looking beyond the behavior we don't like or respect to the person as a whole.

We can't get to know other people unless we also let other people get to know us, which requires self-disclosure as well as a willingness to let people see or observe what we do. Self-disclosure and listening to self-disclosure advance the entire process of getting to know one another quickly and to the point.

Self-disclosure means doing something rarely done at work: talking about ourselves, our thoughts, our feelings, our values. It's rarely done because most people don't like to do that, afraid that people will use what they say against them. Office politicians often abuse the confidential privilege on which self-disclosure relies.

> *[Facilitator: Use an illustration from your own experience, or use the following case.]*

In an illustrative case, at a Fortune 100 company, one woman told a coworker about difficulties she was having with her ex-husband, the stress it caused her. Although the troubled woman capably handled her work, the coworker then used that information to prompt their boss to let her replace the woman on an important project. Still, not talking about ourselves to other people prevents them from know-ing who we really are and accepting us for who we are, warts and all.

None of this suggests that we have to tell everyone about ourselves. Intimacies between us and our significant others, for example, are private, and few *reasonable* people want to know about those anyway. Nor does it mean answering every ques-tion people might ask us. Someone might want to know those intimate details, and we're within our rights to say, "I'm sorry but that information is between us alone." We are entitled to keep stuff about ourselves to ourselves. Nor does it suggest that we have the right to know everything we want to know about other people. Prying into anyone's personal life works both ways. They, too, have the right to privacy.

People at work come together as strangers. The extent to which coworkers share information about themselves, however, determines their ability to work together effectively. They should exchange ideas about their work, their values with regard to the work they do, the importance to them of their roles in the organization, and their thoughts and feelings about the unit's goals. They should exchange their thoughts and feelings about what's important to them, personally as well as professionally, what kind of rewards provide incentives, the kinds of support they look for from other people. Unless we know what other people think, feel, or value, we're bound to run across their ships' bows like a warning shot from a cannon. That shot could trig-ger an unnecessary conflict with which no one wants to deal.

[Facilitator: Use an illustration from your own experience, or use the following case.]

Two coworkers, assigned to work on a project, struggled with one another for weeks until a third party suggested they talk about how they individually approached a project. It turned out that one person took a broad, visual approach to the work. The other took a structured, linear approach to the work. Once they understood one another, they could agree on an approach that worked for both of them.

Likewise, the extent to which people share information about themselves determines the degree to which they accept and affirm one another. If diversity means anything at all, it means differences, and differences can breed contempt *unless people practice accepting and affirming one another.* No one ever said self-management is easy.

[Facilitator: Use an illustration from your own experience or continue with the case.]

In the example of the two coworkers with two different approaches to work, they both felt anger and resentment toward each other while struggling for control of the project. Behind each other's backs, they talked to other people in disparaging ways about each other. After they talked out their differences and resolved the problem, the anger and resentment evaporated and they learned to respect each other as indi-viduals. The result was a project that incorporated the best of both approaches.

Instructions to Participants

This activity is an exercise in self-disclosure and acceptance and affirmation in which you work with another person to do two things: (1) disclose information about yourself to another person, and (2) listen to another person without interpreting what that person said or forming a value judgment about that person.

[Facilitator: Distribute the Acceptance/Affirmation Instructions and Self-Disclosure Statements now. Read the instructions aloud.]

INSTRUCTIONS FOR THE
ACCEPTANCE/AFFIRMATION EXERCISE

1. Separate into pairs, preferably with someone you don't know or don't know very well.

2. Everyone has a list of fifteen open-ended statements that begin with the pronoun "I."

3. Each person reads aloud and completes one statement at a time. Do not change roles with the other person until you have said all that you feel you can about the given statement within two minutes.

4. As you listen to the other person speak, you may interrupt only to ask questions to clarify something, such as "What do you mean by that?" or to ask the person to elaborate, such as "Tell me more about that," or to ask the person to talk about his or her feelings, such as, "How did you feel when that happened?"

5. When one person has completed a statement, the other person completes the same statement.

6. Do the same with each self-disclosure statement in the handout.

7. You have forty-five minutes to complete this activity, after which we'll discuss how you felt in the exercise and what you think you learned from it: about yourself, as well as about the other person and about self-disclosure.

PROCESSING QUESTIONS

1. How did you feel about talking about yourself this way?

2. What did you learn about yourself when talking that you didn't realize before?

3. What did you learn about the other person that you didn't know before?

4. How did you feel about just listening and not judging the other person's self-disclosure?

5. What insights did you gain about the value or importance of accepting and affirming other people?

SELF-DISCLOSURE STATEMENTS

INSTRUCTIONS

Nothing stops you from trivializing the exercise. However, you gain nothing from it if you do. An example might be, "I'm the kind of person who usually keeps busy." Nothing's wrong with that statement in itself, but it doesn't tell anyone very much. An explanation of why you keep busy and how you feel about being busy would help the listener fully appreciate what you think and feel.

1. I'm the kind of person who usually . . .

2. I like . . .

3. I do . . . on my job.

4. I usually . . . when things don't go well for me.

5. I have responsibilities on my job for . . .

6. I don't like . . .

7. I had a first impression of you that . . .

8. I usually tell people about myself . . .

9. I have many acquaintances and . . .

10. I feel satisfied with . . .

11. I feel unsatisfied with . . .

12. I want to achieve . . .

13. I wish I could . . .

14. I'm glad I did . . .

15. I'm glad I didn't . . .

Exercise 15.5. Trust

Instructor's Notes

There are actually two exercises here: (1) an exercise for intact work groups or teams, and (2) an exercise for people who don't know each other very well. The two exercises are distinguished not by the instructions but by the materials used in the discussions between people. Therefore, Trust Statements for Participants Who Work Together and Trust Statements for Participants Who Don't Work Together are different and should *not* be used with any group other than the one specified in the title.

Separate the participants into pairs. In a workshop where people ordinarily work together, have the participants find partners whom they don't know very well or at all. In a workshop where people don't work together, save this exercise until after they have had some experiences with each other in the workshop.

Learning Objectives and Outcomes

By the end of this exercise participants will be able to:

▶ Test their willingness to trust people.

▶ Express their trust for at least one person they don't know all that well.

Self-Management Skills Involved

▶ Openness and honesty
▶ Trust
▶ Communication

Requirements

Time:	Approximately sixty minutes
Materials:	Trust Statements for Participants Who Work Together worksheet
	Trust Statements for Participants Who Don't Work Together worksheet
	Flip chart and multicolored markers
Preparation:	Photocopy the appropriate worksheet for each participant in your workshop.
Room Setup:	Any arrangement that allows pairs of participants to talk with each other

Lecture Notes

If we don't trust people, how can we:

▶ Depend on people to do their jobs?

▶ Rely on people to support our efforts?

▶ Expect people to tell us the truth?

▶ Expect people to trust us?

Trust is an essential element of respect for others. Self-managed people trust other people. It's risky, but it's worth it. According to Rosalie Maggio, in her book *Quotations From Women on Life,* the movie actress Geena Davis is supposed to have said: "If you risk nothing, then you risk everything."[1] Davis may not have been talking about trusting other people, but she might as well have been.

Each and everything in our lives involves other people in some way. We have to trust them to do what they are supposed to go in our relationship with them, and we can't take responsibility for seeing to it that they do it. The vendors or customers with whom we deal, our coworkers, the people reporting to us, and the people to whom we report—family members, government officials, social leaders, the whole world around us have responsibilities for maintaining social order and commerce. Unless we take the risk of trusting other people, we put ourselves in the position of the main character in the movie "Conspiracy Theory," and in that way we risk everything.

[Facilitator: If you haven't seen that movie, I suggest you view it to explain it to participants who haven't seen it; or, have a student in the class explain it; or, just omit the reference to it.]

This doesn't mean to trust without question. Only infants do that. People earn our *distrust* by what they do and say. Otherwise they need not earn our trust until they do something to prove they're not trustworthy. Just like anything else in self-management, we need to practice trusting people. That's what this exercise is all about.

[Facilitator: Distribute the appropriate worksheet and then read aloud one of the two following explanations. Explanation 1 should be provided to people working together in the workshop for the first and only time. Explanation 2 should be provided to people who work together regularly.]

Explanation 1

Assume that the trust statements refer *only* to your relationship in this workshop. Two possible outcomes can happen. You will reinforce existing trust levels or you

---

[1] Rosalie Maggio, compiler, *Quotations from Women on Life* (Paramus, NJ: Prentice-Hall, 1997) 82.

will uncover areas in which trust levels can be improved. Since the exercise is designed for the purpose of helping you build trust, accept what your partner says as a form of instructive feedback, not as criticism. If you feel anger or resentment when your partner says something such as "I didn't check that I trust you to take this workshop seriously because you're always cracking jokes," ask yourself why you feel the way you do. Don't attack the other person. Instead, ask him or her what he or she thinks you should do to repair the relationship. This type of discussion is practice for building greater trust in other relationships.

Explanation 2

During this exercise one of three things, or all of them, can happen. One, you will reinforce the trust level between you and your partner. Two, you will uncover areas in which trust levels can be improved. Three, you will uncover areas of distrust or mistrust that need additional attention after you leave the workshop.

Since the exercise is designed for the purpose of helping you build trust, accept what your partner says as a form of instructive feedback, not as criticism. If you feel anger or resentment when your partner says something such as "I didn't check that I trust you to take this workshop seriously because you're always cracking jokes," ask yourself why you feel the way you do. Don't attack the other person. Instead, ask him or her what he or she thinks you should do to repair the relationship. This type of discussion is practice for building greater trust in other relationships.

Processing Questions

1. Explain why you were truthful or untruthful in talking with your partner about trust.

   Typical answers: I was truthful because I thought that it would help us make our relationship stronger. I was untruthful because I didn't think my partner could accept how I felt without getting angry.

2. What did you realize about yourself with regard to trusting another person?

   Typical answer: I'm less trusting than I thought.

3. How truthful do you think your partner was with you and what gave you that impression?

   Typical answers: I thought my partner was truthful because some of the things she said hurt a little. I thought my partner wasn't as truthful as he could be because I felt he was too complimentary, and it made me uncomfortable.

4. What conclusions do you draw from the exercise about the value or importance of trusting other people?

   Typical answer: If we don't trust each other at work, whom can we trust?

Facilitator's Notes

If an argument breaks out during one of these discussions, which to date has not happened, mediate by asking the person becoming angry or resentful why he or she feels the way he or she does. You might get one or more of the following possible answers:

▶ The other person's tone of voice seemed sarcastic or antagonistic.

▶ The other person used offensive language.

▶ What the other person said hurt my feelings.

▶ I feel bad about what the other person said, but I can't accept responsibility.

Discuss the response with both parties, and in the case where the "other person's" tone of voice or language was in fact offensive, discuss how those things create distrust or mistrust. In the case where the person getting upset owns up to hurt feelings or inability to accept responsibility, discuss how those things also create distrust or mistrust.

TRUST STATEMENTS FOR
PARTICIPANTS WHO WORK TOGETHER

INSTRUCTION

Thinking about the person with whom you are working in this exercise, and calling upon your experiences with this person, place a check mark on the space provided in front of the statements with which you completely or strongly agree. Leave blank any space in front of a statement with which you cannot completely or strongly agree. After both of you have finished checking your lists, begin talking with each other about each item that each of you has left *blank*. Explain why you didn't check off the blank items. Explain what you think has to happen before you can trust the other person in this item.

_____ 1. I trust you to do your job well.

_____ 2. I trust you to help me when I need help, that I can depend on you.

_____ 3. I trust the information you give me is true and accurate, that I can rely on you.

_____ 4. I trust that you will tell me honestly what you think of me and what I say or do.

_____ 5. I trust that you are willing to let me tell you honestly what I think of you and what you say or do.

_____ 6. I trust that you will give me accurate and honest feedback about my work.

_____ 7. I trust that you will accept accurate and honest feedback from me about your work.

_____ 8. I trust that you will keep my confidence and not gossip about me to other people.

_____ 9. I trust that you believe I will keep your confidence and not gossip about you to other people.

_____ 10. I trust that when we disagree, we can talk things over and resolve our differences to our mutual satisfaction.

_____ 11. I trust that you will always uphold your end of any agreement or assignment we have.

_____ 12. I trust that you will always tell me the truth, even if it's something you don't think I'll find flattering.

TRUST STATEMENTS FOR
PARTICIPANTS WHO DON'T WORK TOGETHER

INSTRUCTION

Thinking about the person with whom you are working in this exercise, and calling upon whatever experiences you have had with this person, place a check mark on the space provided in front of the statements with which you completely or strongly agree. Leave blank any space in front of a statement with which you cannot completely or strongly agree. After both of you have finished checking your lists, begin talking with each other about each item that each of you has left *blank*. Explain why you didn't check off the blank items. Explain what you think has to happen before you can trust the other person in this item.

_____ 1. I trust you to take this workshop seriously.

_____ 2. I trust you to participate fully and enthusiastically in this workshop.

_____ 3. I trust you to be open and willing to work with me on this exercise.

_____ 4. I trust you to be truthful.

_____ 5. I trust you to give me accurate and correct information.

_____ 6. I trust you to give me accurate and helpful feedback about what I say or do.

_____ 7. I trust you to believe that I will give you accurate and correct information.

_____ 8. I trust you to believe I will give you accurate and helpful feedback about what you say or do.

_____ 9. I trust you to work with me to draw insightful conclusions from this exercise.

_____ 10. I trust you to keep anything we say in this workshop in confidence.

Follow-Up Activities for Developing Trust

Learning Objectives and Outcomes

By doing this activity, participants will take steps to:

▶ Evaluate or assess their willingness and ability to trust other people.

▶ Take corrective action to improve trust levels when needed.

Self-Management Skills Involved

▶ Evaluating or assessing one's own feelings of trust

▶ Openness to feedback from other people

▶ Openness to making changes in one's own behavior

Requirements

Time:	Thirty minutes to prepare participants for follow-up activity
Materials:	Instructions for Follow-Up Activities for Developing Trust handout
Preparation:	Photocopy the handout.
Room Setup:	None

[Facilitator: Distribute Instructions for Follow-Up Activities for Developing Trust.]

INSTRUCTIONS FOR FOLLOW-UP ACTIVITIES
FOR DEVELOPING TRUST

1. Make a list of the people with whom you work. Refer to the instructions in the Trust Statements for Participants Who Ordinarily Work Together handout with regard to each person on your list.

   For each person, identify the statements you did not check and think about why you left the statements blank.

   When the opportunity arises, ask each person with whom it's important to speak, to discuss this issue with you.

   Explain that you are working on an assignment designed to help you improve your trust levels with other people and that you would appreciate the person's help.

2. Give everyone you meet the benefit of the doubt and continue trusting them until they do something to earn your distrust.

3. See to it that you are trustworthy.

4. Explain what you're trying to do to improve your own trustworthiness and ask people to give you feedback about their level of trust in you. Ask them also what they think needs to happen for them to be more trusting of you.

5. For areas in need of improvement, set goals for changing the conditions under which people do not completely trust you.

SELF-MANAGED TEAMS

"Abracadabra" is a *magic* word. "Self-managed team" is not. Yet, in the common wisdom of management, *self-managed team* resonates as if it were magic. Corporate cultures often, in my experience, replace sound management with hocus pocus. They form teams, tell them to work independently, but don't prepare or train people to function as teammates—and they superimpose a team leader on a team that is self-managed in name only.

Dubbing a team "self-managed" doesn't make it so, and genuine self-management doesn't guarantee effectiveness. Successful self-managed teams (SMTs) are driven by willing self-managed people trained to work in such a team, and they must have the company's full support.

Semiautonomous teams often masquerade as SMTs. These work groups, which aren't in themselves ineffective, report to a supervisor or team leader appointed by management, the employees perform separate functions and frequently get together to solve problems, make decisions, and carry action plans to management for approval. Instead of the autonomy required for making a team self-managed, the team's head has final authority over decisions and actions.

The team's leader also transmits mandates from upper management, and sees to it that the team carries out objectives and does work designed by management. The leader assigns work, monitors progress, hands out rewards. Thus, the leader differs little from a traditional first-line manager in a command and control organization. While this arrangement can be efficient, it doesn't drive problem-solving decisions to where they belong: where the work is done.

In contrast, an SMT gets direction or objectives and a mandate for *autonomy* from management; that's the real meaning of *empowerment.* Instead of an appointed leader, the team, if it so decides, elects its leader, and it distributes responsibilities that have previously been the province of managers to each of the team's members.

The team may ask one person to manage the budget, another to communicate to groups external to the team, and so on. How an SMT organizes itself and designs its work are team decisions, not management fiats.

To take on and follow through on that kind of responsibility requires that team members use self-management skills. Self-management training is therefore essential for people to understand what an SMT is, what values it must have, the generic activities that go into making a team successful, and the specific activities of group decision making and problem solving.

ORGANIZATION OF SECTION IV

The exercises in Chapter 16 deal with the values, attitudes, and activities the organization and its SMTs must accept to make SMTs effective. All effective or high-performance teams are created to achieve specific, well-defined goals that one individual working alone, or any group of individuals working independently of one another cannot achieve. Synergy so defined has a unique application in SMTs: No one person manages or leads an SMT, yet everyone manages or leads it in his or her own way and in his or her own capacity. That means everyone takes responsibility for his or her individual assignments *and* for the tasks and processes of the team. Without values to live by no one takes responsibility for anything.

Chapter 17 provides activities that help teams work through the six common experiences all teams have during their lifetimes: Introducing, Stage Setting, Probing/Testing, Creating, Producing, and Maintaining. The uniqueness of an SMT occurs after initial formation. Management creates the team and provides direction. Together, management and the team members set the stage that guides how the SMT will function. From there the team takes over all the responsibilities for managing the team's experiences.

The exercises in Chapter 18 help team members apply self-management values and attitudes in the service of adopting, clarifying, and managing the roles each person plays in the team. The team members also coordinate the relationships between individuals and between the team and organizational structures. A synergistic whole, represented by the intersection of the interlocking circles of a Venn Diagram, emerges.

SELF-MANAGED INDIVIDUALS AND SELF-MANAGED TEAMS

Team training books fill bookstore and library shelves; we really don't need another one. Instead, these exercises focus on unique issues related to self-management in the service of a team. They also assume that the participants are either already in SMTs or are about to be organized into one. This training works well with SMTs experiencing difficulties or barriers to productivity or to team member relations, as well as with newly formed groups.

This training also works best if the participants have been through self-management training. They know the concepts and skills involved in self-management, and they can apply what they know and can do as individuals to what has to be done to make their SMTs work well as a group (be effective) as well as get the job done (be efficient). Whereas the exercises in the previous chapters, even when organized as team activities, focused on the individual, these exercises focus on the dynamics of the team. The shift in learning objectives changes from *self*-management to the management of a team. The following exercises take the same values and skills involved in self-management competencies and apply them to managing a work group that has no manager involved in its daily pursuits.

16

Values of Self-Managed Teams

B y reading this chapter, you will be able to facilitate two exercises that will help participants apply self-management competencies and values to the activities of SMTs.

Exercise 16.1. Identifying Values of SMTs

Instructor's Notes

Exercise 16.1 is designed to help participants identify team values and to relate their self-management competencies to managing the team. It is also designed to encourage people to (1) work independently, (2) work in small subgroups, and (3) work for the benefit of the whole team. To those ends, divide the group into four teams with from two to four people in each subgroup. Conduct Part 1 before referring to Part 2. Conduct Part 2 and Part 3 as one continuous exercise.

Each subgroup or team will draw its own conclusions about the values of teams. Use their reports to the whole group about their agreed-upon beneficial values or valued activities as the basis of the discussion. For example, after a team reports out, you could ask, "Why did your team think that a flat organization is of value to the team?" Or, "This team said a flat organization is of value to the team. What do the rest of you think about that?"

The subgroups should have an extra handout from Parts 2 and 3 of the exercise to use for preparing "master copies" of the teams' conclusions that you can collect after they are completed by each subgroup; reproduce the master copies for distribution to all the participants. That way everyone has copies of what everyone else has said.

During the discussions after Part 1 and Parts 2 and 3 of the exercise, tie the activity back to actual conditions where the participants work. For example, ask, "How do you see these values or valued activities reflected in your daily operations?"

Learning Objectives and Outcomes

By the end of this exercise participants will be able to identify:

▶ The personal and organizational values that make SMTs successful

▶ The relationship between self-management competencies and the values of successful SMTs

Self-Management Skills Involved

▶ The ability to identify one's own values

▶ Communication, especially the ability to exchange ideas with other people

▶ The ability to accept other people's opinions or values

Requirements

Time:	Approximately ninety minutes
Materials:	Values of Self-Managed Teams worksheet
	Value Definitions/Actions worksheets for Teams 1, 2, 3, and 4
	Flip chart with assorted markers
Preparation:	Photocopy the worksheets.
Room Setup:	U-shape or other arrangement for intact teams that will encourage discussion

Lecture Notes

We measure a team's efficiency by its results—the most readily accessible measure of an SMT's performance. However, focusing only on results neglects the social side of an SMT's life, the aspects of SMT performance that measure the team's effectiveness (vision, assumptions, values, interpersonal relations, paradigms, attitudes). In popular jargon, we distinguish between what has to be done (task dynamics) and how things get done (process dynamics). Whether we talk about task dynamics or process dynamics, values and attitudes drive the life of an SMT.

A value is a belief or feeling people consider to be worthwhile or desirable; an attitude is a readiness to act on a value. In our context, the personal and organizational values and attitudes of an SMT make it unique in relation to other workplace organizations. SMTs foster synergy—the ability to achieve specific, well-defined goals that one individual working alone, or any group of individuals working independently of one another cannot achieve—by removing artificial barriers between management and nonmanagement ("they" or "them"). Self-management values and attitudes combine "I" and "you" into "us," the whole that makes the results greater than the sum of its parts.

[Facilitator: Open a discussion by asking, "What are some of the values of everyday life?" Answers could include The Ten Commandments, the Sermon on the Mount, the Way of Taoism, and the Declaration of Independence.]

Values form a code of *espoused* values that often lie hidden from other people's perceptions or that, when spoken or written, are declaimed loudly but aren't visible in behavior. For an SMT to succeed the members must not only "talk the values talk," they must also "walk the values walk." In an SMT, do as *I do* is as important as do as I say.

In this activity, we have two questions to answer: (1) What are the personal and organizational values that drive SMTs? (2) What are the actions or behaviors to which we must commit to make espoused values concrete?

[Facilitator: Separate your team into subgroups of from two to four people. Distribute the Values of SMTs worksheet and read the instructions aloud. Allow more time for group activity if needed. Use your own discretion for the amount of time to extend.]

Discussion After Part 1 of the Exercise

1. Each subgroup reads its list of words.
2. As a team reads its list, the other subgroups check items they did *not* list.
3. Ask, "What is the value of breaking down into smaller groups and then comparing results?"

   Typical answer: People feel freer to talk in a small group, and the small groups can then contribute to a larger group answer?"

4. Ask, "What accounts for the differences between the groups and how significant is the fact of differences?"

Typical answer: People have different ideas or values, and by comparing the differences, and resolving them, you can produce a higher quality outcome or result.

Instructions to Participants, Part 2

[Facilitator: Distribute the Values Definitions/Actions worksheets to each team.]

1. In the handout Value Definitions/Actions each team has eight or nine words or phrases to define.
2. As a group, define those terms.
3. Make your definitions sufficiently comprehensive to include both the individual and the organization.
4. You have thirty minutes to complete this part of the exercise.
5. Elect a scribe/reporter whose duties will include:
   — Making a master copy of the definitions of the words or phrases
   — Writing the definitions on your flip chart
   — Reporting your team's findings to the assembled group

Instructions to Participants, Part 3

1. As a team, use your handout to list five or more behaviors or actions you believe are necessary for making each of these values concrete or visible. For example, say you define "flexibility" as a willingness to do the team's work differently. A behavior might be, "Research and identify alternative methods for solving old problems."
2. Design your lists to include both individual and organizational actions, and distinguish them. Following through on the example, you could refer to individuals by saying, "Each person makes an effort to research new methods" and refer to the organization by saying, "The organization should make additional resources available."
3. You have ten minutes for this part of the exercise.
4. The scribe/reporter will have the following duties:
   — Add the group's action decisions to the master copy of the handout.
   — Write the action lists on the flip chart and report to the whole group.
   — Hand in the master copy of the handout to be duplicated for distribution to all the participants.

Discussion After Part 3

1. What beneficial values or activities do you find on the job that help you work as an SMT?

   Typical answers vary with the organization, but some answers commonly relate to what the organization does to undermine self-management, creating semiautonomous teams and not SMTs. Groups complain that too many beneficial values are espoused and not implemented.

2. What can you or the organization do to increase the degree to which everyone "walks the walk"?

   Typical answers relate to the kind of answers given to question 1.

Values of SMTs

INSTRUCTIONS

1. Individually, on the next page, under the heading "My Vote," place a check mark after each word or phrase that you think is a beneficial value or behavior for an SMT.

2. After everyone is finished identifying their candidates, compare votes.

3. As a team, form a consensus concerning the words or phrases you think should be included in the team list of beneficial values or activities for an SMT.

4. Where there is disagreement, resolve the disagreement to either discard the word or phrase or include it as a team agreement.

5. You have five minutes for the individual voting and fifteen minutes for achieving team consensus.

Values	My Vote	Team Vote	Values	My Vote	Team Vote
Self-esteem/Self-respect			Motivation		
Bureaucracy			Courage/Risk taking		
Vertical organization			Trust		
Cooperation/Collaboration			Honesty/Integrity		
Availability/Accessibility			Creativity/Innovation		
Dependability/Credibility			Commitment		
Quality			Empowerment		
Results/Customer focus			Competence		
Leadership			Problem solving/Decision making		
Continuous improvement			Feedback		
Continuous learning			Hiding errors		
Strategy			Motivation programs		
Cross-training			Foresight/Insight		
Job enrichment			Quickness/Decisiveness		
Cost center			Flexibility		
Thinkers vs doers			Responsibility		
Authority to follow through			Drive		
Self-confidence			Lack of trust		
Profitability			Capability		
Individual effort			Caring		
Adherence to rules			Diversity		
Command and control			Hierarchy		
Internal competition			Individual rewards		
Respect for others					

VALUES DEFINITIONS/ACTIONS: TEAM 1

Value	Definition	Actions/Behaviors
Self-esteem/Self-respect		
Cooperation/Collaboration		
Availability/Accessibility		
Dependability/Credibility		
Quality		
Results/Customer focus		
Leadership		
Continuous improvement		
Drive		

VALUES DEFINITIONS/ACTIONS: TEAM 2

Value	Definition	Actions/Behaviors
Continuous learning		
Strategic		
Cross-training		
Job enrichment		
Authority to follow through		
Motivation		
Courage/Risk taking		
Trust		
Respect for others		

VALUES DEFINITIONS/ACTIONS: TEAM 3

Value	Definition	Actions/Behaviors
Honesty/Integrity		
Creativity/Innovation		
Commitment		
Empowerment		
Competence		
Problem solving/Decision making		
Feedback		
Foresight/Insight		
Self-confidence		

VALUES DEFINITIONS/ACTIONS: TEAM 4

Value	Definition	Actions/Behaviors
Quickness/Decisiveness		
Flexibility		
Responsibility		
Profitability		
Individual effort		
Capability		
Caring		
Diversity		

Exercise 16.2. The "I" in the Word "Team"

Instructor's Notes

Divide intact teams into subgroups of two to four people. The exercise is designed to help everyone join in the discussion and to ensure that everyone can identify his or her own needs as well as to suggest how the team can help him or her be a more productive team member.

Learning Objectives and Outcomes

By the end of this exercise participants will be able to:

▶ Explain the values involved in the relationship between "I" and "Team."

▶ Explain the relationship between "I" and "Team."

▶ Identify their needs with regard to team membership.

Self-Management Skills Involved

▶ The ability to identify one's own needs

▶ The ability to consider one's own needs as important as anyone else's

▶ Communication, especially the ability to listen to other people express their own needs

▶ The ability to empathize with other people's feelings about their own needs

Requirements

Time:	Approximately sixty minutes
Materials:	Instructions for the "I" in the Word "Team" Exercise handout
	The "I" in the Word "Team" worksheet
	Flip chart with assorted markers
Preparation:	Photocopy the handout and worksheet.
Room Setup:	U-shape or other arrangement for intact teams that will encourage discussion

Lecture Notes

The common wisdom of teams is bound up in the slogan, "There is no I in the word team." I beg to differ. Without a group of "I's" pooling their resources and strengths, there is no team.

Yes, the individual frequently sacrifices his or her own needs and always considers the needs of the group, but the group ignores the needs or interests of the individual at its own peril. An SMT, composed of self-managed people, considers individuals' rights, needs, and interests as well as the team's. Otherwise, no one would want to work in one.

In this exercise, you will look at: (1) the value of each individual member, (2) the relationship of the individual to the team, and (3) the relationship of the organization to the team.

[Facilitator: Distribute The "I" in the Word "Team" Instructions handout and worksheet now. Read aloud the instructions for the individual activity and the group activity.]

INSTRUCTIONS FOR THE "I" IN THE WORD "TEAM" EXERCISE

INSTRUCTIONS: INDIVIDUAL ACTIVITY

1. At the top of the "I" in the word "Team" worksheet in one sentence explain your interpretation of the value of the individual to the team.

2. In the chart, make a list of what you need from the team to help you:
   - Be a productive member of the team.
   - Feel more content or satisfied working in the team.
   - Satisfy personal needs or meet personal goals.

3. In the chart, make a list of what you need to give to the team to help:
   - The team become more productive.
   - Improve the quality of team life.
   - Satisfy the team's needs or meet its goals.

4. Make a list of what you can and should do by or for yourself to:
   - Become more productive.
   - Be a more effective team member.
   - Satisfy your personal needs or meet your personal goals.

5. You have fifteen minutes to complete this part of the exercise.

INSTRUCTIONS: GROUP ACTIVITY

1. Give each participant an opportunity to read his or her lists to the group.

2. Discuss but don't debate what people have said. The objective is to learn about what your team-mates think is important to them, even if you disagree. Focus on ways in which you can help one another meet his or her own needs while meeting those of the team.

3. You have twenty minutes to complete this part of the exercise.

4. Elect a scribe/reporter.

5. As a team, make a list of three or more insights you have gained from the exercise about the value of the "I" in the word "team."

6. Share the insights with the entire class.

The "I" in the Word "Team"

The value of the individual to the team: _____

_____

What I need from team	What team needs from me	What I can do on my own

Follow-Up Activities for Building a Stronger SMT

Instructor's Notes

Encourage SMTs to do regular progress checks as to how they are functioning as a team, to assess how well the team and the organization are "walking the talk," and to reevaluate what individuals need from the team and what the team needs from its members.

Learning Objectives and Outcomes

By doing these activities participants will take steps to:

▶ Identify and reinforce their team strengths.

▶ Work to improve areas in which the team needs to take corrective action.

Self-Management Skills Involved

▶ Risk taking and trust

▶ Decision making

▶ Openness, honesty with oneself and with one another

▶ Communication, especially giving feedback to teammates

Requirements

Time:	Five minutes to read instructions plus discussion time
Materials:	Instructions for Follow-Up Activities for Building a Stronger SMT handout
Preparation:	Photocopy the handout.
Room Setup:	Any arrangement in which the team meets (e.g., a conference table)

[Facilitator: Distribute the Instructions for Follow-Up Activities for Building a Stronger SMT handout and read them aloud.]

INSTRUCTIONS FOR FOLLOW-UP ACTIVITIES
FOR BUILDING A STRONGER SMT

1. Periodically, use the handout Values of Self-Managed Teams to assess how well the team and the organization are "walking the talk." Identify strong areas on which to build. Strengths could include the value *flexibility*. Ask, "How can we use flexibility as a way to improve the quality of our outputs?" Identify areas in need of improvement. For example, if the organization doesn't value implementing decisions at the point of action, ask, "What can we do to increase the organization's willingness to let the team make and act on its own decisions?" An action plan that includes the following points will help you and the team change the culture in which team values need to be strengthened or created.

   — Current conditions in need of change, identifying indicators and contributing factors

   — An explanation of why they need to change

   — Change goals

   — A suggested action plan, including the team's responsibilities for helping make the change happen and steps for monitoring the change

2. Periodically, use the handout The "I" in the Word "Team" to reevaluate what individuals need from the team and what the team needs from its members. Identify strong areas on which to build. Strengths might include "supports individual effort that benefits the team." Ask, "How can we use that support of individual effort to advance both individual and group growth?" Identify areas in need of improvement. For example, suppose the team doesn't support individual effort, what can the team do to provide individuals with the support they need. An action plan that includes the following points would help the team recognize the importance of individuals as well as the importance of the team as a whole.

   — Current conditions in need of change, identifying indicators and contributing factors

   — An explanation of why they need to change

   — Change goals

   — A suggested action plan, including the individual's and the team's responsibilities for helping make the change happen and steps for monitoring the change

17

Six Common Team Experiences That Turn Values Into Action

By reading this chapter, you will be able to facilitate an exercise that will help team members grasp the six common experiences teams have and how an SMT manages those experiences.

Exercise 17.1. Six Common Experiences of Teams

Instructor's Notes

The exercise works best if you say very little in setting up the activities. The more the participants draw their own conclusions, the better. The six experiences are Introducing, Stage Setting, Probing/Testing, Creating, Producing, Maintaining. The self-management skills involved also reflect the values an SMT must apply in order to be effective.

Divide the team or class into subgroups of three or four people each. Walk the participants through the six experiences as described in Instructions to Participants, and, since the activities are designed as self-discovery exercises, offer few or no explanations until after the entire exercise is completed.

Learning Objectives and Outcomes

By the end of this exercise participants will be able to:

▶ Explain the six common experiences of teams that turn values into action.

▶ Explain unique situations that occur when SMTs undergo those experiences.

Self-Management Skills Involved

▶ The ability to recognize one's own strengths and the contributions one can make to the team

▶ Communication, the ability to exchange information about oneself and the ability to contribute to and to influence team problem-solving activities

▶ The ability and the willingness to learn more about other people, to accept their contributions to team problem-solving activities, and to be influenced by other people when appropriate

Requirements

Time:	Approximately two hours (length depends on discussion time allowed)
Materials:	Objectives of the Exercise overhead
	Methods You Will Use in the Exercise overhead
	Roles You Will Play overhead
	Task envelopes with the birthday cake worksheet, the Instructions for the Birthday Cake Activity handout, and the Observer's Guide for the Birthday Cake Activity handout
	Solution to Cutting the Birthday Cake overhead
	Flip chart with lined paper and multicolored markers
Equipment:	Overhead projector and screen
Preparation:	Prepare the overheads.
	Photocopy the handouts and worksheet.
	Stuff task envelopes with the birthday cake worksheet, the Instructions for the Birthday Cake Activity handout, and the Observer's Guide for the Birthday Cake Activity handout.
Room Setup:	Round tables for groups of three or four people

Lecture Notes: Introducing (five minutes)

[Facilitator: These instructions are to be provided without a handout.]

Instructions to Participants

1. Raise your hand if you are sitting at a table where you know half or more of the other people.
2. Those of you sitting at tables with people you know, change places and sit with people whom you don't know at all, know only slightly, or would like to know better.
3. Introduce yourselves to one another following this outline.
   — Name and title
   — Most important job activity
   — Expectations from this workshop
   — Anything else about yourself you would like your partners to know

Lecture Notes After the Activity Is Over

This is the experience called Introducing. Whenever a new team forms or new people come into the team, you go through this experience.

Discussion Questions

1. What does this activity tell you about the Introducing experience of teams?

   Typical answer: It's important to know something about the people with whom you work, especially if your team is just beginning to form.

2. What difference would it make if a new group doesn't get time and opportunity to learn about one another, even at this superficial level?

   Typical answer: We couldn't communicate very well with each other.

3. What happens when a new person enters the group?

   Typical answer: Here's another person, and we'd better take some time to get to know her, give her a chance to find out about us, but sometimes we don't do it or don't do it well enough.

4. What are some of the expectations you have of the workshop?

[Facilitator: Let people answer as you write the answers on a flip chart.]

Lecture Notes: Setting the Stage (two minutes)

[Facilitator: The overall purpose of this exercise is to undergo the six common experiences of teams, not just to hear about them. Put up the Objectives of the Exercise overhead now, but do not go into any detail about the experiences.]

Instructions to Participants

You have just undergone one of six experiences of teams. Introducing is an important activity that helps facilitate team communication. In the overhead, the Introducing experience is listed first, but as we discussed, introducing takes place every time someone new enters the team. As we continue the exercise, here are the outcomes to expect: Introducing, Stage Setting, Probing/Testing, Creating, Producing, Maintaining.

[Facilitator: Put up Methods You Will Use in the Exercise overhead now.]

In the Introducing part of the exercise, you've already used two of the methods that you will use during the exercise. You talked with one other person in a small group discussion and we've held a large group discussion about what you did. In a few minutes you'll be engaged in a group problem-solving discussion and make decisions as a group.

[Facilitator: Put up Roles You Will Play overhead now.]

Even if you've worked together before, because we've restructured your team into subgroups, you are acting as a newly formed team. The remainder of the roles are listed on the overhead: Members of a newly formed team, Problem solvers, Decision makers, Evaluators of experience, Planners.

Lecture Notes After the Activity Is Completed

Talking about objectives, roles, and methods as we just did illustrates the experience called Setting the Stage. In this stage, as an SMT, you should also design and develop objectives, methods, without the controls from outside management that my instructions and materials represented.

Discussion Questions

1. How would you feel if I hadn't explained the objectives and methods of this exercise and the roles you will play?

    Typical answer: At a total loss as to what we are doing and what is expected.

2. During your introductions to one another, you discussed your expectations for this workshop. How did talking about your expectations help set the stage for the workshop?

    Typical answer: I now have an idea of what at least one other person thought he/she would get out of being here, and at least one other person has an idea about what I want. Maybe we can help each other meet those expectations.

3. If, by the end of this workshop, we won't have met those expectations, how do you think you will feel?

   Typical answer: Especially since we told you our expectations, we'd feel let down if you don't help us meet them.

Lecture Notes: Probing/Testing (ten minutes)

[Facilitator: These instructions are to be provided without a handout.]

Instruction to Participants

1. Elect a timekeeper and divide the ten minutes equally among each person.

2. Everyone at the table will describe one thing about himself or herself (skills, knowledge, aptitudes, etc.) he or she doesn't think anyone at the table would know. For example, if you think that no one knows you have a hobby, such as woodworking or camping, or that you really do like to crunch numbers, that's what you talk about. Nothing obvious, such as "I have hazel eyes."

3. When listening to a person tell the one thing, do not interrupt. Write it down if you wish.

4. When he or she has finished, you may ask questions to clarify something you don't understand or ask the person to expand on or elaborate on something he or she has said.

Lecture Notes After the Activity Is Completed

This experience is called Probing/Testing. Whereas Introducing scratches the surface of getting to know people, Probing/Testing pushes the envelope of superficial work relationships.

Discussion Questions (no more than five minutes)

1. What did you learn about the people at your table that you think is valuable information about them?

   Typical answers: [Varies from group to group. People usually talk about hobbies or skills that other people might not have had an opportunity to see or previously hear about.]

2. How will that information help you and the team work together more effectively?

   Typical answer: The more we know about one another, especially about one another's preferences, their values, and how they like to work or don't like to work, the better we can work together.

Instructor's Notes: Creating, Producing, and Maintaining

Distribute task envelopes to each table and have the participants place them in the middle of the table. Do *not* offer the envelope for only one person to handle. Each group will have to self-select if it wants one person to manage the process.

In this part of the exercise, the teams will have a problem to solve and tasks to perform: dividing a birthday cake among fourteen people using only four straight cuts with a knife. That is the only instruction the participants will receive. They have to make the decisions as to how to do it, especially whether the pieces will be of equal size and if they can cut the cake horizontally.

As simple as the activity seems, *many people do not solve this problem.* Even groups of engineers have difficulty with it because they fail to make the decisions above. In some classes, no one solves the problem.

Participants learn the importance of listening to one another's suggestions. They also see that producing is a complex process, even with a problem as apparently simple as this.

Lecture Notes: Creating, Producing, and Maintaining (forty-five minutes)

Instructions to Participants

1. Each team has a task to perform.
2. Each team has a sealed envelope in the middle of the table.
3. Open the envelop and read the team's mission as described on the Birthday Cake Activity worksheet. Do *not* continue with the task until completing the next step, which I'll explain when you're ready.

[Facilitator: Allow no more than three minutes for the teams to read the mission statement.]

4. Turn to the additional instructions attached to the Birthday Cake.

[Facilitator: Read aloud from the instructions handout.]

Discussion Notes After the Whole Exercise Is Completed

The last part of the exercise consisted of three experiences: Creating, Producing, and Maintaining. By deciding on a method or group of methods for completing the task, you engaged in creating activities. By completing the task, you engaged in producing. After cutting up the cake, when you decided on what was effective or what wasn't effective for solving the activity's problem, you engaged in one type of maintaining activity. When you agreed on what you can do in the future to be more effective at solving problems, you engaged in another maintaining activity. In the exercise as a whole, you engaged in all six common experiences of teams: Introducing, Stage Setting, Testing/Probing, Creating, Producing, and Maintaining.

[Facilitator: You can use the overhead Objectives of the Exercise as a guide for this discussion. It's advisable for you to ask the participants to identify the activities that mark each of the experiences, taking each experience one at a time. Best answers should include the following.]

▶ *Introducing.* Getting to know one another at a superficial level, when a new group forms or when new people enter the group.

▶ *Stage Setting.* Finding out why the group has been formed, setting goals for the group, looking at methods and resources, identifying individual roles; writing a group charter or constitution.

▶ *Probing/Testing.* Getting to know one another better: strengths, weaknesses, interests, values, attitudes, personal resources.

▶ *Creating.* Designing outputs, designing group processes, designing methods.

▶ *Producing.* Doing the work of the group.

▶ *Maintaining.* Seeing to it that the group's resources are available and accessible, reporting, communicating internally and externally, planning for the future, building relationships with groups outside the team.

Lecture Notes to Use as a Wrap-Up to the Whole Exercise

Every team experiences these activities throughout its lifetime. They may not experience them in the sequence we just followed, and they may not experience one or more of the activities. It's likely that if a team doesn't undergo any one given experience, the team will face many difficulties, often called Storms, disagreements or conflicts that if left unresolved can destroy the team's effectiveness or the team itself.

Storms can occur at any time in the life of a team. They can also occur during any one of these six experiences. Disagreements or conflicts can occur even during Introducing activities.

[Facilitator: Describe your own experience of such a conflict, but if you haven't one, use the following.]

For example, in a newly formed cross-functional team in a division of a multi-national financial corporation, most of the people had never worked together and didn't know each other very well. During the first meeting, two people who previously had had difficulties with each other began an argument that led to one of the two, whose skills were essential to the team's success, walking out and refusing to work with the team unless the other person was cut loose. The division head had to step in and mediate the situation to everyone's satisfaction.

Now, if these six experiences are common to all teams, what does it matter if the teams are self-managed?

> *[Facilitator: Ask the participants to distinguish between SMTs and other teams, especially semiautonomous teams. If they have trouble doing so, offer the following explanation taken from Chapter 18. If you have already provided the class with this explanation, use the notes as a reminder. If you haven't used this explanation before, you can provide the whole lecture.]*

Semiautonomous teams dominate environments where teams exist. In many of these work groups, the employees perform independent functions and get together to solve problems, make decisions, and carry out action plans. However, the team reports to a supervisor or team leader appointed by management to oversee the process. Instead of autonomy in the broadest sense, the team's head has final authority over decisions and actions.

The team's leader also carries mandates from upper management to the team, seeing to it that the team carries out objectives and does work designed by management. The leader assigns or delegates the work, monitors progress, and hands out rewards. In short, the team's leader differs little from the traditional first-line manager in a command and control organization.

On the other hand, a genuine SMT gets its direction and a mandate for *autonomy* from upper management; that's the real meaning of "empowerment." Instead of an appointed leader, the team, if it so decides, elects its leader, and the team assigns responsibilities that have previously been the province of managers to each of the team's members. For example, the team may assign budget management to one person, or assign the responsibility for communicating to groups external to the team to another person, and so on. How an SMT organizes itself and designs its work are team decisions, not management fiats.

Let's take each experience and talk about how an SMT might have to manage it.

> *[Facilitator: If your participants have difficulty coming up with answers similar to these, help them out.]*

Introducing.   When a new SMT forms, someone from management sets up the initial meeting. However, after the initial meeting, when adding or replacing members, an SMT does its own interviewing, selecting, and hiring. They therefore go through all the ritual introducing processes of inducting new members. If the company forms an SMT out of an established work group, the initial introducing is not needed at all because everyone already knows everyone else.

Stage Setting.   In a semiautonomous team, management designs the team's objectives and work to be performed. The work is assigned or delegated, and the team takes all its direction, form, and expectations from management. When a new SMT forms, someone from management sets the stage or contributes to the experience by explaining its expectations. Management then turns the team loose to develop its own structure and team expectations. Often, the team writes a charter or constitution to identify members' expectations of one another.

Probing/Testing. A semiautonomous team engages in very little probing/testing because management gives the team its goals, methods, and structure. What probing/testing does go on focuses only on interpersonal relationships. Members of an SMT probe and test not only for interpersonal relationships but also for how the work can get done most effectively and by whom. They probe and test for how best to get the work done and how best to manage the team's processes.

Creating. In a semiautonomous team, usually, management not only creates the goals, it also creates the objectives (milestones) and the methods for achieving them. If management gives the team the mission to design the outputs, the team may do so, but typically the design is given to the team. In an SMT, management will create goals (give direction), but it will give the team the autonomy to set objectives and methods for achieving them. Most frequently, the design of work and outputs is the team's responsibility.

Producing. A semiautonomous team does what management asks it to do. An SMT does so also, but as a result of team decisions as to how to get it done.

Maintaining. A semiautonomous team may often solve its own problems and make decisions about how to support the team, but then the team must seek the approval from management before moving forward. Management gives an SMT the authority to act on its own decisions as to how to support the team, and, when necessary, reorganize it.

OBJECTIVES OF THE EXERCISE

By the end of the exercise, you will be able to explain:

1. The six common experiences of teams

   ▲ Introducing

   ▲ Stage Setting

   ▲ Probing/Testing

   ▲ Creating

   ▲ Producing

   ▲ Maintaining

2. How an SMT manages these experiences

Methods You Will Use in the Exercise

▲ Large group discussions

▲ Small group discussions

▲ Group problem solving

▲ Group decision making

Roles You Will Play

1. Members of a newly formed team

2. Problem solvers

3. Decision makers

4. Evaluators of experience

5. Planners

BIRTHDAY CAKE ACTIVITY

You belong to a larger team, with fourteen members (including yourself). One member, not present, has a birthday anniversary today. Your mission, as a group, is to divide this cake among *all* fourteen members. You have a straight-edged knife, and you can make only *four straight* cuts with that knife. You have five minutes to complete this task from the time the facilitator says to start.

INSTRUCTIONS FOR THE BIRTHDAY CAKE ACTIVITY

1. Before beginning work on the task, each person will state one way, different from other ways already mentioned (if possible), he or she would like to see the group function. For example, you could say, "I'd like the group to let each person make his or her guess as to how to do this."

2. As a group, decide on the method or methods to adopt for completing the task as instructed. For example, you could decide, "Let's use a trial-and-error method in which we each cut the cake in a different way."

3. One person takes notes on the Observer's Guide about how the team functioned.

4. Discuss what was learned from the activity and the note taker will report briefly to the whole group. The discussion should include:

   How we decided on a method for completing the task. Did we each make a suggestion, or did we agree with one person on how to go about completing the task?

   How well did we stick to that decision? Did we follow our own decision, or did we go off with people doing something different from what we decided?

   What helped the team do its work effectively? Did we share ideas, did we listen to other people, did we let other people influence our own thinking?

   What hindered the team from doing its work effectively. Did we not listen to each other's ideas, did we let people shoot down ideas before we considered them properly?

   What would we do differently to be more effective in the future?

OBSERVER'S GUIDE FOR THE BIRTHDAY CAKE ACTIVITY

INSTRUCTIONS

To know what you're to look for while the group attempts to solve the problem and perform the tasks of cutting the birthday cake, read the questions before the activity begins. In the spaces provided, jot brief answers to each of the questions.

You will also participate in the activity, and taking notes as the group works will make it easier to complete the form and give *specific* feedback when the activity is over. It's important to note who did what to help or to hinder the team. This observer activity is a role that an SMT should rotate among its members from one meeting to another.

How did the group decide on a method for completing the task?

How well did the group stick to that decision?

What helped the team do its work effectively?

What hindered the team from doing its work effectively?

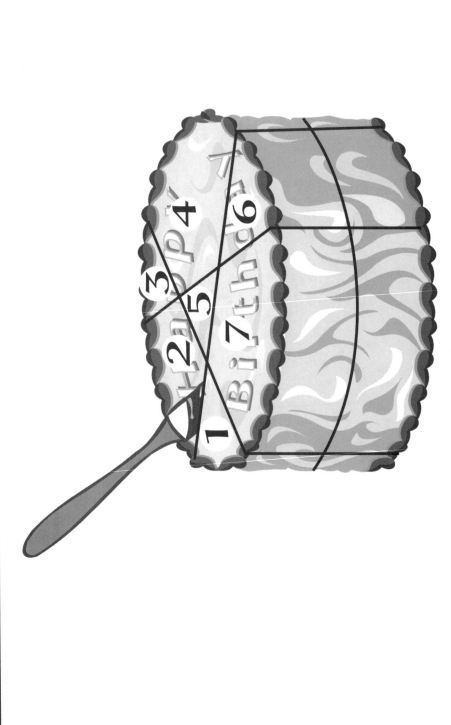

Fourteen pieces: Three vertical cuts and one horizontal cut that slices the seven pieces in half.

Follow-Up Activities for Managing the Six Common Experiences of Teams

Instructor's Notes

Provide the participants with this opportunity after they have completed the whole exercise.

Learning Objectives and Outcomes

By doing these activities participants will take steps to:

▶ Identify and reinforce their team strengths.

▶ Take corrective action to manage experiences that require attention, for example, improve the level to which people probe/test.

Self-Management Skills Involved

▶ Risk taking and trust

▶ Decision making

▶ Openness, honesty with oneself and with one's teammates

▶ Communication, especially giving other people feedback

Requirements

Time:	Five minutes to read instructions plus discussion time
Materials:	Instructions for Managing the Six Common Experiences of Teams handout
	Checklist for Managing the Six Common Experiences of Teams handout
Preparation:	Photocopy the handouts.
Room Setup:	Any arrangement in which the team works (e.g., conference table)

[Facilitator: Distribute the instructions and checklist handouts. Then read the instructions aloud.]

INSTRUCTIONS FOR MANAGING THE SIX COMMON EXPERIENCES OF TEAMS

1. As a team, produce a team charter or constitution that anticipates issues that can cause friction in the team and how to manage them. Take into consideration:

   - Chronically late or absent members

   - Passive members or uninvolved members

   - Dominating, carping, or complaining members

   - Distracting or overly long discussions, especially about trivia

   - Missing information or failure to involve people who could supply that information

   - Lacking preparation or failing to properly follow up on the part of a member

   - Domineering task orientation by the team that overwhelms individual members

   - Domineering process orientation by the team that prevents the group from meeting its work-related goals

   - Methods for rotating meeting assignments: facilitator, process observer, maintenance (e.g., note taking)

   - Methods for processing the effectiveness of the group, including progress toward task goals as well as maintenance of relationships

2. At the end of each meeting, conduct a discussion of the group's effectiveness. Check not only on task progress (Producing) but also on how well the group handled Introducing new members (if needed), Probing Testing, Creating, and Maintaining. Some teams make a chart of the six common experiences and a checklist of activities for each one. They then rate themselves as to how well they did the items in the lists. (See Checklist for Managing the Six Experiences.) Some of the problems the team can surface might include a failure to create close working relationships with new members, resources needed but not available, failure to test methods and results.

3. Rotate assignments in the group, not only during meetings but also in daily operations. For example, for one month one person writes production reports, another person maintains inventories, another communicates with management, and so on. The next month, other people perform those functions.

CHECKLIST FOR MANAGING THE SIX COMMON EXPERIENCES OF TEAMS

Experience	Possible Activities
Introducing	Interviewing, selecting, and hiring Inducting and introducing new members
Setting the Stage	Develop structure Identify and discuss team expectations Write a charter or constitution
Probing/Testing	Discuss interpersonal relationships Discuss how the work gets done and corrective actions needed Discuss who is doing what and what changes might have to be made Discuss how best to manage the team's processes
Creating	Set objectives and methods for achieving goals Design of work and outputs
Producing	Identify team production requirements Identify resources needed Do the work Test effectiveness of how the work is done and results achieved
Maintaining	Evaluate effectiveness of the work done and results achieved Take corrective action Evaluate what resources the team has and what they need Acquire resources needed and distribute to team members

18

Roles and
Role Management

By the end of this chapter, you will be able to facilitate two exercises that will help participants identify the roles they play in an SMT and the role the organization must play to support SMTs. These exercises are best suited for intact SMTs and not for general audiences. If you do work with a generic audience, you may want the participants to refer to their experiences and role(s) on their team in the workshop. The exercises work very well together as a set that leads to the visual model illustrating the interdependence of team members, SMTs, and the organization used in Exercise 18.2.

In some cases, your workshop may involve workers from a business's site but who work in different, interactive teams. Mixing them in workshop teams will allow them the opportunity to clarify roles across team lines and to improve interaction between their teams.

Exercise 18.1. Roles We Play

Instructor's Notes

The purpose of this exercise is to help the participants identify the roles they play and the roles other people expect them to play. It's important to separate the participants into teams of four to six people, preferably all on the same work team or on the same cross-functional team.

When lecturing, make the experience interactive, encouraging people to discuss action roles and to supply illustrations. When talking about role expectations, ask people to explain what roles they expect another person on the team to play.

Learning Objectives and Outcomes

By the end of this exercise participants will be able to explain and apply:

▶ The four key aspects of a role: Role Concept, Role Expectations, Role Acceptance, and Role Behavior (or Performance)

▶ Roles and responsibilities in their SMT

▶ Team expectations of each of its members

▶ Individual member expectations of other team members

Self-Management Skills Involved

▶ The ability to identify the team roles a person should play as well as those he or she does play

▶ The willingness to accept feedback from other people even if it doesn't agree with our perceptions of ourselves and the team roles we play

▶ Communication, the ability to give other people feedback about the team roles they play

▶ The willingness to accept other people's perceptions of the team roles they play

Requirements

Time:	Ninety minutes to two hours
Materials:	Four Key Aspects of Team Roles handout
	Task Action Roles handout
	Process Action Roles handout
	Instructions for Completing the Team Role(s) Grid handout
	Team Role(s) Grid worksheet

Preparation: Photocopy the handouts and worksheet.

Room Setup: Groups with no fewer than four people, preferably at round tables

Lecture Notes

In 1961 psychologist Gordon Allport, talking about personality development, described behavior as roles we play in our relationships with other people. We can describe our behavior on work teams the same way.

We each have at least one role we play in our group. Sometimes we don't even know we're playing the role or roles, we "just do what we have to do" without analyzing or discussing what we do. People take for granted that we will do our jobs and do them well. However, not consciously managing the roles we play will lead to problems when other people don't expect you to play those roles or expect you to play different roles than you think you should play.

[Facilitator: Distribute the Four Key Aspects of Team Roles handout now.]

Team roles involve the tasks a member performs and how the member contributes to producing desired outcomes; these are called task roles. Team roles also involve the things a member does to help the team manage how people work together and how problems are solved or decisions made; these are called process roles.

We can further subdivide roles into three types:

1. **Skill Roles.** Individual members with specific skills no one else has are expected to apply these skills for the benefit of the team. These are usually task roles that contribute to producing the team's outcomes; however, some process roles also require skills, such as facilitation skills.

2. **Knowledge Roles.** Individual members with specialized knowledge no one else has are expected to use and share that knowledge for the benefit of the team. Again, these are usually task roles, but some process roles also require special knowledge, such as methods for resolving conflicts.

3. **Action Roles.** Everyone is expected to perform one or more roles to assure the fulfillment of the group's mission and goals; this set of roles also include leadership roles. Both process and task roles can be action roles.

If we don't clarify roles, confusion can interfere with the group's progress or success. If we adapt Gordon Allport's ideas to the work situation, we can then find ways to avoid barriers to team functioning. Allport divided roles into four distinct aspects:[1]

---

[1] Adapted from Gordon W. Allport, *Pattern and Growth In Personality* (New York: Holt, Rinehart and Winston, 1961).

1. *Role Concept.* What you think your role or roles on the team should be.*
2. *Role Expectations.* What other people think your role or roles on the team should be.
3. *Role Acceptance.* What team role or roles you're willing to accept.
4. *Role Performance.* What team-oriented behaviors you think you already perform.†

Now, we can apply these four aspects of roles to any group of people working together. However, only in an SMT does it matter that everyone on the team carefully and consciously identify and assume team performance roles. If roles the team needs are absent, the team will fail—at best the team will be efficient but it will not be effective.

Efficient teams get the results they are required to produce, they do the team's job correctly. They are task-oriented. When an SMT manages its task dynamics (the aggregate of task roles) properly, the team is efficient, no doubt, and will fulfill its mission. However, to ensure that the team is effective, we have to manage the team's relationships also.

Managing the relationships of the team members—how it solves problems, makes decisions, includes all the members, and other such matters—makes a team effective. It does the right job the right way for creating and maintaining team cohesion. This requires managing the process dynamics of the team (the aggregate of all relationship roles).

Since every team needs to ensure that tasks get done and that the team works effectively, to the satisfaction of everyone involved, in an SMT, all the team members have to understand and apply all of the dynamics of the team and the roles that each of its members must play. There is no manager or appointed leader to watch over those dynamics.

[Facilitator: Distribute the Task Action Roles handout now.]

The Task Action Roles handout consists of a table that lists the task action roles most teams look to their members to perform. In an SMT, it's advisable not only to know what to look for but also to consciously ensure that those roles are played.

[Facilitator: Make this part of the lecture interactive by using the handout as a guide to discuss the definitions of the task action roles, their importance to the participants' teams, who should play such roles, when, where, and how. Draw the discussion of task action roles to a close with the following.]

In small teams, some, if not all, the members have to play multiple roles. Sometimes people's preferences make it easy for the team to assign roles; some people enjoy seeing to administrative details, other people enjoy coming up with new ways

---

*Allport called this Role Conception, but I think that's an awkward 1960s phrase.

†Allport called this Role Behavior, but I think that's another awkward 1960s phrase.

of doing things that make the team more efficient, and so on. Keep in mind, however, that if no one assumes any one specific role in the table, the team's efficiency could suffer. If no one *wants* to take on the unassumed roles, the team must devise a way to delegate the roles to team members, even if it means drawing straws for them.

Now, some people might have some specific skill that they can contribute to meeting the demands of the team's process dynamics, such as the role of facilitator. Some people might have specific knowledge they can share with the group as to how the group might work together well, such as knowledge of group dynamics. Everyone, however, is also expected to play one or more Process Action Roles, including leadership roles, in order for the team to work effectively as well as efficiently. That's what we discuss with the Process Action Roles handout.

> *[Facilitator: Distribute the Process Action Roles handout and make this part of the lecture interactive by using the handout as a guide to discuss the definitions of the process action roles, their importance to the participants' teams, who should play such roles, when, where, and how.]*

So much for talking about roles, now it's time to adopt this information as tools for making our teams more effective as well as more efficient. Remember, as an SMT only team members can manage these team dynamics.

> *[Facilitator: Distribute the Instructions for Completing the Team Role(s) Grid and the Team Role(s) Grid worksheet now.]*

Instructions to Participants: Individual Activity 1

1. Using your action roles handouts to guide you, write your role concept in the top box of the Team Role(s) Grid. That is, what do you think your role or roles on the team should be?
2. Using the action role handouts, write what you expect from other team members in the second box. Those are your role expectations, what role or roles you think other people on the team should play. Be specific.
3. You have fifteen minutes to complete these two steps.

Instructions to Participants: Group Activity 1

1. When everyone on your team has stopped writing, each person takes a turn explaining his or her role concept and role expectations.
2. Discuss the role concepts and role expectations and follow these guidelines.
   — Don't argue about a role concept.
   — When talking about expectations of team members, if you disagree with a person's role concept, say so, and describe your expectation(s). Explain your reasons for disagreeing.

— Remember: Other people have the right to reject your expectations of them as much as you have the right to reject their expectations of you.

— Discuss differences of opinion with regard to both essential and nonessential roles on the team, and reach agreement by consensus. Majority voting is not allowed.

— As people tell you their expectations of you (or of team members in general), write notes in the third box. This box will consist of Role Expectations also, but this time, what other people think your role or roles on the team should be.

3. You have thirty minutes for this part of the exercise.

Instructions to Participants: Individual Activity 2

1. After the general discussion with the team, in the fourth box, write the expectations other people have that you're willing to accept. This Role Acceptance is crucial to team success, and if other team members have expectations of you that you think you cannot or do not want to fulfill, you have to discuss those expectations with the team and arrive at a mutually acceptable resolution.

2. In the fifth box, write the expectations you think you already meet well and those in which you think you need to improve. This is Role Performance. You may find out, after telling the team what you think you do well, that you may not be doing what you think you do.

3. You have fifteen minutes to complete this part of the exercise.

Instructions to Participants: Group Activity 2

1. Each person takes a turn explaining his or her position on Role Acceptance and Role Performance.

2. In the turn, discuss each person's Role Acceptance and Role Performance and follow the same guidelines as in the previous group activity.

— If you disagree with a person's interpretations, say so and explain your reasons for disagreeing. Be specific. Focus on behaviors and why they are important to the team.

— Remember: Other people have the right to reject your expectations of them as much as you have the right to reject their expectations of you.

— Discuss differences of opinion with regard to essential and nonessential roles on the team and reach agreement by consensus. Majority voting is not allowed.

3. You have thirty minutes for this part of the exercise.

Discussion Questions

1. How comfortable or uncomfortable were you discussing these issues and what made it comfortable or uncomfortable for you?

   Typical answers: (1) Very uncomfortable, because we don't usually talk about these things, and it seems strange to do so. (2) Comfortable, because while we don't talk about these things often enough, we do try to work through differences of opinions. The structures you gave us will help clarify the roles we play.

2. What did you learn about the value or importance of discussing team roles?

   Typical answer: If we don't discuss team roles, we can get tied up in unnecessary, sometimes trivial, squabbles about who's supposed to do what.

3. What use do you need to make use of the information from this discussion?

   Typical answer: We should periodically stop and take a look at the action roles in the handout and see who's doing what and what roles still need to be assumed by members of the team.

FOUR KEY ASPECTS OF TEAM ROLES

THREE KINDS OF ROLES

1. Skill Roles. Individual members with specific skills no one else has are expected to apply those skills for the benefit of the team.

2. Knowledge Roles. Individual members with specialized knowledge no one else has are expected to use and share that knowledge for the benefit of the team.

3. Action Roles. Everyone is expected to perform one or more roles to assure the fulfillment of the group's mission and goals; this set of roles also include leadership roles.

FOUR ASPECTS OF TEAM ROLES

1. Role Concept. What you think your role or roles on the team should be.

2. Role Expectations. What other people think your role or roles on the team should be.

3. Role Acceptance. What team role or roles you're willing to accept.

4. Role Performance. What team-oriented behaviors you think you already perform.

TASK ACTION ROLES

Individual Task Behaviors	Descriptions
Activity management	Chairing, coordinating, resource management, meeting management
Initiating	Making suggestions or proposing new ideas, getting things started
Information seeking	Asking questions for clarification or accuracy
Information giving	Offering data or authoritative information
Opinion seeking	Asking for views as to values or to the relative merits of ideas or generalizations
Giving opinions	Stating view as to values or to the relative merits of ideas or generalizations
Elaborating	Interpreting, explaining, or explicating facts or opinions; drawing conclusions
Shaping or orienting	Identifying progress toward goals defining positions, organizing activity
Consensus seeking	Polling the group for its readiness to make decisions or to resolve disagreements
Consensus taking	Making decisions or resolving issues; formulating a position; agreeing to abide by group decisions
Summarizing	Pulling together related ideas, opinions, or suggestions; restating them; coordinating activities of subgroups or members
Reporting	Taking minutes or recording discussions, decisions, and so forth
Representing	Communicating the group's progress or decisions or actions to the external environment
Maintaining	Providing materials and performing routine tasks, for example, distributing agenda, timekeeping, and so forth

PROCESS ACTION ROLES

Individual Process Behaviors	Descriptions
Gatekeeping	Taking interest in other people's opinions or feelings; opening channels of communication
Listening	Paying attention to what other people are saying
Expediting	Keeping discussions on track yet encouraging everyone to contribute, for example, "Let's take a minute to hear everyone's opinion on this subject."
Encouraging	Praising, rewarding, reinforcing; openness to other opinions or feelings (even if they differ from the majority's)
Harmonizing	Negotiating (reconciling disagreements, mediating), or relieving tension including appropriate humor)
Yielding	Giving up an unpopular viewpoint, foregoing status, admitting mistakes, meeting other people half way
Observing	Heeding the group's process, calling attention to possible damage to effective functioning; expressing feelings present in the group; calling attention to group reactions to what is going on; diagnosing problems
Accepting	Respecting people's rights to express themselves and to meet their own needs; respecting or promoting differences among people; using differences between people as starting points of rational problem solving
Cheerleading	Giving the group permission to feel good about what it is and does, how it functions, or its successes

INSTRUCTIONS FOR COMPLETING THE TEAM ROLE(S) GRID

1. Roles to clarify: Identify real work roles.

2. Individual Activity 1
   - Box 1: Write what you think your roles on the team are.
   - Box 2: Write your expectations of *other* team members; be specific.

3. Group Activity 1
   - Discuss what you have written with your team.
   - In Box 3, as other people tell you their role expectations of you, write notes concerning other people's role expectations that you have not included in your initial role concept (Box 1).

4. Individual Activity 2
   - In Box 5, identify others' expectations that you are willing to accept. If you are willing to accept everything in Box 4, leave Box 5 blank.
   - In Box 6, list roles you think you already do well and those you do but can improve upon.

5. Group Activity 2
   - Discuss role acceptance and role performances.
   - Explain what role(s) you reject and why.
   - If the group thinks the roles you reject are essential for the team, negotiate a resolution.

TEAM ROLE(S) GRID

Role Concept (The way you see your team role(s))

Role Expectations (My expectations of other people)

Role Expectations (Other people's expectations of me)

Role Acceptance (What role(s) you are willing to accept)

Role Performance (The role(s) you think you already play)

Exercise 18.2. Creating Organizational Synergy

Instructor's Notes

Do not use this exercise unless at some time previously you have facilitated the exercise called The "I" in the Word "Team" with the participants of this workshop. That way they work through what they need from the team, what the team needs from them, and what they can do on their own before looking at what the team needs from the organization.

Separate the participants into teams of five or six people, preferably those on the same work team or on the same cross-functional team.

Learning Objectives and Outcomes

By the end of this exercise participants will be able to explain:

▶ What their team needs from the organization to be successful

▶ What the organization is providing, but not adequately

▶ What the organization is providing effectively

▶ What the organization is not providing at all and should

Self-Management Skills Involved

▶ The ability to recognize what the participant or the team needs from the organization, both what they have and what they still require

▶ The willingness to speak up for oneself and for the team

▶ Communication, especially the ability to give feedback to the management of the organization

Requirements

Time:	Approximately forty-five minutes
Materials:	Synergistic Organization overhead
	What We Need From the Organization worksheet
Equipment:	Flip chart, multicolored markers
	Overhead projector and screen
Preparation:	Prepare the overhead.
	Photocopy the worksheet.

Optional: Produce preprinted charts (see What We Need From the Organization worksheet). You could enlarge this to poster size flip charts for the group activity.

Room Setup: Groups with no fewer than five people, preferably at round tables

Lecture Notes

Synergistic organizations depend on the relationships that exist between the individual members and the team, and between the team and the organization. Only then can all the elements work together to focus sufficient energy on common goals.

[Facilitator: Put up the Synergistic Organization overhead and distribute the What We Need From the Organization worksheet now.]

The overhead represents a synergistic organization. Only when what the individual, the team, and the organization bring to the table correlate with one another, as depicted by the overlapping circles, can the whole achieve the synergy expected from combining the parts. When everyone is pulling the same direction, we get results that not only satisfy the customer but that satisfy us and the organization as well.

In a synergistic organization, goals flow from the strategies of management to the teams. Team goals flow to individual goals. When so aligned, action toward accomplishing those goals produces a unity of effort that can only lead to positive results. On the other hand, if the goals of the organization, the goals of the team, and individual goals aren't aligned, everyone pulls in different directions and the whole becomes less than the sum of its parts. It's as if we took one of the circles in the diagram and moved it off to the side, thereby depriving the whole of an essential part.

[Facilitator: Draw on your own experiences for illustrations. If you lack a good example of an organization that lacks synergy, use the following.]

A major, global financial institution had a training unit that offered courses based on what its own leadership thought would be good for managers to take. In the diagram, they would be represented by the circle labeled team. The training unit conducted no organizationwide training needs analyses and did nothing to align its course content and productivity goals with those of the larger organization. The training unit measured success by the number of people who had enrolled in its courses, and, even then, the targets the training unit set were based on increasing enrollments by whatever means possible, not in relation to changes in the larger organization. The result: The training offered failed to increase organizational synergy, and when it came time to downsize, because the training unit really didn't fit with organizational goals, it was among the first units to be cut.

In previous exercises, we have looked at what you need from the team, what the team needs from you, and what you can do on your own. In this exercise, we will add the organization to the picture.

Instructions to Participants: Individual Activity

1. Using the categories in the diagram and the handout What We Need From the Organization, in the first column list five specific, actionable things that the organization needs to do to support an SMT. Include things the organization does and things that it doesn't do but you think it should.
2. In the second column, opposite the item that the organization should do, place a plus sign (+) for what the organization does and does well.
3. For what the organization does but you think it could do more or do more effectively, place a plus sign (+) over a minus sign (–).

[Facilitator: On a flip chart, write +/–.]

4. For the things you think the organization should do but doesn't do at all, place a minus sign (–).
5. You have fifteen minutes to complete this part of the activity.

Instructions to Participants: Group Activity 1

If there are two or more groups in the workshop:

1. Elect a scribe who will write the group decisions about what the team needs from the organization on a flip chart.
2. Compare lists and ratings.
3. Make a comprehensive list of things the organization should do to support an SMT and rate the items.
4. Come to a consensus around disagreements as to what to include on the list.
5. Come to a consensus around disagreements as to the ratings of the items.
6. Put the team lists and ratings on flip charts.
7. You have thirty minutes to complete this part of the activity.

[Facilitator: Allow more time if needed.]

8. Report to the whole group.

Instructions to Participants: Group Activity 2

If there are two or more groups in the workshop:

1. In your small group, go around the room to the other flip charts.
2. Discuss in your small group any item on a chart that your group did not include in its own chart.

3. If you agree that any item you didn't include should be included, return to your chart and add the item or items you agreed on and rate them plus, minus, or plus over minus.

4. You have ten minutes to do this.

Discussion Questions

1. How did this exercise help you evaluate your organization's role in supporting an SMT?

   Typical answer: It made us take the time and effort to think through some of the team problems and to identify those things we need from the organization that we might not be getting. It also helped us recognize what we are getting from the organization and didn't recognize sufficiently.

2. How do you feel about the organization's support of SMTs?

   Typical answer: [Answers will vary by organization. If the teams are getting what they need, they'll feel supported, if not, they'll feel let down.]

3. Which of those things that you think the organization should do but is not doing or not doing as effectively as you think it should are most important and need immediate attention?

   Typical answer: [Answer will vary by organization depending on answers to the exercise.]

4. For those things you think the organization should do but are not doing or not doing as effectively as you think it should, what is your next step?

   Typical answer: Pass the information we just gathered to management.

5. How can you best communicate your ideas to the organization?

   Typical answer: We have a formal communication system in which our team represents itself to management. We need to make better use of it.

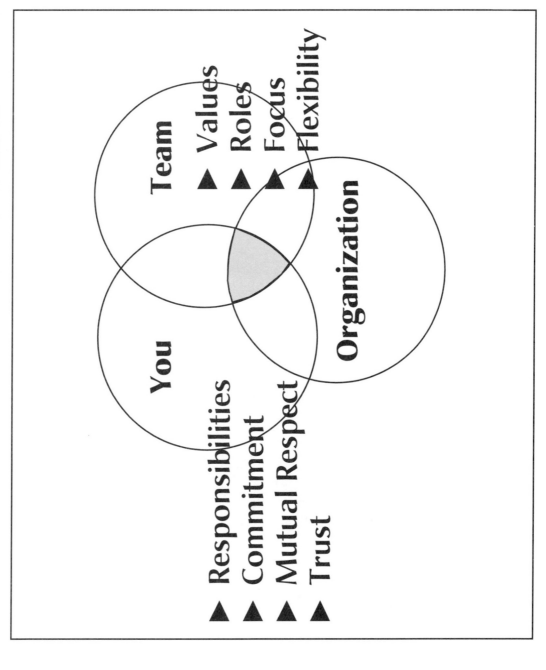

WHAT WE NEED FROM THE ORGANIZATION

What We Need From the Organization	Rating
Values (Example: Employee satisfaction as well as customer satisfaction.)	
Roles (Example: Be available, accessible for discussing problems and solutions.)	
Responsibilities (Example: Make resources available.)	
Focus (Example: Be customer focused.)	
Commitment (Example: Dedication to quality rather than expediency.)	
Mutual Respect (Example: Treat employees like adults.)	
Trust (Example: Provide opportunities to make our own decisions.)	
Flexibility (Example: Try out new ideas.)	
Other	

Follow-Up Activities for Managing Team and Organizational Roles

Learning Objectives and Outcomes

By doing these activities participants will take steps to:

▶ Identify and reinforce their team strengths, particularly in relation to action roles.

▶ Take corrective action to manage team roles that require attention, for example, ensure that at least one person takes a responsibility no one else wants.

▶ Identify and reinforce organizational synergies.

▶ Take corrective action whenever they identify areas in need of improvement, for example, a unit's goals do not properly align with organizational goals.

Self-Management Skills Involved

▶ Risk taking and trust

▶ Decision making

▶ Openness, honesty with oneself and with one's teammates

▶ Communication, especially giving feedback to other people and to the organization

Requirements

Time: Five minutes to read instructions plus discussion time

Materials: Instructions for Follow-Up Activities for Managing Team and Organizational Roles handout

Preparation: Photocopy the handout.

Room Setup: Any arrangement in which the team works (e.g., conference table)

[Facilitator: Distribute and read from the Instructions for Follow-Up Activities for Managing Team and Organizational Roles handout.]

INSTRUCTIONS FOR FOLLOW-UP ACTIVITIES FOR MANAGING TEAM AND ORGANIZATIONAL ROLES

1. Use the Team Role(s) Grid back on the job; set aside periodic meetings to reproduce the exercise you did in the workshop. Become conscious of and observe your own and other people's activities; you don't always realize that you or someone else is doing something no one noticed before. Contrarily, people may think they're performing a role they are in fact not doing. Periodically check with one another as to concept and expectations.

2. Use the Task Action Roles and Process Action Roles to identify which, if any, are missing from the self-management of the group. Design a plan for guaranteeing the missing roles are filled, where needed. For example, if no one wants to assume a needed role, use a lottery or other method for filling it.

3. Create a team spokesperson position, which will rotate monthly among the members, to carry team issues and needs to management.

4. On a periodic basis, or as needed, do a needs audit, similar to the exercise handout What We Need From the Organization, listing specific, actionable issues. Be sure to include items the organization does, as well as things it doesn't do.

5. After completing the needs audit, create change plans to include:
   - Current conditions, identifying indicators (symptoms of problems) and contributing factors (possible causes of the problems)
   - An explanation of why they need to change and change goals
   - A suggested action plan, including the team's responsibilities for helping make the change happen and steps for monitoring the change

Index